THE LONDON MARATHON

THE HISTORY OF THE GREATEST RACE ON EARTH

THE LONDON MARATHON

THE HISTORY OF THE GREATEST RACE ON EARTH

JOHN BRYANT

arrow books

Published by Arrow books in 2006

3 5 7 9 10 8 6 4 2

Copyright © John Bryant 2005

First published by Hutchinson in the United Kingdom 2005

Arrow Books
The Random House Group Limited
20 Vauxhall Bridge Road, London SW1V 2SA

Random House Australia (Pty) Limited
20 Alfred Street, Milsons Point, Sydney
New South Wales 2061, Australia

Random House New Zealand Limited
18 Poland Road, Glenfield
Auckland 10, New Zealand

Random House (Pty) Limited
Isle of Houghton, Corner of Boundary Road & Carse O'Gowrie,
Houghton 2198, South Africa

The Random House Group Limited Reg. No. 954009

www.randomhouse.co.uk

A CIP catalogue record for this book
is available from the British Library

The Random House Group Limited makes every effort to ensure that
the papers used in its books are made from trees that have been legally
sourced from well-managed and credibly certified forests. Our paper
procurement policy can be found at:
www.randomhouse.co.uk/paper.htm

Mixed Sources
Product group from well-managed
forests and other controlled sources
www.fsc.org Cert no. TT-COC-2139
© 1996 Forest Stewardship Council

Typeset by Palimpsest Book Production Limited,
Polmont, Stirlingshire
Printed in the UK by CPI Bookmarque, Croydon, CR0 4TD

ISBN 0 0994 8435 8
ISBN-13 9780099484356 (from Jan 2007)

Dedicated to the many thousands, fast and slow,
who have run the London Marathon.
They all know what it is to win.

Contents

Foreword

Sir Steve Redgrave

It was the morning of 22 April, 2001. Ahead of me were some familiar landmarks – Tower Bridge, the Millennium Eye and, of course, Buckingham Palace. But on this day I was not on my way to be greeted by the Queen or sightseeing with my family.

I was caught up in a mass of bright colour, alongside the great and the good, the old and the young, the able-bodied and the disabled, all blending together in a carnival atmosphere on the streets of London.

'Good luck Steve,' 'Where's your boat, Steve?' and 'Keep up, Steve!' These were just some of the words of wisdom, encouragement and leg-pulling that accompanied my first London Marathon.

It doesn't matter that you have five Olympic Gold medals, it doesn't matter if you are royalty, an athlete at the pinnacle of your career, or a fundraiser dressed as a hot-dog and juggling goldfish. Those 26.2 miles around the streets of London treat everyone with the same respect – with all but a very select few focusing on achieving nothing more than their own, very personal, goal.

Mine was to finish, and to raise as much money as possible for charity. The London Marathon will never be a race that I or nearly 30,000 others are ever going to win. The event is so special simply because that fact doesn't deter people from all walks of life and from all around the world putting in months of rigorous training. That is one of the many things which makes the event so extraordinary.

For the record, my first finishing time was four hours, 55 minutes and 36 seconds. Ask anyone what their time was and they will tell you to the second – it is something to be very proud of after all.

I

On the Line

*The difference between the mile and the marathon is
the difference between burning your fingers with a match
and being slowly roasted over hot coals*
Hal Higdon

I am standing on the start line like a teenager on a date,
all hope and anticipation. The spitting rain shivers off my
shorts and trickles down my all too naked legs. Someone
behind is treading on the backs of my shoes, and hundreds
more are pushing me forward. I am already breathing too
fast and there's a taste of panic round my lips.

I am nervous, uncertain, excited. I fiddle with my watch,
strain for the boom of the cannon and wonder if this, at
last, will be the one I've been waiting for. Perhaps out on
the road I'll find what I've dreamed about for so long –
the elusive, perfect marathon.

I ought to be a lot more confident, less fearful of the
distance. I am young, fit and fast. I've been an athlete for
years, racing everything from the mile to the marathon. But
lining up with so many thousands for this first London
Marathon in 1981 is like nothing I've ever seen.

I woke up long before the alarm, pulse already racing,
and joined the hordes spilling off the train and trudging
towards Greenwich Park. In the swelling rain we are a
billowing sea of bin liners.

Among the crowd I spot the odd familiar face, a fellow
club runner or two, but most are strangers to me. Where,
I wonder, have they all come from? I thought I knew most
marathon runners and believed I knew all about marathons.
I've run them before – tough marathons, fast marathons.

3

In Harlow once, on an undulating course, I hit the wall, that invisible barrier that every marathon runner dreads, but I still dragged myself home in 2 hours and 21 minutes.

Marathons like that were high-class races, with fiercely fast fields. But only a few dozen runners would ever show up, maybe a hundred or so at most for a championship event. They were grim affairs, full of hardened, anorexic-looking men, proud of their athletic club vests, their reputations as runners and their exclusive membership of a brotherhood of suffering.

The biggest race in Britain, the most impressive field we ever saw, was the National Cross Country Championship. That had over a thousand and we thought it was huge. But here is a race – a road race – that has attracted entries from many thousands. Something very strange has happened to my familiar world of running – and it seems to have happened overnight.

In the years to come we athletes, who once enjoyed the privileged loneliness of the long-distance runner, will reckon we can blame the sudden appearance of this horde on a man in a Richmond pub – a man with a pipe and a pint.

Back in the 1970s, across the Atlantic, the American evangelists of a new fitness cult were urging their converts to put down their pipes and beer and jog, jog, jog their way to health and happiness. Their proudest pilgrimage was a new and spectacular annual ritual, the New York Marathon, in which legions of fun runners took to the streets and closed down the city for a 26-mile procession that was half race, half carnival.

Here in Britain, too, there was a scattering of such middle-aged fanatics who enjoyed and preached the joys of jogging. Of these none was more colourful or eccentric than Chris Brasher, that man with the pipe and the pint – a once-upon-a-time Olympic gold medal winner, sometime pacemaker for the first four-minute mile and, by the 1970s, long-serving athletics and Olympics correspondent of the *Observer*.

His idea of a perfect day was to get some exercise, the madder and tougher the better, and to round it off by embroidering accounts of it over a few beers. It was actually in a pub, the Dysart Arms – used by members of his running club, the Ranelagh Harriers – that Brasher and his friend John Disley first heard tales of a New York marathon.

Thousands, they were told, could be seen running through the city streets, with hundreds of thousands more cheering them on. Some of the Ranelagh men had raced there, returning with wonderful accounts of this new world of running. The New York Marathon, Brasher decided, could be a very good story indeed – so he set off to run it himself and to write about it for his newspaper.

Brasher and Disley, his one-time steeplechasing partner, climbing companion and business associate, came back from New York in 1979 bubbling with enthusiasm for the idea of a big-city race on a scale they had never seen before. Brasher wrote of it in the *Observer*:

To believe this story you must believe that the human race can be one joyous family, working together, laughing together, achieving the impossible.

Last Sunday in one of the most trouble-stricken cities in the world, 11,532 men and women from forty countries, assisted by over a million black, white and yellow people, laughed and cheered and suffered during the greatest folk festival the world has seen.

I wonder whether London could stage such a festival? We have the course, a magnificent course, but do we have the heart and the hospitality to welcome the world?

His question was answered that wet morning of 29 March 1981 when 7,055 runners (in those days only 300 of them were women) set out to run the first London Marathon over a course designed and masterminded by Disley.

Brasher and Disley had been encouraged to think that they could dare to take on the planning of a marathon through the streets of London because they had already successfully organised the World Orienteering Championships in 1976, at Aviemore in Scotland. They had picked up the tricks of promoting this event as they went along, recovering quickly from their mistakes and learning above all the advantages of organising the championships free from the bureaucracy that dragged so heavily on athletics at the time. 'We wanted nothing to do with committees, governing bodies and officials,' said Disley. 'We wanted to get on with it and sweep aside any problems. Orienteering was new, and we could get away with doing it our way.'

For those orienteering championships Disley had been the Event Director and Brasher the Course Director. When it came to planning the London Marathon they decided to exchange duties. It was an inspired piece of role swapping and together they were able to get their marathon on the road.

Dealing with the police, the keepers of the royal parks, and the local politicians who ruled the boroughs of London was never going to be smooth, but Brasher was not a man who allowed himself to be slowed down by the weight of too much diplomacy. Along with Disley, he harnessed the help of Donald Trelford, the then editor of the *Observer*, and a whole army of well-wishers, to bulldoze his way through brick walls of bureaucracy and clear the ground for his dream.

Early in 1980, Trelford met with Brasher and Disley to do battle with anyone who might object to their ideas – including the Greater London Council, the police and the athletics governing bodies. Later that year Brasher and Disley went back to America to visit the Boston Marathon, the world's oldest marathon outside the Olympics, and to revisit the New York City race, hungrily devouring any detail they could find of how such races were organised and financed.

Afterwards they roughed out a budget showing that their marathon needed around £75,000. They badly needed a backer, and an old friend, BBC sports commentator and agent Peter West of West-Nally, a public relations company, found one. Gillette had just ended a sponsorship deal with cricket and were looking for other games to play with their money. They had heard about the running boom in New York and were shrewd enough to wonder if the London Marathon might catch on and be worth sponsoring. They came up with an offer of £50,000. It helped to buy 2,000 foil blankets, 75 portable lavatories, and 50,000 plastic cups.

At a second meeting with the Greater London Council and the police, Brasher was finally given the go-ahead to stage the race, but with one tough warning from the Council leader, Sir Horace Cutler, who told him: 'Never ask the ratepayers to bail you out. You'll not get a penny from the ratepayers.'

Brasher and Disley celebrated their breakthrough over a drink and together they scribbled out some rather grand-sounding aims:

1. To improve the overall standard and status of British marathon-running by providing a fast course and strong international competition.
2. To show to mankind that on occasions the family of man can be united.
3. To raise money for the provision of recreational facilities in London.
4. To help London tourism.
5. To prove that when it comes to organising major events, 'Britain is best'.
6. To have fun and provide some happiness and sense of achievement in a troubled world.

Romantic these dreams might have sounded, but the race immediately caught the popular imagination. More than

20,000 hopefuls applied for a starting number. The excitement, the uncertainty and hype in the months leading up to the event were infectious. Nobody foresaw what was about to hit London.

I had a taste of what was to come when I was sent by the *Daily Mail* to run in the New York Marathon in November of 1980, just months before the London race. New York had gone marathon crazy. The papers were buzzing with race previews, shops and restaurants offered special discounts for runners, a passing cab driver, spotting me training, urged, 'Burn some rubber on marathon day.' On the streets of the city I discovered a new breed of runner – men and women who ran not to compete or to win, but because they believed in and preached the magic effects of exercise.

Of course, there has always been magic in movement. And there have always been those who have known the secret of this magic. You would have seen them in the mists of pre-history working up a sweat over the steps of some ancient tribal dance. And you can see them today, loping around the Serpentine, scrambling up the peaks of Yorkshire, or simply plodding the roads and paths of their local park.

The secret that every runner knows – the real magic in movement, the thing that keeps them going after the novelty of losing a little weight and gaining a little breath wears off – lies in what it does to the mind. For while running makes the heart grow stronger, shapes the body and provides an invaluable reservoir of energy for work or play, to thousands of addicted runners those are only the side-effects. They run because it makes them feel good and induces the euphoria that was being hailed in America as the 'jogger's high'.

The New York Marathon, the brainchild of a man called Fred Lebow, had caught the wave of recreational joggers who had taken to the streets in search of this magic euphoria, to lose weight, to follow fashion, or simply to ward off the effects of age.

They were encouraged and inspired by Frank Shorter winning the Olympic marathon for the United States in Munich in 1972, and by evangelists of the new aerobic movement like fitness guru Kenneth Cooper, running coach Arthur Lydiard, and the best-selling author of *The Complete Book of Running*, Jim Fixx.

The New York Marathon was a glorious celebration of their enthusiasm. It was the first of the new generation of big-city marathons. The Boston Marathon had existed for the best part of a century but the New York Marathon was invented to cater for the 1970s jogging boom. Here was a race that encapsulated a sporting revolution – it was open to all runners of all shapes and ages, no matter what their ability.

And when the New York Marathon changed its course from four laps of Central Park to take in all the New York boroughs to coincide with the bicentennial celebrations in 1976, the race took on the aura of a carnival. Press and television made stars of its also-rans. It became trendy to run it, and people applied in their thousands for the chance to do so.

I came back from America and wrote about the festival atmosphere, the bands that played on every street corner, the battles at the front of the field and the tales of the eccentrics in the shuffling pack. In Britain celebrities like the disc jockey Jimmy Savile and the gossip columnist Nigel Dempster were eagerly signing up for Brasher's marathon. Thoughts of the blisters and the hard effort were swept aside; the event was making headlines and there were plenty who wanted to be part of the story.

There was certainly no shortage of pre-race publicity for that first London Marathon. To illustrate the enormity of the marathon distance, sports writer Ian Wooldridge accompanied Brasher round the London course in a chauffeur-driven limousine a few days before the race, stopping wherever possible at pubs and wine bars en route. When they eventually reached the finish at Westminster Bridge, Wooldridge wrote that Brasher, who could only just stand, clambered into a Gore-Tex running suit to trot off into the night towards his home in Richmond.

By race day, the marathon hype, much of it generated by the energetic Brasher calling in favours from his friends in journalism and broadcasting, had attracted coverage on national television. And as I joined the thousands of new marathon runners trudging their way to the start that March morning, the helicopters were clattering overhead and the cameras were rolling.

2

The Great Suburban Everest

It felt like an elephant had jumped on to my shoulders
and was making me carry it the rest of the way in.
Dick Beardsley, on hitting 'the wall'

I look around me nervously as we glance at our watches
and wait for the shock of the cannon that will send us on
our way. The place reeks of liniment. You can smell the
anticipation and excitement.

There are more than 7,000 starters here and I wonder if
they know what they are taking on. How many, I wonder,
can hope to finish? Traditionally the marathon was always
seen as a man-killer of an event. It existed at the outer rim
of what was considered possible even for the toughest and
hardest-trained of athletes. It was reckoned to be the ultimate – a trial open only to the veteran, the race-hardened,
the eccentric, the foolhardy, the hero.

Are these people aware that the human body is not designed
to run marathons? Just consider what it does to you.

During the course of 26 miles, 385 yards, or 42,195
metres, the average runner's feet hit the ground over 30,000
times. Each step sends a shock the equivalent of three times
your body weight through your legs, your thighs and your
spine. Slapping your foot against the road can rupture small
blood vessels in the feet and legs and can reduce your levels
of haemoglobin, needed to carry oxygen through your blood
cells. An average 160lb person will be subjected to as much
as 640lb of pressure per footstep, every time the foot hits
the ground.

The finest runners can romp through the marathon in just a fraction over two hours, at an average speed of close to 13 miles per hour and a total energy expenditure of around 3,000 calories. And although it takes much longer for non-elite runners to complete the distance, the total cost in fuel consumption is about the same.

But fast or slow, the physiological stresses can become so severe that sometimes, however determined a runner might be, the body can take it no more, and giving up is the only option. Hypothermia – a catastrophic drop in body temperature – dehydration or simply physical damage such as blisters can bring anybody to a standstill. As Paula Radcliffe discovered in the Athens Olympic Games in 2004, even the finest and toughest can be humbled by this race.

'I knew I was in big trouble,' Radcliffe wrote of her experience at the 36km point in Athens. 'I could hardly pick my legs up at all; they were like sore lead weights. I felt so empty. It got to the point where I couldn't put one foot in front of the other. And I stopped.'

So why do they do it? Can it ever be good for you? Dr Dan Tunstall Pedoe, the London Marathon's Chief Medical Adviser throughout its 25 years, reckons, 'The training is good for you but I wouldn't say running a marathon is good for you. It depletes your glycogen, damages your muscles and it takes a long time to recover.'

But even with all this suffering, amazingly most runners reach the finish high on a wave of excitement and adrenalin, their agony dulled by endorphins, the chemicals released by the brain to deaden pain.

Most runners would like to claim they do it for health and fitness, but the haunted, hollow-eyed stare of many of those who stumble across the finish line tells a different story. Reduced to a survival shuffle, they can hardly be said to be improving their health.

And they certainly don't do it to win. It's not for the glittering prizes, as with most sport. On the contrary, most competitors start these races with the avowed aim of being also-rans. Surely these huge city marathons have to be the greatest example of the philosophy of Baron de Coubertin, the founding father of the modern Olympic Games, who was fond of proclaiming: 'It's not the winning, it's the taking part.'

The London is unique as a sporting event in that thousands of those who go the distance take part because it means something to them personally. It's not something second-hand they experience by sitting in the stands or watching it on TV.

But why the marathon? What is so special about this strange, accidental distance? What is it about 26 miles, 385 yards?

All over the world the marathon has a mystique about it that may have much to do with its legendary origins – the great tales of heroism and suffering that hang around it. But more probably its widespread popularity comes from the fact that it provides a challenge pitched just at the right level of possibility.

To gain personal satisfaction and perhaps some prestige among fellow runners, friends or the crowds that line the route, there is no need these days to run the marathon fast. 'No one gives a damn if I run well in other marathons,' complained one veteran of two dozen Londons. 'All that impresses most people is that I actually finish the London Marathon, no matter how slowly.'

Brasher loved to call the marathon 'The Great Suburban Everest' – a peak that every man or woman might aspire to. Just about anyone, he believed, can conquer the distance. But the reality, he said, is that relatively few are prepared to make the effort, and when they do it almost invariably hurts – and hurts a lot.

The reason it hurts so much, and the reason why so many come back for another attempt, is 'the wall', that dreaded physiological and mental breaking point that lurks around every corner after the 18-mile mark.

Runners mutter that even when you reach 20 miles the

race is only half over. The truth is that this point marks the end of the beginning. After 20, the collapse of controlled effort, the disintegration of smooth and easy running comes all too suddenly. This is where the marathon, the suffering, the true effort really begins – at the wall.

This is the point at which hundreds of runners crack and where the distance starts to bite. Any reasonably fit runner can knock off 20 miles. I was used to turning out for 15- or 20-mile races without a thought, without lengthy preparation, without elaborate rituals of tapering, diet and rest.

But somewhere around 18 miles the human body, when exercising vigorously, or even when running comfortably, simply runs dangerously low on glycogen, the sugar-based fuel that keeps the human engine ticking over. When the tank is nearly empty, all hell breaks loose. If you are lucky you can still run, burning only fat – but it slows you down and it floods you with pain.

Marathon runners live in dread of it. They plan every training run, every meal to get round it. They learn the painful lesson that poor pacing can send them crashing into the wall, and the shadow of it haunts their every footstep.

But pain is the whole point of the marathon. It defines the experience. Fast or slow, there is plenty of pain for everyone; and through sharing, pain offers the ordinary runner the chance to experience something that is normally tasted only by the elite. Most of us never get the opportunity to line up alongside an Olympic champion, to play in a Cup Final or to swim the Channel.

But here is Brasher's suburban Everest, and for a moment at the start you line up with the greats. The finish for everyone lies somewhere beyond the wall, but you know that, if you can handle the pain, you can probably make it.

The night before that inaugural London Marathon, Dave Bedford – former world record holder for the 10,000 metres, one-time wild man of British athletics and now Race Director of the London Marathon – decided *he* could probably make it.

'I'd had quite a few pints when someone bet me £250 that I couldn't do the marathon the next morning,' said Bedford. 'It was in my nightclub, The Mad Hatter in Luton. I hadn't run for twelve months, but the bet seemed too good to turn down so I took up the challenge. To prepare, I switched from drinking beer to pina coladas and phoned Chris Brasher to try to get a number. I then went for a curry in The Light of India in Luton only to realise that the clocks were being brought forward by an hour that morning. I left Luton at 6.30 a.m. It's not preparation for a marathon that I would recommend.

'I thought I'd have an easy run in around three hours, but the tandoori king prawns got the better of me by Tower Bridge. I was caught on television with my head over a drain and Brendan Foster commentating saying, "There's Dave Bedford, not looking as fit as we might have expected." Did I hit the wall? Well, the last three miles took me 45 minutes, I couldn't face the post-race drinks party, and I went to bed for two days. And, by the way, I'm still waiting for the bet to be paid.'

Chris Brasher was another who couldn't resist the temptation of running in that first London Marathon. 'I went to bed after midnight,' he said. 'I set my alarm for 5 a.m. but around 2 a.m. the phone rang. It was Dave Bedford and he was obviously drunk, saying that he wanted to run. I told him to do whatever he wanted to do, turned over and went back to sleep. The phone rang again at 4 a.m. This time there was a problem with the finish gantry. Apparently, there was a danger that it would chop off the heads of the mounted soldiers during the Changing of the Guard, and somehow we had to get the timing of the ceremony moved forward.

'There was a bit of panic but we managed to get it altered and I got up, still determined to run. I wanted to savour the meal we had prepared just as a chef wants to sample what he has cooked. I wasn't aiming for any particular time but I crossed the line in 2:56 with a huge sense of relief.

Afterwards I had a few drinks and dozens of people came up to me and said that the experience of taking part made it one of the great days of their lives. What they said to me then made it one of the greatest days of my life too.'

That first London Marathon seemed so innocent, so exciting, so big. Almost everyone wanted to be part of it and the whole day began to take off like some extended street party. Television coverage helped to make it an instant success and, despite the drizzle, the people of London were curious to see what was going on and turned out in their thousands to watch.

Not everyone was so enthusiastic. There was a desperate shortage of portable lavatories at the start, and a few scuffles broke out between local residents and runners lurking round their back gardens. Some of the sporting press were wary of what they regarded as a Brasher-led *Observer* publicity stunt. One sports writer turned down the invitation to attend the race on the grounds that he was employed to cover athletic events, not circuses.

But when it was all over the event had somehow made a surplus of over £12,000 and 6,255 people had managed to finish the race – an amazing 88 per cent of the starters. The quality at the front of the field was good, with 144 runners completing the course in less than two and a half hours, and there were nearly 5,000 who crossed the line in under four hours.

Overnight the marathon had become an event for ordinary but determined people. With the suddenness of the starting gun, it seemed, running had become a fashion, an enthusiasm, a cult, an obsession – and for many a life-changing experience. It was strange to find my personal, almost hidden passion suddenly being shared and enjoyed by thousands.

Those who had taken part limped to their offices and factories next day proudly displaying their blisters and their medals. Thousands more who had witnessed it, in London or through television, took to the streets, the meadows, the towpaths and the woods.

The Times greeted the event with a leading article and the *Daily Mail* seized the moment by setting up an elaborate newspaper spoof.

Three days after the first London Marathon was April Fool's Day. I had entered my brother for the race but he didn't run, so we had a spare number. Since the world seemed to have gone marathon mad, we pinned the number on to a Japanese male model and took a picture of him running. This the *Daily Mail* published on 1 April, with a joke report that a Japanese athlete who could not speak English believed he was in a 26-day, rather than a 26-mile, race. According to the report he was last seen on Sunday evening heading north.

The story generated hundreds of calls to the paper, from people who were sure that they had spotted the unfortunate runner at points all over the country. There was even an approach from the Japanese Embassy wanting to know if they could help with the search. To keep the joke going, the *Mail* dropped the 'lost runner' on the outskirts of St Albans and he padded into town shortly before noon on 1 April.

He was spotted by delighted street traders who, having read that he spoke no English, tried to flag him down with cries of '*Finito*' and '*Kaput*'. Unable to stop the relentless runner, one enterprising shopkeeper dragged a waiter from the local Chinese restaurant in the hope that he would have better luck in overcoming the language barrier.

Like the April Fool's Day runner, the London Marathon was to prove unstoppable. In the days after the race, thousands of novice joggers were out on the roads, vowing that they too would have a go at the marathon next time. Marathon mania had taken hold overnight and suddenly a new and permanent fixture had appeared on the national sporting calendar.

That first year I was lucky enough to win a large engraved trophy as the first media man home. Along with it came a week's free car rental and a few gallons of champagne. I didn't know whether to be pleased with my run or not. I had hit the wall badly and staggered home in 2:45. Twelve months earlier I would have been desperately unhappy with my time, but this race was different. Friends and colleagues seemed to think it was wonderful that I had run at all.

I wondered what might have been. How I might have run much faster, how I might have achieved my potential. Others saw my finisher's medal and treated me as if I were a hero. There was a part of me, the unfulfilled athlete, that still dreamed of winning a marathon; but around me were hundreds who were convinced that they were already winners.

At the finish of every London Marathon one of the great ritual statements is: 'Never again!' The runners say it, but it's not true. They come back because this time they think they won't end up hitting the wall. You always believe that next time you can beat it. You can run round it, over it, past it, somehow. You'll get fitter, you'll drink more, you'll get the pace right, the shoes right. You will always think that this time you will be the hero you were meant to be – so you come back, year after year if you can get in. You come back because you know you can do better. You're like a surfer searching for the perfect wave.

Up at the front in that first London Marathon a couple of runners were running perfect marathons of their own. An American, Dick Beardsley, and a Norwegian, Inge Simonsen, ran silently together, stride for stride. As they neared the tape their eyes met and they caught the spirit of that unforgettable day.

These two winners crossed the line together in 2:11:48 – smiling and hand in hand.

3

Once a Winner . . .

Great is the victory, but the friendship of all is greater.
Emil Zatopek

The gesture of sportsmanship as Beardsley and Simonsen crossed the finish line put their picture straight on to the front pages. The TV commentator David Coleman found the perfect words to capture the moment. 'There it is,' he said, 'the hand of friendship.'

'It wasn't premeditated,' Beardsley remembers. 'We had been hammering each other for so long yet we'd been glued together, it just seemed right. We became real good friends after that race. Because it was the first one it was special, and we were lucky to do it.'

In the Boston Marathon the following year Beardsley came a close second, in a legendary photo-finish with Alberto Salazar, in 2:08:53. That was such a tough race that both men seemed scarred by the effort. 'I lost a part of me on that Boston course,' said Beardsley. 'When you run that hard it's as if the brain remembers the pain and won't let you go there again.'

At the start of the 1980s, Beardsley was part of an elite pack of athletes spearheading the great new running boom. He could travel the world on tickets paid for by race promoters and his relaxed, outgoing personality made him much in demand as an athlete and a speaker.

Sportsmen are notoriously superstitious, and Beardsley had a catalogue of rituals that he performed to bring him luck before every race. He would always spit twice on the starting line and then wipe the spit away with his foot. Next he would slide his wedding ring off and on his finger exactly four times, always within a minute of the start. He insisted, too, on racing in the same shoes, shorts and singlet that had served him well in previous races. But one year he had run so many good races that his kit wore out. Superstitious as ever, Beardsley hung his old running kit and shoes in the window of his hotel. 'If I couldn't wear them,' he said, 'then at least they could watch how I did.'

These days, 25 years on, Beardsley still considers himself lucky – lucky that he's not in prison, lucky that he's still alive and lucky that he can run at all.

In March 1997, at the age of 41, he came up before a Minnesota court for sentence after pleading guilty to forgery. He faced a possible prison term for writing prescriptions on a doctor's pad for more than 1,600 controlled painkillers. He was given 240 hours' community service and a $1,000 fine.

Beardsley's marathon fall from grace resulted from a catalogue of accidents that started while working on a tractor on the dairy farm that he'd bought to fulfil his childhood fantasy.

On the morning of 13 November 1989 he was up early to milk the cows and load corn. As he perched on his tractor's slippery towbar, the leg of his overalls got caught in the power take-off, a rotating shaft connected to the tractor's engine. The power take-off trapped his left leg and started to spin him wildly, smacking his head against the barn floor with each revolution. Beardsley screamed for help but his wife Mary was in the house, too far away to hear. Somehow the tractor engine spluttered and died and Beardsley crawled out to the yard, where Mary found him.

The superbly fit athlete, who'd won the marathon with a smile in London, had suffered a punctured lung, a broken right wrist, smashed ribs, concussion, fractured vertebrae and a mangled left leg.

'I got caught up in a rotating shaft and almost had my

left leg torn off at the knee,' he said. 'I was really lucky – twice they were going to amputate.' Two weeks after the accident his leg became infected and he was given more surgery and heavy doses of painkillers. Incredibly, through all his problems, Beardsley dreamed of a comeback to running and did endless leg lifts in a bid to keep fit and strong as he lay on his hospital bed.

By 1992 he had built up his strength sufficiently to return to farm work and also to get back to his running. But after a race, while he was driving home with his wife and his son, Andy, Beardsley suffered the first of three more life-threatening accidents when his car was rammed on the driver's side by a motorist who had gone through a halt sign. While his wife and son escaped uninjured, Beardsley was back in hospital with spinal and shoulder injuries – and pumped full of more painkillers. He came out unable to cope with the tough labour of farm work and got a job as a farm reporter for a local radio station.

Six months after his car had been written off, Beardsley, still trying to fight his way back as an athlete, went for a run in the snow and was struck from behind by a hit-and-run driver. Once again he was back in hospital, this time for 16 days, with neck and back injuries. Three weeks later at home he became dizzy, passed out and fell down 15 stairs. The pain did not stop, and neither did the accidents. Just one month later Beardsley lost control of his car in a blizzard and it flipped over several times before landing upside down. He had to be cut free, and suffered fractured bones in his back as well as head injuries.

Even while convalescing, the disasters continued. He collapsed and fell down the stairs again and at one point was kicked by a cow while he was dozing in a barn. After 19 operations, with rods and screws holding his back together, and with even easy running out of the question, he grew ever more dependent on painkillers. When his father died of cancer, Beardsley scoured the house for any painkillers left unused. The pressure on him grew worse as his son Andy, distressed by his grandfather's death, attempted suicide. When his ransacked supply of painkillers dried up, Beardsley took to writing his own prescriptions, picking them up from a dozen different dispensaries around his home in Minnesota.

He kept his secret hidden, leading a double life, seeming almost as normal as ever. Later, when his doctors found out how much he had been taking, they shook their heads in horror and told him he had been just weeks away from death.

On the morning of 1 October 1996, Dick Beardsley presented a forged prescription at the Walmart Pharmacy in Detroit Lakes, as he had done many times before. The pharmacist was a friend who had been on fishing trips with Beardsley, but he had grown suspicious, and this time the game was up. Beardsley was arrested on narcotics charges and the story made headlines across America.

Beardsley feared he would be sent to prison, but was sentenced instead to detox treatment and lengthy stays in psychiatric hospitals. He said he was relieved to get caught and fortunate to be given help to fight his addiction. His belief that, despite all his troubles, he was lucky even prompted him to write a song about himself while lying on a hospital bed.

'It seemed like every time I walked outside something happened,' he said. 'The song "Lucky" is about how lucky I am to have had the life I have had, the friends I have had, and to have God in my life. I think about that song every day.'

Beardsley is a man who does not give up easily. In 2002 he ran five marathons and in 2003 he ran six – setting a post-accident personal best of 2:45:58 in Toronto. Every September he is the inspiration and organiser of a popular half-marathon in Detroit Lakes.

In October 2004, Dick Beardsley, approaching the age of 49, ran another marathon. It was a small, unheralded race in Mason City, Iowa, called the 'On the Road for

Education Marathon'. The event had been set up by a student as a project to help his school and the local community, and to win the boy the rank of Eagle Scout. The course goes off road, along rough, winding trails beside the Winnebago River.

Beardsley reckoned it was a race and a cause worth supporting, and believed that if his luck held out he might do well in the masters' (over 40) age group. But to his surprise and delight he won. Almost a quarter of a century after his victory in London he was a winner again. This time he'd covered the 26 miles on dirt trails in 2:51:34. Nearly two minutes behind him in second place was a man 28 years his junior.

'A race like that gives you good memories,' said Beardsley, 'and the London gave me some of the best memories of all. I'd love to run it again, everyone there treated me so well, and it was such fun.

'But it's the race I am running every day now that can never be finished,' he added. 'The day I say I've got my addiction beat, I'll be in greater danger than when my leg got caught in that power take-off. I can't let that day come.'

4

You Can't Beat
a Local Hero

*The marathon has everything. It has drama. It has
competition. It has camaraderie. It has heroism. Every
jogger can't dream of being an Olympic champion, but
he can dream of finishing a marathon.*
Fred Lebow

The hand-in-hand finish of the first London Marathon gave
the race a fine and enduring image. But, as the Greeks
found when one of their boys won the first Olympic
Marathon in 1896 in front of more than 60,000 wildly
enthusiastic spectators, you can't beat a local hero if you
want to please the crowd.

No event has sparked as much myth and legend as the
only race that was actually invented for the first modern
Olympic Games in Greece – the marathon. Mystery and
half-truth surround the ancient Greek who inspired the
event, and there are equally mysterious questions hanging
over the performance of the modern Greek who carried off
the first Olympic marathon medal.

Nearly a century later, in 2004, when the Olympic
Games returned to Athens, the opening ceremony was overshadowed by the scandal of a Greek Olympic sprint champion, Kostas Kederis, who failed to show up for a drugs
test. Back in 1896 there were no regulations about drugs and
no drug testing. But there were other ways to cheat in the
struggle for Olympic victory – and there were those who
wonder if the first marathon winner was one of the boldest
cheats of all . . .

*   *   *

The ancient Greeks were no strangers to long-distance running but they did it as a means of communicating, not as competition. They had their Olympic Games, dating back to 776 BC, but they had no endurance event.

They raced in a stadium with long straights, called *stades*, reckoned to measure 192 metres. There were none of the sweeping bends of today's running tracks. To run more than one *stade* the athletes would career around a pole, executing a hairpin turn of 180 degrees to race the straight again. They ran naked and barefoot, kicking up the sand. At the end of the straight they would push, pull and trip opponents as they jostled for the inside position, swinging round as close as possible to the turning pole – which stood on a wide-based plinth to stop them grabbing the pole itself. Their longest race was 24 times the length of the *stade* – around three miles.

But the Greeks did use long-distance foot soldiers as messengers. These were tough, wiry professional runners who could tackle any distance and any terrain. They were essential cogs in the Greek war machine.

One of these messengers, according to legend, a man called Pheidippides, started it all when he ran from the battlefield of Marathon to Athens with news of victory over the invading Persians. 'Rejoice, we conquer,' was the message he was supposed to have gasped, before dropping dead with exhaustion. He had covered around 25 hilly miles on a hot summer's day.

There are certainly records which confirm that at least parts of this story are based on fact. The historian Herodotus (485–425 BC) wrote a detailed account of the Battle of Marathon, but he made no mention of Pheidippides' run. As he was a sort of gossip columnist of the day, with a great eye for detail, it is unlikely he would have failed to include such a colourful story.

He did, however, record that a man called Pheidippides was sent to run the 150 miles across mountainous country from Athens to Sparta to try to enlist Spartan support against the Persians. He covered the distance in well under 48 hours, but what happened to him next is a mystery.

The 25-mile (40km) run from Marathon to Athens actually comes from a separate story related by Plutarch some 600 years later. Plutarch told of a messenger named Eucles who ran to Athens to announce victory. It was Eucles, say modern historians, not Pheidippides, who hit the wall with the words 'Rejoice, we conquer,' before he keeled over and died.

Whatever the truth, it is Pheidippides who is immortalised as the local hero today on the marble stone, just beyond the southern tip of the village of Marathon, which bears the words: 'Starting point of the marathon'.

In 1889, Baron Pierre de Coubertin was commissioned by the French government to report on the state of physical education and sport in the national school system. Out of his research sprang his romantic proposal to reinvent the ancient Olympic Games for the modern world.

In June 1894 an international Olympic Congress was convened to consider the idea. One of its leading figures, Michel Breal, a linguist and historian from the Sorbonne, wrote to Coubertin saying, 'If the organising committee of the Athens Olympics would be willing to revive the famous run of the Marathon soldier as part of the Games, I would be glad to offer a prize for this new marathon race.' The prize, Breal proposed, should be a fine silver cup.

Coubertin delivered the letter to the Greeks, who embraced the idea with patriotic fervour. The official programme for the 1896 Games said that the marathon was 'evidence of the Greek dedication to freedom as a nation and the sacrifice of the individual to maintain that freedom'.

But despite all their enthusiasm for the Games, and for the newly invented 'Marathon race', by the time the runners set off on the 25-mile journey to Athens, the Greeks had won nothing. It was the final event of the Games, and their

last hopes rested on the 14 local heroes selected to represent them from two trial races. There were generous prizes
being dangled to try and guarantee a Greek victory.
Georgios Averoff, the main backer of the Games, offered
his daughter in marriage plus a million-drachma dowry for
the winner, if he were a Greek.

The Greeks needed a victory badly. And they needed a
local hero if they were to salvage any national pride at their
Olympic Games. In Spiridon Louis, it seemed, they had
found the answer to their prayers.

Louis was 24 years old, the son of a working family from
Maroussi, a suburb of Athens. His village was famous as
a fine source of spring water, and twice a day Louis would
accompany his mule as he took barrels of water into Athens
to sell. It was an eight-mile journey each way, and perhaps,
walking or trotting beside the animal, Louis had discovered the perfect method of training.

The fifth day of the Athens Games, marathon day,
dawned in glorious sunshine. Long before the stadium
opened at 10 a.m. the Greeks were out in huge numbers,
abuzz with talk of the race. Every seat was taken and thousands scrambled on to the hills looking down over the
finish, or lined the route of the marathon as it dipped down
into the city. The road itself, between Marathon and Athens,
was narrow, unpaved, rutted and thick with dust.

The day before the main event the contestants had been
taken back along this road to the village of Marathon,
where they had been lodged at inns and houses overnight.
Most of the Greek runners went to a church service on the
morning of the marathon, and the priests offered up prayers
for a home win.

Some of the competitors went for a morning trot to try
out the new shoes they had been given. When they got back
from their warm-up run a doctor tested their reflexes by
tapping their knees with a hammer. They were all judged
to be fit enough to run and they were offered milk and
beer to drink in the hours before the start. The organisers

had also arranged for two soldiers on horseback to accompany each runner, and for horse-drawn medical wagons to follow the field.

There were 18 starters, 14 of them Greek, including Spiridon Louis from Maroussi. Louis had served in the army under Colonel Papadiamantopoulos, the official starter for the race, who had urged his man to take part in the trials for the Greek marathon squad. So keen was the Colonel that he should run that Spiridon had taken part in a last-minute trial just five days before the marathon to secure his place.

With the Greeks were four foreigners – Gyula Kellner of Hungary, Edwin (Teddy) Flack of Australia, Arthur Blake of the USA, and Albin Lermusiaux of France. The Frenchman insisted on running in white gloves – in honour, he said, of the King of Greece. Flack had already demonstrated his talent for the sport by winning the 800m and 1500m, while Blake and Lermusiaux had finished second and third in the 1500m.

A photograph taken as the contestants lined up for the 2 p.m. start shows the runners wearing an odd assortment of singlets, shirts and cloth caps. Children clung to roofs to catch a glimpse of the four rows of strangely dressed men waiting for the Colonel on his horse to fire his pistol. After speeches in Greek and French from the starter, the runners started in bright but cool conditions, with the Frenchman in the white gloves haring off at a crazily aggressive pace.

He was pursued out of the village by Flack, Blake and a group of four Greeks. Flack had planned to run comfortably until about five kilometres from home, then to use his speed to outkick anyone still with him, but Lermusiaux was soon out of sight. After six kilometres Flack decided to speed up rather than lose contact with the leader altogether.

Even so, by the official 15km mark at Pikermi, the Frenchman was three kilometres ahead of the field and was timed at an impressive 52 minutes. Way behind at this stage was Spiridon Louis, who was handed a beaker of wine and a hard-boiled egg by his stepfather to keep him going.

After Pikermi the course starts to climb, and the runners started to wilt. Blake gave up at around 20km, his feet covered in blood. At 25km, at Harvarti, Lermusiaux was the first man through a decorated arch built over the road by the villagers in honour of the runners. But he was paying heavily for his early pace and Flack was gaining on him every minute.

The Greek Louis, though, was reported to be more than six minutes down on the leaders. As they approached the 32km mark, Lermusiaux hit the wall badly and was over-taken by the Australian. Flack now had a very comfortable lead, and with only around six kilometres left in the race a messenger cycled off to the stadium to report that Flack's victory now seemed certain.

But a mile or so later Louis suddenly appeared at Flack's shoulder, looking 'very fresh and running well'. They ran side by side as the road dipped downhill towards the city of Athens, and five kilometres from the finish Louis was handed some slices of orange by the girl he was later to marry.

Then, at almost the same spot where Paula Radcliffe was to give up the chase 108 years later, Teddy Flack ground to a standstill, defeated and broken by the surprising speed and freshness of the Greek, who seemingly had come from nowhere. Flack was disorientated and angry. It was reported that he hit out at a Greek spectator who came to his assistance, believing that he was trying to stop him from continuing.

Back in the stadium, the Greek royal family had arrived early enough to see the first track and field events of the day. The final of the 100m was won by Tom Burke of the USA, the only man to use a crouch start, and the high jump by Ellery Clark, a baby-faced law student, again an American. The crowd of 60,000 were subdued, politely applauding the victories of the foreigners, still unaware that Flack was no longer in the lead.

But even as Flack was being brought to the finish in a hospital wagon, trotting alongside the leader on his white horse was Colonel Papadiamantopoulos, the official starter and the man who had been Louis' mentor. The Colonel offered Louis cognac as he ran, then, as they hit the street that led to the stadium, he leaned down to tell him that he would gallop ahead with the good news.

The shouts of '*Hellene, Hellene!*' (A Greek, a Greek!) rippled around the stadium as soon as the breathless Colonel delivered his message to the royal box.

From outside the stadium a cannon boomed to announce that a runner was in sight, and at two minutes to five, Louis appeared, his white vest with its number 17 drenched in sweat and covered in dust. The crowd erupted. The roars from the stadium were echoed by the thousands perched on the hills outside. Hats were tossed in the air. Flags and handkerchiefs fluttered like doves. Women threw jewellery at Louis like fans at a rock concert, and the Crown Prince Constantine and Prince George leapt from their seats to run alongside the local hero as he strode down the straight to the tape.

His time was 2:58:50. A full seven minutes behind him came another Greek, Vasilakos, to take second place, followed by a third Greek, Belakas. Fourth was the only foreigner to finish, the Hungarian Kellner, who ran in tired and angry, shouting that Belakas had never overtaken him and must have ridden in a carriage, or taken a short cut in the final stages, to have come home third.

The Crown Prince was deputed to sort out the row and rapidly concluded that Belakas had indeed cheated. The Greek was immediately stripped of his third place. Louis, though, was hailed as a hero, and presented with a silver medal, instead of the now traditional gold, and a crown of olive branches.

As he already had a wife in mind, Spiridon turned down the offer of a bride, but he accepted free meals for life, haircuts for life and a plot of land. When asked by the King of Greece what royal reward he would like, he chose a horse and cart to replace his donkey. Spiridon reckoned he'd done enough travelling on his own two feet.

Since his legendary victory there have been plenty of questions about how the local hero managed it. Did the first Olympic marathon champion triumph by cheating?

One afternoon in February 1996 I sat down to lunch with a man named Nicholas Robertson – the grandson of Sir George Robertson, who had competed in the discus in those far-off Olympic Games of 1896.

George Robertson had been 23 at the time of the Athens Games, an Oxford classics scholar and a hammer thrower. There was no hammer at these inaugural Olympics, so he tried his hand at the discus and finished in sixth place. He also composed and delivered an ode in ancient Greek, which won him the prize of a wreath of olive leaves.

Unbelievably, at the lunch table, his grandson produced – now fragile, brittle and browned – the leaves from the wreath won a century before. He also related a rich catalogue of family lore and memories that cast a surprising light on the legend of Spiridon Louis.

George Robertson, a classic Corinthian Oxbridge all-rounder, had not stopped at the discus and Olympic ode competition. He had also entered the tennis, and in this tournament his doubles partner was Edwin Flack.

Edwin 'Teddy' Flack was an Australian accountant based in London. A member of the Thames Hare and Hounds cross-country running club, he had done most of his training on Barnes and Wimbledon Commons and had become the toast of Athens by winning both the 800m and the 1500m. His proven ability to run made him one of the favourites for the marathon, and no one knew Flack's form better than Robertson, who shared a room with him in Athens throughout the Games.

Robertson's grandson had trawled through family memories, postcards and letters home from his grand-father while at the Olympics, and what he'd uncovered cast many doubts on Spiridon's marathon achievement. The half-remembered family accounts of cheating were strengthened by a radio interview recorded on 9 March 1964, between Rex Alston of the BBC and Sir George Robertson, who by then was 91.

'Anyone could enter the Olympics just by showing up,' Sir George told Alston. "As a classics person I thought I had better go and see what they were like. I shared a flat with Flack of Australia and there were some queer stories about the marathon but I don't know if I ought to tell.'

'Oh yes,' urged Alston, 'you tell them.'

'Well, it was a remarkable race. The marathon was accompanied by a lot of Greek officers on horseback. And my friend Flack was accompanied also by the butler of the British Ambassador on a bicycle – you see what a funny sort of a race it was.

'And when they were about three miles from Athens, the butler said, "I think I will go back and see where the others are." And he went back about a mile and there wasn't a soul in sight so he came back to Flack and said, "You'll win this thing on your head."

'And, as a matter of fact, soon after that happened, up turned Louis still running and proceeded to win the marathon. Where he came from none of us had any idea. There was not a soul who could be seen on the road except Flack, and yet he turned up.

'Louis is long dead,' said Sir George, 'and I don't know what the truth of the matter was.'

One man who spent decades searching for the truth was Swiss author and journalist Noel Tamini. He even named a running magazine in honour of Louis. Yet as he studied the Greek water-carrier and his enigmatic running career, Tamini found doubts jogging in the shadow of the legend. In a remarkable article carried in the London Marathon programme in 1997, Noel Tamini, too, questioned the performance of his hero.

There was something strange about this athlete who wasn't an athlete, who appeared out of nowhere, who won this great race and who then never ran another step.

The mystery confronted me again one day in 1986 when a reader of the running magazine I had started in 1972 wrote to me. My magazine was called *Spiridon* in honour of the great man's place in the marathon tradition, so what the reader wrote made me sit up. He had read a book by a French academic, Michel Deon, which reported claims that Spiridon had cheated.

While living in Greece, Deon had met a man from Spiridon's home village of Maroussi who had known the marathon-runner well. The man was a poet, called Katsimbalis, who told Deon that Louis, familiar with the local landscape, had taken a short cut through the forest, followed by six fellow Greeks, and had 'thus crowned the Games with a symbolic victory which linked ancient and modern Greece with a golden laurel wreath'.

Deon asserted that many people in Greece confirmed the rumour. 'Isn't it miraculous,' said Katsimbalis, 'that after Flack had been assured that there was nobody in sight behind him, Spiridon suddenly surged past him? He overcame the deficit in a quite surprising manner. I have to believe there was some cheating at a given point. Louis, though a great walker like all peasants, knew nothing about running or racing. It's a great shame for the honour of the sport which I love, but I know the Greeks too well.'

Robertson and Tamini are not alone in questioning the performance of Spiridon Louis. In August 2004, Althea Richardson revealed that she had her grandfather's handwritten account of the 1896 marathon race and the Athens Olympics, in which her grandfather had taken part in the bicycle race. He wrote that he was:

one of a small band of cyclists who accompanied the runners from the start at the village of Marathon itself to the stadium in Athens. There were also several Greek mounted army officers included in the following. The eventual winner, a fine Greek peasant, was several times assisted by one or other of these officers, who gave him a stirrup to cling to, then setting their horses at a fast trot, helping him along as much as a kilometre at a time.

As far as man can say, and it was also the general opinion at the time, Flack, an Australian, should have won this race as at thirteen kilometres from the stadium was leading strongly, but was caught up by the Greek 'assisted'.

Norris McWhirter, the co-founder of the *Guinness Book of Records*, is another who has pointed a finger at Spiridon Louis, denouncing him as a cheat in his *Book of Historical Records*, published in 2000:

Sir George Robertson was incredulous that Spiridon Louis could have won it. Robertson believed Louis hitched a ride on the stirrup of a cavalry horse. Harold Abrahams conducted an interview with Sir George in 1964 and the truth came out, but Abrahams never published it. Now it is time for the story to come out. I think it's the greatest sports scoop ever.

Whatever the truth, the romantic story of Spiridon Louis was, for many, too good to question. In Athens, George Robertson and Teddy Flack reckoned it would be ungallant to upset their hosts by voicing their suspicions, and the excitement and enthusiasm that surrounded the triumph of the Greek hometown hero meant that the marathon race was taken up and imitated in Europe and America. The first Boston Marathon was run less than a year later, in April 1897, and the inspired innovation of Michel Breal rapidly became a sporting institution.

The Greeks had ached for their Olympic victory, and the world was happy to let them have it. Both the Games and the marathon race were a huge popular success and guaranteed a future by the performance of this unlikely local hero.

5

The Best of British

*All top international athletes wake up in the morning
feeling tired, and go to bed feeling very tired.*
Brendan Foster

There were no short cuts for the runners at the front of
the London Marathon. But by the second race, in 1982,
they had a couple of local heroes of their own.

After Dick Beardsley and Inge Simonsen had crossed the
line together, Squire Yarrow, the race referee, growled to
John Disley, 'If they try that again I'm going to pick a
winner – or disqualify them both.'

But while the men's race was close enough for a dead
heat, the first women's race was by contrast a procession.
At the front was Joyce Smith, a veteran of track and
cross-country racing who had taken the traditional path to
the marathon late in her career. She started out as a school-
girl long-jump champion and won the English National
Cross Country Championships in 1959 at the age of 21.
She made her marathon debut 20 years later with a British
best of 2:41:37.

By the time of the first London Marathon she was 44
years old and a mother of two children, but she ran 2:29:57
for a new British record and a time that put her third on
the world rankings. She came in seven minutes ahead of
the New Zealander Gillian Drake, with Briton Gillian
Adams another three minutes behind in third.

Smith won again in 1982, almost unchallenged in
2:29:43, while London celebrated its first local men's hero
in the marathon, Hugh Jones. He ran a fantastic race to

record 2:09:24, finishing almost three minutes ahead of the Norwegian Oyvind Dahl, with Britain's Mike Gratton in third.

Hugh Jones was a member of the same running club as Chris Brasher, the Ranelagh Harriers, and Brasher had arranged a sponsorship deal for him with New Balance, a sports shoe company. In the hour before the race, according to Jones' coach Alan Storey, the runner agonised over whether to race in the colours of New Balance or Ranelagh Harriers. In the end he pulled on the New Balance vest – $4,000 was a lot of money to an athlete in 1982.

Brasher had also roped in the manager of his sports shop, Grenville Tuck, to make the running over the early miles. But once he dropped back, the red-haired Jones found there was no opposition and ran on alone with 19 miles still to cover to the finish. By the 15-mile mark he was already more than a minute clear, and even today his time looks impressive. 'Since those days we have got rid of some of the bad surfaces such as Wapping High Street with its cobbles,' said John Disley, 'and we have lost probably four or five bad turns. I would think the course is about a minute and a half faster.'

Alan Storey was equally impressed by the performance. 'Maybe Hugh's time was worth 2:08.30 in better conditions in a competitive race,' he said. 'It was good then, and against British standards now it looks formidable.'

Jones, a student at the time of his victory, was straight out of the British harrier tradition. 'I used to run to primary school in north-west London,' he said. 'It was only three quarters of a mile but I did that run four times a day. I did the return journey in double-quick time during the dinner hour. It was a good few years before I realised that this was the basic conditioning that primed me for a lifetime in sport. At the age of 11, in a Boy Scout cross-country race around a windswept reservoir, I finished ahead of older kids without making anything more than a casual effort. It was only then that I knew I had a talent.'

By the time of his marathon win in 1982, Jones was running twice a day – covering 120 miles in the hard weeks and around 90 miles when he wanted to take it easy. Before the London race he had already run for England in the World Cross Country Championships and won the AAA Marathon Championship, where only 65 runners lined up for the start.

The 1982 London Marathon was a huge contrast. 'Vast crowds and TV coverage lent a feverish buzz to the occasion,' said Jones. 'My final burst over Westminster Bridge to the finish was shown on the national evening news.'

These days Jones is General Secretary of the Association of International Marathons and his duties include course measurement around the world. He is also a formidable veteran runner and, like Dick Beardsley, is still winning marathons 25 years on, with a victory in the 2004 Sahara Marathon. In 2003 he popped up as coach to Tony Blair's spin-doctor, Alastair Campbell, helping him complete the London.

'But back in those early days of the 1980s,' said Dave Bedford, 'Hugh Jones was just a university student who turned up to run in the marathon.' Jones was certainly happy-go-lucky and had a refreshingly unsophisticated approach to the problems of distance running. When he was told he had one leg shorter than the other and warned that this could lead to long-term injury, he took himself off to an old-fashioned shoemaker known as John 'the Boot' in Richmond. When you stepped into his repair shop and looked at the endless rows of battered boots and shoes you felt that you had somehow gone back in time. The shop had a wonderful Dickensian feel about it, and you half expected Mr Pickwick to step through the door to see if his shoes were ready yet.

John the Boot, a small man with a twinkle of mischievous energy about him, said that he could solve Hugh Jones' problem by building up one shoe. 'The trouble was that Hugh was a bit absent-minded and very much the amateur.

He'd forgotten which leg was shorter and I built up the wrong shoe. Once we got it right he was flying and I got more runners coming to see me about their shoes than I could keep up with.'

There were more runners everywhere. By 1982 over 10,000 of them had got through the finish of the London Marathon in under four hours, and each year there were thousands waiting to get their hands on a coveted number. In 1984 the organisers took 20,000 entries, in 1986, 25,000, and by 1989 they were accepting more than 30,000 each year.

Brasher and Disley were constantly on the lookout for ways to increase the size of the field. One evening in a Kingston pub, the Duke of Cambridge, Brasher and I, refreshed by a few beers after a run, came up with the craziest solution yet.

We reckoned that since the roads were closed along the route, and since there was some dual carriageway at around halfway, we could have two completely different starts. One half of the field would start as usual at Greenwich; the other half would start at the finish near Buckingham Palace and run back towards Greenwich. One lot would wear red numbers, and the other blue. It seemed a great idea that evening, but in the chill of the morning, even Brasher conceded that the chaos when the two fields met running in opposite directions might cause some problems. The marathon now has three separate starts, the red, the green and the blue, which allows many thousands to get over the start line quickly before the courses merge after three miles.

Up at the front of the London in those early years the hard-training local British heroes kept delighting the London crowds, somehow managing to run great times whilst still holding down full-time jobs.

The 1983 race was won by Mike Gratton, from Gerry Helme, in 2:09.43. 'Work can be a problem,' said Gratton, 'but if someone really wants to get to the top they can organise it. I was a PE teacher and used to run into school in the morning and home to the track in the evening. My Wednesday used to be teaching geography in the morning, the cross-country club at lunchtime, sixth-form hockey all afternoon and then a 15-mile run in the evening. I followed that by a few pints in the Royal Dragoon in Canterbury just to deaden the soreness. I didn't own a car, I just ran everywhere.'

Like Jones, Gratton put in the miles and reaped the rewards, though both of them had to wait a while for the money. They each remember that it took almost a year before they could collect their prize money. 'But that was just the eccentricity of Chris Brasher,' said Gratton.

In 1984, Olympic year, Gateshead's Charlie Spedding won the race and selection for the Olympic Games in 2:09.57. Spedding, a pharmacist from Durham, had taken time out from his career to concentrate on running and work for Nike Sportswear. 'Those were great days for British marathon running,' he said. 'It was only the second marathon I had run and I had also won the first. I suppose I had found my distance.

'In London I planned an even pace to run 2:10, and at Tower Bridge, around 12 miles, I couldn't even see the leaders. I convinced myself they were going too fast and when they started coming back to me I was flying past people. I was running with Kevin Forster, a clubmate, and at about 20 miles we caught the leaders. Then I made one effort and I was away. I ran my race and won $10,000 – more than I had ever won before.'

Victory in London took Spedding to the Los Angeles Olympics, where he won the bronze medal. The following year London still saw the British up front, with an epic duel between Spedding and Steve Jones of the RAF. 'It was just the two of us,' said Spedding. 'We raced each other hell for leather, side by side.'

The official account of the race euphemistically states that 'Jones stopped off briefly to rid himself of stomach cramps.' Spedding recalls that at around 23 miles Jones asked him how he could relieve his bowels, 'although he didn't quite use those words'. 'You'll have to stop, Steve,' said Spedding. Jones slowed but he didn't stop. 'He did what he had to do but kept moving. In years gone by he'd have been beheaded for doing that outside the Tower of London,' said Spedding. In the final mile Jones managed to pull away to win by 17 seconds in 2:08.16, then the fastest time ever recorded in Britain.

It was a triumph for British marathon running, but in the years that followed, local winners were to become an endangered species. The worldwide status of the London Marathon inevitably attracted competitors from all over the globe, and soon the British were finding themselves outgunned by top runners from Japan, Norway, Denmark and Portugal.

In the women's race there hadn't been a British winner since Joyce Smith in 1982. Then, in 1989, there was a victory for 33-year-old Veronique Marot, a Leeds solicitor with a charming French accent and an enchanting habit of lighting the odd cigarette to round off a tough race or training session.

Marot was born in Picardy in France, but took British nationality in 1983 at about the same time she started training for the marathon. She had already dabbled at fell walking, mountaineering and rock climbing. She set a British record in London of 2:25.56, which stood until Paula Radcliffe broke it in 2002.

In 1990, the year after Marot's victory, there was at last another British men's winner when Allister Hutton, a 35-year-old laboratory technician from Edinburgh who had twice previously finished third, demolished opposition that included the world record holder from Ethiopia, Belayneh Densimo, with a brave demonstration of front running.

Hutton's win in 2:10:10 was said to have earned him around $50,000 in prize money and bonuses. He recalls running his race to shouts of 'Come on, Jock!' from characters straight out of *EastEnders*, and the fun there was to be had with his British rivals like Steve Jones and Charlie Spedding.

'We were not really running for money or prizes,' said Hutton. 'You would do your race and you would go and have a drink and a laugh. It was great fun. I remember after the race sitting in the restaurant at St Katherine's Dock overlooking the course. As you sat there with a few beers you knew you'd done your bit, while the poor souls underneath were still plodding on with the race.'

Like Hugh Jones before him, Hutton was coached by Alan Storey, and in 1991 this maker of champions became part of the organising team when he was appointed general manager of the marathon.

Britain's last victory in the men's race to date came in 1993, when 35-year-old Eamonn Martin crossed the line looking less exhausted than his exuberant and excited coach Mel Batty, a former world record holder for 10 miles, whose own liquid replacement regime at the post-race celebration had to be seen to be believed.

On the Thursday morning before the race, Martin had been at the birth of his son, also named Eamonn, but by the Friday he was at a pre-marathon press conference talking confidently of his prospects over 26 miles.

It was Martin's debut at the marathon but he'd served a long apprenticeship as a track runner. He worked full time as a components testing engineer with Ford and so he was delighted when a £250,000 deal was agreed with the marathon sponsors, Nutrasweet, for him to run in the next two London races. It was said that it had taken an extended series of lunches between Bedford and Martin's coach, Batty, to seal the deal and that each lunch took longer than Martin's winning time in the marathon.

But by the time of the tenth anniversary of Martin's win in 2003, it was a very different story. The years that had passed without a win in the men's event were a sad reminder to the organisers that while they might have created the world's greatest mass marathon, the race had failed to achieve

Brasher and Disley's goal of raising the standard of British running. Despite the marathon's huge investment in sport in London, its support of Britain's endurance squad and its financial commitment to a high-performance centre for distance running at St Mary's College, Twickenham, British distance runners were just not winning.

It was so bad that in 2003 one of the fastest Britons lining up in Greenwich on marathon morning was a woman, Paula Radcliffe. 'Maybe it sounds a bit sexist, but how can it be that a woman can run a marathon faster than a man?' asked Bedford. 'It's preposterous. If I were 25 years old again and running and I couldn't beat Paula's time I'd give up. You would think it would spur men on, but if you're only good enough to beat Paula Radcliffe, what good is that? It doesn't say much about you as a British male marathon runner, does it? It embarrasses them and so it should. I'd be embarrassed.'

Chris Brasher agreed. The year before his death he said that the failure of the top British men runners was his greatest disappointment. He accused them of being defeatist, and of convincing themselves that they couldn't beat their African counterparts. 'They've got discouraged by the success of the Africans and they think they can't compete,' he said. 'If you think you can't compete then forget it and do something else. To be a world or Olympic champion at marathon running you have really got to graft. You've got to be mentally and physically tough so that nothing can put you off.'

Brasher and Bedford are part of a chorus of criticism. Eamonn Martin reckons today's runners need more competition – tough cross-country and track races. 'You've got to get out there and learn your trade,' he said. 'The present lot hide. They kid themselves that they're doing lots more training, then they get injured. Athletics is about competition. Some of the present lot run away from it.'

Seb Coe, now Lord Coe, who won two Olympic gold medals in the 1980s, said, 'I am not sure there are distance runners around at the moment who are as emotionally tough and committed as people like Brendan Foster and Dave Bedford. Some of this is psychological.'

Nick Bitel, Chief Executive of the London Marathon, blames the decline in standards on young Britons being unfit and obese.

'Times have certainly changed,' said Hugh Jones. 'Socially things have turned around since people of my age grew up. It's exceptional now for kids to do any sort of exercise and it's that early conditioning as a child that produces runners among adults. I used to run to primary school. In those days most kids would walk it, now every mother drives them.'

Allister Hutton reckons, 'It's just that people are too lazy now to get off their backsides and do hard work. That's the reason we don't have good runners any more in the middle and long distances. The source has just dried up. Nobody is interested in doing the training that's necessary, or even the training we were doing 15 years ago. You have to be hungry for it and that hunger doesn't seem to exist any more. All the best British marathoners of recent years, people like Steve Jones, Charlie Spedding, Eamonn Martin and Liz McColgan, came from a successful background in track. The short answer is that today they're too bloody lazy.'

His fellow Scot, Liz McColgan, who won the London Marathon by over two minutes in 1996, said, 'There is a lack of application, there is nothing fancy or secret about it.'

'Britain just doesn't have the same number of people running endurance events as it used to,' says Alan Storey. 'You need the raw material. Twenty-five years ago the top ten UK clubs would have 10 to 20 runners training twice a day running 100 miles a week. We're nowhere near that figure now. We're not going to have a production line of future marathon stars coming through. That is not to say that Britain can't have a London Marathon winner in the next 10 years. London is won by "freaks" these days and who is to say we can't produce a freak?'

'When there is a British winner,' said Dave Bedford, 'it adds just that edge to it. It gives a real buzz to the race, but we never make it easy for British runners. We don't set it up for local heroes. London has to be as hard to win as the Olympic Games.

'I won't say harder because I think the Olympic Games is a bit of a lottery. London is not a lottery. Everyone knows the conditions, the weather, the course, but every time there has been a British winner it gives me, and the event, an incredible shot in the arm. There's not been a British men's winner since Eamonn Martin, but if you look at the women's race during that same period we have had Liz McColgan from Scotland, and Catherina McKiernan from Ireland. So from that point of view the event hasn't been without serious home interest.

'But when we put the field together it's about trying to create a race. We don't really want pacemakers out there for just one person. The magic of the marathon is that it is a race.'

Mike Gratton sees a glimmer of hope in the performance of Tracey Morris, who, in 2004, broke through in the London from the ranks of the also-rans to win a place on the Olympic team for Athens.

'I think Tracey has possibly started the cure for underperformance in British distance running,' he said. 'If there are enough people out there who think, "If Tracey can do it so can I," then there may be a belief that it is achievable and they will train for it. It's the desire to get to the top that's the problem, not the infrastructure. There hasn't been enough belief that it is attainable and worth the extraordinary effort that is required.'

But the evidence from the mid pack, from the average runners, suggests that standards may have slipped there, too. David Fereday, at the age of 67, is one of that elite, perhaps obsessive, group who've run in every London Marathon. These days there are only 29 of them left.

Fereday hopes to keep at it for at least four more years

and to break four hours at the age of 70. He takes a meticulous, scientific approach to his racing and training, recording every training session and the time of every mile he covers. He produces complicated graphs containing the secrets of his training and his racing hopes. He knows about marathon running – what goes right and what goes wrong.

'One interesting statistic,' he says, 'is how my best time of 2:44 from way back in 1985 compares position-wise today. In 1985 that time placed me 850th in the London. These days that same time would place me much higher, around 250th.

'This represents a dramatic fall in the standard of club runners,' he says, 'and the pathetic standard of our top 5K, 10K and marathon men. The guys just aren't there taking up road-running these days. It's nothing to do with the national governing bodies of the sport,' he adds, 'there just ain't the blokes at the sharp end.

'You go to a road race these days and it seems there's hardly anybody under 40, and only the odd one under 30. There are just loads of grizzled old veterans – and the over-40 age group is usually well outnumbered by the over-50s.

'But then,' he says with a grin, 'what sane individual wants to go through the pain of hitting the wall? It just isn't normal, and as for getting out on the road each night after work to train – I think today's young runners would just say, "Forget it!"'

6

With a Pipe and a Dream

*Chris Brasher has done more for the corporate spirit of
London than anyone since Adolf Hitler.*
Sir Christopher Chataway

The first time John Disley came across Chris Brasher was
in a climbing hut in North Wales. He couldn't see him but
he could certainly hear him.

'I was lying in bed one morning in this hut in Snowdonia,'
said Disley, 'when I was woken up by this disembodied
voice bellowing instructions from the kitchen area on how
to make porridge. It was Chris Brasher. He was a student.
He had just been made president of the Cambridge
University Climbing Club and there he was barking out his
orders to one of his clubmates.

'I realised later that he knew no more than anyone else
about making porridge but what he was doing at breakfast that day with that poor lad was what he was successful
at doing most of his life. He was spelling out right from
the start: I am the boss.'

It was that relentless self-belief that was to be Chris
Brasher's trademark throughout his colourful career.
Decades later the balding, bespectacled Mr Toad-like figure,
polka-dot scarf knotted at the neck, pipe clenched defiantly
in his jaws, was still telling the world to do it his way –
whether it was stirring the porridge or serving up the world's
greatest marathon.

During the course of a routine office row with his editor
at the *Observer*, Donald Trelford, who did so much to back

47

the London Marathon at its birth, Trelford asked Brasher, 'Are you so big-headed because you won an Olympic gold medal, or did you win a gold medal because you are so big-headed?' 'He looked chastened,' said Trelford, 'a rare occurrence. He chewed on his filthy pipe and growled, "Good question, I don't know the answer."

'There was something of the great Victorian about him,' said Trelford. 'A manic energy and bustling single-mindedness that brooked no opposition in pursuit of diverse interests and campaigns that included the environment, mountaineering, fly-fishing, racehorse breeding and the technology of running shoes which, when his firm was bought by Reebok, also made him very rich.'

There were three great achievements in Brasher's life, any one of which would have been enough for most men – setting the pace in the first sub-four-minute mile, winning an Olympic gold medal, and getting the London Marathon up and running. His was a lifetime of improbable achievements as athlete, mountaineer, journalist, environmentalist, businessman.

'Chris was the engine room of the London Marathon,' said Dave Bedford. 'Brasher had all the power and enthusiasm, but when it came to setting up the logistics and overseeing everything, John Disley was the man. They were a great double act.'

The two founding fathers of the London Marathon certainly presented a contrast in style and personality. Disley was modest, methodical, analytical, thoughtful, with the shy introversion of the typical long-distance runner. Brasher was brash, explosive, extroverted, ebullient, imaginative and seemingly over-brimming with self-confidence.

Some loved his roaring log fire of a personality, others were wary of the blazing enthusiasms that could crackle with impossible demands. But whatever you made of this maverick enthusiast, you could never ignore him.

Brasher was born in what is now called Guyana and was first forced to run cross-country at Oakley Hall Prep School, near Cirencester, when all other games were cancelled in the ice-bound winter of 1941. He was seven years old, uncertain, shy and hobbled by a stutter.

'At morning prayers,' he remembered, 'all the boys would sit around and the master would get us to start reading the Bible. Each boy had to read a paragraph. For days I would be terrified by this, trying to imagine what words I would have to read. I kept looking through and looking ahead. I know perfectly the shortest paragraph in the Bible, just two words – Jesus wept. Sadly I never got to read that paragraph, but in any case it would have taken me about four minutes.'

Brasher never completely managed to lose the stutter, but usually he could control it, though once, when he was working for the BBC, it came back. 'I was interviewing the Duke of Windsor,' he said, 'about the eminent heart surgeon Michael Debakey. The Duke had been a patient of Dr Debakey, but when he was answering my first question he stuttered a little. That jolted me back to my school days and I stuttered too. The Duke of Windsor thought I was taking the mickey. He was not amused.'

The stuttering prep school pupil went on to Rugby School, where everyone (including Brasher himself) tipped him to win the famous cross-country race, the Crick. But he lost and the defeat left such a deep scar that plenty of his schoolmates reckoned that losing the Crick run was a key driving force in his subsequent life and character.

Only days before he died at the age of 73, he told me that he failed because of a stomach upset. Wartime rationing meant food was scarce, and an elderly aunt, knowing of the importance of the race, had brought an egg to the school to fortify him. The egg was bad. He ate it anyway, and lost the race.

What Brasher needed was a coach to channel his dogged determination into athletic achievement. In the early 1950s he found one in Franz Stampfl, an Austrian refugee and inspirational motivator who produced champions from running tracks in London for a shilling a session.

'Franz could make you feel anything was possible,' said Brasher, 'and I loved his philosophy of life. If you've got a talent, use it, don't waste it, don't abuse it. Enjoy yourself and never compromise. If you are willing to go out and die, Franz was the man to prepare you.'

Brasher improved steadily as a cross-country runner and a miler while a student at Cambridge, but he hardly looked the part. Clem Thomas, who was to captain Wales at rugby and was Brasher's contemporary at St John's College, described his appearance then as 'a gaunt guy in glasses who looked a real little swot'.

His introduction to the steeplechase, the event that was to take him to the Olympics, came in Greece during an athletics tour with Achilles, the combined Oxford and Cambridge club. 'The track,' he said, 'was just two long straights, ancient Greek style, and you had to career around a statue at each end. I was getting left behind badly at each turn until I realised what the Greek runners were up to. The statues were of naked men, classical heroes, complete in every anatomical detail. If you grabbed the right part you could swing around the statue at great speed. With that technique I could keep up easily.'

Brasher first galloped and huffed into the public consciousness as the unlikely-looking, teeth-gritting pace-maker who led the first 2½ laps of Roger Bannister's history-making sub-four-minute mile in 1954. Bannister generously said he couldn't have accomplished it without his pacemakers and that Brasher and Chris Chataway had done the donkey work. But Brasher always reckoned that the fame that followed left him feeling a bit of a fraud. 'The four-minute mile was Bannister's achievement really,' he said. 'That is why I pushed myself so hard at the Melbourne Olympics two years later. I desperately wanted and needed to prove something to myself.'

For the 1956 Olympics Brasher trained as never before. He gave up cigarettes, girlfriends and climbing. For a year his ambition to do well at the Games became an all-consuming obsession. 'I remember getting my spikes from Sandy Law, a cobbler in Wimbledon,' he said. 'Sandy planed the leather thinner and thinner to make them lighter. "These are only going to last four races," he said. "Take more off, Sandy," and then, "These will only last two races." But I said, "Take more off, Sandy, take more off." Those spikes weighed 3¾ ounces and there was nothing lighter for years. Not until the synthetic materials came along.

'I was determined to leave nothing to chance. I even had contact lenses made in case it rained at the time of the race. They were huge and painful to put in, but it was all part of being ready.'

Six weeks before the Olympics Brasher travelled out to Australia with his friend Chataway. The rest of the Great Britain team would arrive later and have less time to acclimatise. Stampfl was now living and working in Australia, and under his guidance Brasher trained to a peak, running personal bests of 4:06 for the mile and 8:45.6 for two miles shortly before the Games.

But even so, nobody really gave him a chance. He was the third string in the 3000m steeplechase behind John Disley, the 1952 bronze medallist, and Eric Shirley, and Britain hadn't won a gold on the athletics track since 1936.

Before the start, Disley turned to Brasher and said, 'Chris, if I don't win I hope you do.' Disley was not fully recovered from an earlier illness and knew he was not at his best, but Brasher's performance was to amaze him. Against the odds, against the predictions, Brasher, the scrubber, won the gold.

It was a new Olympic and British record. But first Brasher had to survive a protest and a disqualification. He had used his elbows, they said, and impeded another runner. Brasher went straight to the appeal jury and protested. The other athletes said he had won fairly and they would throw their medals back if they were promoted above him.

'Can you imagine that sort of thing happening these days?' asked Brasher. 'But back then nobody had shoe contracts and the athletes could say exactly what they felt.'

After he collected his gold medal – 'Blind drunk,' he said, 'totally blotto from trying to keep up with the British press' – he retired from competitive running and went on to enjoy life in business, in broadcasting and in newspapers (at the *Observer* he was twice voted Sports Journalist of the Year).

In 1959 he married the tennis star Shirley Bloomer, and by the 1960s he was working both for his paper and for the BBC as a reporter on the *Tonight* programme, and then as editor for the BBC's *Time Out* series. Later he was made Head of Features for BBC2. He led an action-packed life as a reporter, taking part in the Monte Carlo Rally, going down the Cresta Run and filming on mountains with the climber Joe Brown.

John Disley, who had finished sixth in that Olympic race, demonstrated his talent for organisation while still in Melbourne by helping to form the IAC – the International Athletes Club. The aim of the club was to break the archaic and paternalistic hold that people like Jack Crump and Harold Abrahams had over athetics in Britain and to improve the lot of the international athlete. In 1959 Disley married the international sprinter Sylvia Cheeseman and subsequently worked as an organiser of outdoor activities and Inspector of Education in Surrey.

It was the sport of orienteering that brought Brasher and Disley back together. Both had tried this new form of running in the forest with map and compass while they were on trips to Scandinavia in the 1950s, and the first public mention of the sport in Britain was probably in an article by Brasher, in the *Observer* in 1957. He wrote: 'I have just taken part for the first time in one of the least known sports in the world. It is hard to know what to call it. The Norwegians call it Orientation . . .'

Disley introduced orienteering into schools in Surrey, but he felt that it needed publicity, so he roped in former international running friends like Bannister, Gordon Pirie, Bruce Tulloh and Martin Hyman to sample it. With the new sport beginning to take off in Britain, Brasher and Disley formed a club called the Southern Navigators and helped to set up the British Orienteering Federation.

In order to popularise the sport in Britain, they pressed for the World Orienteering Championships to be staged in Scotland in 1976. The event took place near Aviemore and was featured in a BBC documentary narrated by Brasher. It was the first event in Britain to use properly prepared professional orienteering maps, and the championships were so successfully organised that they established for Britain a place in the world orienteering scene.

'We got a lot of confidence and a lot of experience from organising those World Orienteering Championships,' said Disley. 'We learned a lot of lessons and a lot of tricks and when it came to putting on a marathon through the streets of London, we weren't the innocents who knew nothing. We knew it could be done and we knew that we could probably do it.'

The two men lived close to Richmond Park and both were back into running with the Ranelagh Harriers, an old established club based at the Dysart Arms in Petersham. There they found their fellow club runners in the bar dreaming and talking of the marathon.

Brasher said he had been fascinated by the marathon ever since he had watched the finish of the race in the 1960 Olympic Games. 'I was standing with the crowd on the Via Appia waiting for the runners in the marathon,' he said. 'I remember two lines of soldiers, one on each side of the road, each soldier carrying a lighted torch. Then out of the darkness came two Africans with Abebe Bikila in the lead – barefoot on the ancient cobbles, just a whisper of feet – an Ethiopian conquering Rome 21 years after Mussolini conquered Ethiopia.

'Almost 20 years later I was in a pub in Richmond with members of my running club and we were talking about the New York Marathon. I told them I would never run a marathon, it was far too boring. But the others said it was amazing, and that the crowd in New York just wouldn't let the runners stop. I reckoned I'd better see for myself, so there and then we decided that we would run a tour to the 1979 New York race.'

Always a man of fierce and sudden enthusiasms, Brasher simply fell in love with the marathon as he ran through the streets of New York. It was a new affair, a new passion. He became obsessed with its legends, its lore, its characters, its demands – and how it might offer the perfect way to slake the thirst for adventure that he believed everyone ought to have.

The article he wrote for the *Observer* on 28 October 1979 on his return from New York was a long and passionate love letter.

It is mad for an overweight, middle-aged matron to attempt the toughest event in the athletic calendar. And yet there were matrons and maidens, old men and young boys, doing just that: over 11,000 of them running 26 miles, 385 yards through the streets of New York and another 7,500 running the same distance through the streets of Chicago – all on the same Sunday in October.

For mile after mile the route is yards deep in spectators. It is like running through the nations of Europe. There are Scotsmen and Irishmen, Scandinavians and Spaniards, a full mile of Hasidic Jews in formal black coats, wide-brimmed toppers, beards and ringlets – men and boys, but few women or girls.

At the eight-mile mark I overtook a dinner-jacketed waiter carrying a tray with a bottle of Perrier water steady as a rock. He can't be running the whole distance, I thought. But he was and he did.

And so to the throbbing music of Harlem, and into Fifth Avenue and a lovely smile from a big black gentleman, and a dazzler from a dazzling girl. Ahead are the soaring towers of Manhattan and the sun is in your face burning up the day, broiling the tarmac.

You know now that you will indeed make it to the finish in Central Park at the Tavern on the Green.

And what a welcome it is. I have heard the crowd shouting Sir Gordon Richards home in the Derby; the roar of the winning goal at Wembley; Olympic chants in four continents; but I have never heard such fervour as came from that crowd who cheer you as you approach the finish of the New York City Marathon.

Last Sunday millions of us saw a vision of the human race happy and united, willing their fellow human beings to a pointless but wonderful victory over mental doubts and bodily frailty. I wonder whether London could stage such a festival?

Brasher and Disley worked hard at picking the brains of the New York Marathon's mastermind, a Romanian immigrant named Fred Lebow. His first New York race in 1970 attracted 126 starters, only 55 of whom finished the four-lap course around Central Park. Lebow funded these early races out of his own pocket, even buying cheap wristwatches for prizes.

When the idea of a marathon through the five boroughs of New York was first suggested to Lebow in 1975 he was completely opposed to it. He thought it could never happen. It would cost too much, he said, the police would never wear it, it was an exercise in futility.

But despite his objections, all the necessary sponsorship money was drummed up and police co-operation was guaranteed. Local politicians wanted it to be part of New York's celebration of America's bicentennial in 1976. The marathon that flowed through every borough of New York proved to be a tremendous success, and each year thereafter the numbers who ran and the crowds who watched grew greater.

Back in Britain, Disley produced the draft of a course, a route that used the Thames as a handrail. 'It started in one hemisphere and ran into the other,' he said, 'and took in plenty of historical landmarks. It came down the Royal Mall, curled in front of Buckingham Palace and finished on Constitution Hill.'

The key to getting the enterprise approved was the police, who had to agree to close London streets for the best part of the whole of Sunday. Once permission was obtained, the enthusiasm began to pick up. 'Mind you, we thought at one point we'd have to remortgage our houses to pay for it,' said Disley. 'But once Gillette came in as a sponsor, money was no longer the problem.'

Money, though, was to become a problem again just two years later. In 1983 there was a major storm over the race being used to exploit Brasher and Disley's commercial interests. Towards the end of the 1970s, on the back of their orienteering ventures, they had formed a company, Fleetfoot, to distribute New Balance running shoes in Britain, and Brasher's name in particular became synonymous with the brand.

In the envelope that went out to all race applicants for the London Marathon in 1983 there were two leaflets: one of these gave details of entry, and the other advertised New Balance shoes. Both leaflets were signed by Brasher and Disley. There were plenty who thought this was sharp commercial exploitation, though in fact the company had bid for, and won against competition, a two-year contract with the London Marathon to include a catalogue in the mail-out. But it was a disaster in terms of personal public relations and left Brasher and Disley open to attack.

Investigative journalist Duncan Campbell produced a virulent article in the *New Statesman*, which called into question Brasher and Disley's commercial involvement in the race, and Channel 4 television made allegations of malpractice.

Brasher and Disley came out fighting fiercely to defend their reputations, and when the legal case was settled Channel 4 was £2 million poorer – £380,000 was awarded jointly to Brasher and Disley and costs were reckoned to be more than four times greater. Brasher used some of the money to treat himself to a racehorse.

There are many who believe that the real root of the court case was Brasher's mercurial personality. Campbell certainly found him 'abrasive', and Brasher upset plenty of people with his explosive style of man management. But others point out it was his refusal never to take no for an answer that was the key to Brasher's achievement. 'He had a will-do attitude,' said Nick Bitel, the Chief Executive of the London Marathon. 'If he thought it was right he would do it and get it done. Without those qualities the marathon could never have happened.'

While Fred Lebow is remembered in New York with a statue, Brasher never accepted the knighthood that many thought he deserved. He was offered it while Margaret Thatcher was Prime Minister, but turned it down because, he said, 'that woman never did anything for sport'.

'The success of the marathon,' said Brasher, 'is that at the finish, when it's all over, all the peripheral stuff will be forgotten and a competitor will say, "Christ, that was good." But if you want to achieve that for him or her, if you want to know that the organisation really is good, if you want to know what are the highs and the lows, then you've got to get in and run it yourself.

'That's how you'll discover something new about yourself, about who you are and how you perform when your body and your soul are challenged. That's why I had to run it myself. It made me realise, when I did the marathon, that "ordinary people" are really "extra-ordinary".

'Apart from helping to bring up my family,' said Brasher, 'the marathon is the most satisfying thing I have ever been involved with. I remember when my daughter Kate ran to raise money for the Great Ormond Street Children's Hospital. She had been working very hard at her job, about 110 hours a week, and I knew she hadn't trained properly. I was very worried about her. At the end of the race I went out on to Westminster Bridge looking for her, but there wasn't a sign.

'I wandered down through Parliament Square towards Birdcage Walk and there were all these people staggering home in the last stages of total exhaustion. They had pain written all over their faces, but they came swerving across the road to shake my hand. "Thank you," they said, "thanks for giving us the chance to do this." To tell you the truth I was in floods of tears. Then at last I found Kate and she was fit and fine. You'd give a lot for a memory like that.'

Chris Brasher died in February 2003 – not, as his friends would have expected, by falling off a mountain or nodding off at the wheel of a car after some crazy outdoor adventure, but in his bed, of cancer. Before the start of the 2003 race there was a short silence in his memory. His son, Hugh, lined up at the start alongside Chris Finill, a man who had run in every one of Brasher's marathons. It was a poignant moment.

In that year's London Marathon, as a tribute, I adorned the back of my running vest with the words 'This One's for Chris Brasher'. I'd underestimated the reaction I would get from fellow runners. All through the race they were slapping me on the back as a gesture of solidarity.

I had so many slaps that I finished the race with a bruised back. It was the most unusual running injury I had ever had, but it showed the deep affection these thousands of runners had for the man who had turned his dream into an institution. It was one athletic injury that would have left Chris Brasher himself chuckling with delight.

7

Miles Too Far

*It is horrible, yet fascinating, this struggle between a set
purpose and an utterly exhausted frame.*
Sir Arthur Conan Doyle

You can blame Britain and history for the distance.
Remember that when you hit the wall on the streets of
London.

The marathon really arrived with the London Olympic
Games of 1908, thanks in large part to the first great and
dramatic image of the modern sporting era. A photograph
that defined the marathon for decades to come captured
the desperate struggle for survival of the first runner to
enter the stadium in those Games – Dorando Pietri.

The photo shows a diminutive, mustachioed Italian, staggering on the track, dazed, bewildered, hardly conscious,
in baggy shorts and white vest, his hair grey with dust.
Alongside him, a group of officials in straw boaters, and
policemen in their tall helmets, crouch with hands stretched
like fielders on a cricket pitch, ready to catch him should
he fall again.

Dorando, a confectioner from Carpi, near Modena in
northern Italy, and a self-trained runner, caused what was
to be one of the greatest marathon sensations of all time
with his dramatic collapse. In the debate that followed,
many wondered whether the marathon was truly a man-
killer – whether the distance really was too far.

The last few yards of 'Dorando's distance' were what
had nearly killed him, and it was this marathon, run in
London on Friday 24 July 1908, that was the first ever to

take place over the now familiar 26 miles, 385 yards, or its metric equivalent – 42,195 metres.

The Olympics should have gone to Rome in 1908, but the eruption of Mount Vesuvius in 1906 plunged Italy into an economic slump, and the Olympic Committee turned to Britain to stage the Games. The prospect of a marathon being run in London prompted a series of self-styled 'marathon' races and trials to determine who should be picked to represent Britain. The first of these was in March, over about 20 miles, and organised by Salford Harriers. There were further trials in Liverpool, and in the Midlands, where runners had to cover around 25 miles in a race organised by Birchfield Harriers.

In the south, the marathon trials were organised by the Polytechnic Harriers and South London Harriers, and what was probably the most important one was held on 25 April 1908, in pouring rain which turned to snow, over 22 miles, 1,420 yards, from Eton to Wembley. Every time the 'marathon' was run, the distance was different. There was no fixed length in Britain or anywhere else. The Olympic marathon races of 1896, 1900 and 1904 were all run over approximately 24 to 25 miles, and the distance planned originally for the 1908 marathon was close to 25 miles. But it was then that royalty took a hand in shaping sporting history.

The Princess of Wales thought it would be fun for the royal children, who had a birthday party planned for marathon day, to watch the start of the Olympic race. The original start was scheduled to be in Eton High Street, 25 miles west of the White City Stadium in Shepherd's Bush, but it was now moved to the east lawn of Windsor Castle, adding to the distance, so that the royal children could have a good view. The finish was moved too, so that the runners would grind to a standstill right in front of Queen Alexandra as she sat in the Royal Box. In all, with the extra yards served up to amuse the royal children and the Queen, the distance added up to a painful 26 miles, 385 yards.

This extra mile and a bit, tacked on by royal command, was to prove too much for Dorando. But when the Olympic Committee eventually decided, in 1920, to set an official length, the 1908 distance was the one they settled on. So the marathon distance in the Paris Games of 1924, the *Chariots of Fire* Olympics, was 26 miles, 385 yards, and marathoners have struggled in the footsteps of Dorando ever since.

The runners lined up for that first London marathon in 1908 on a glorious hot July afternoon, perfect for a royal birthday party, but, with temperatures in the eighties, not so good for a marathon. There were 56 starters and they were glad to get out of the cramped stationmaster's office at Windsor railway station where they had changed. Many of them wore hats to keep off the sun, and most doffed them respectfully to the royal onlookers.

Princess Mary raised a hand to signal readiness to Lord Desborough, Punting Champion of All England and the organiser of the Games, who sat in his open Bentley. Desborough rose to his feet in the car, fired his pistol and, watched by four princes and two princesses, the field was on its way.

Dorando's day had begun with a larger breakfast than usual in an attempt to build up his strength. This meal of beefsteak and coffee he was later to blame in part for his collapse. The Italian was given little hope by the sporting press and it was quite a surprise when he reached the stadium ahead of all his competitors in a state of complete exhaustion. One eye-witness wrote:

> It was a spectacle the like of which no man living had ever seen, and that none who saw it expect ever to see repeated. The race itself with 56 of the best men, winnowed from the runners of four continents competing; the arena where it was finished, in the presence of an enormous assemblage with the Queen of England, the royal representatives of several nations,

and hosts of finely dressed men and women from the most fashionable circles of Europe as well as several thousand Americans; and the dramatic and exciting denouement at the end; combined to make it a historic day.

Officially the Olympic race was won by John J. Hayes, of the United States. But the hero of the day, and the man whose name will always be connected with that London marathon of 1908, was the Italian 'Dorando'.*

The contemporary press accounts are nothing if not colourful. The *New York Times* reported that:

The admiration and sympathy of every person in the stadium went out to the gallant Italian who, although he did not win, deserved to win and did more within the limit of his powers than any other man who ran. The crisis in a battle on which the life of a nation hung could hardly have been more impressive than Dorando's entrance into the stadium.

Ten minutes before the megaphone announced 'The runners are in sight', guns had proclaimed the arrival of the leaders at the nearest station of the course. An intense silence overhung the stadium, while thousands awaited breathlessly the approach of the first man.

For ten minutes all eyes were focused on the gate almost directly opposite the royal stand where the contestants were to enter. Finally, after what seemed to be an intolerable suspense, a runner staggered down the incline leading to the track. He was clothed in a white shirt and red knee-length trousers. He stood for a moment as though dazed and then turned to the left, although a red cord had been drawn about the track in the opposite direction for the runners to follow.

*In fact Dorando was his Christian name and Pietri his surname, but in the programme the Olympic authorities wrongly named him as P. Dorando.

It was evident at once to everyone that the man was practically delirious. A squad of officials ran out and expostulated with him, but apparently he was afraid that they were trying to deceive him and fought to go to the left.

At length he turned about and started on the right path along the track. Then followed an exhibition never to be forgotten by those who witnessed it. Dorando staggered along the cinder path like a man in a dream, his gait being neither a walk nor a run, but simply a flounder, with arms shaking and legs tottering.

People had lost all thought of his nationality, and partisanship was forgotten. They rose in their seats and saw only the small man clad in red knickers, tottering onward, with his head so bent forward that his chin rested on his chest. They knew nothing of him as he had not been mentioned among the probable winners, but they realised that his struggle must have been a terrific one to bring him right to the threshold of victory.

Over the 300 yards that Dorando had yet to cover he fell a total of five times, and repeatedly, after the doctors had poured stimulants down his throat, he was dragged back to his feet. Finally he was pushed across the line with one man at his back and another holding him by the arms. While this extraordinary scene was being played out, the American Johnny Hayes entered the stadium in a comparatively fresh state and was trotting towards the finish. In fact he finished less than a minute behind Dorando, but in the tumult and excitement of the moment he failed to get even from his own countrymen the reception he might have expected.

Dorando was sufficiently recovered on the evening of the race to talk to the press about his collapse and disqualification following a protest from the Americans. He said, 'I felt all right until I entered the stadium. When I heard the crowd cheering I knew that I had nearly won. A thrill passed through me and I felt my strength going. I fell down and tried to struggle to the tape but fell down again. I never lost consciousness of what was going on, and had the doctor had not ordered the attendants to pick me up, I believe I could have finished unaided.'

Dorando's collapse was certainly dramatic and sudden – and something of a mystery. Had he merely hit the wall, or were there other, more sinister, factors?

In 1956 the family of Jack Andrews, the Clerk of the Course in 1908, revealed that he had written his own account of the affair, but his notes had never been published. Andrews claimed that at least two people had seen Dorando taking drugs – strychnine and atropine – during the race. Four years later veteran athlete Joe Binks said that Dorando had stopped at several refreshment stalls along the route and 'gargled with chianti'. Just outside the stadium, and three minutes ahead of anybody else, Dorando, it was said, shared a bottle of wine with his coach. Binks noted, 'Dorando was already suffering from heat exhaustion and the effect of the wine knocked him bow-legged.'

Hayes, the actual winner, ran a very cautious race. He started slowly and ran steadily for the first 19 miles (30km), at which point he pushed into third place behind the South African Hefferon. At Wormwood Scrubs, Dorando was 3½ minutes ahead of Hefferon, who was in turn 2½ minutes ahead of Hayes. But by then both the Italian and the South African were limping badly, while Hayes was comparatively fresh and still running strongly.

When the American reached the long level of the Scrubs, through which the runners made their way along cow paths, he could see the two leaders ahead of him but he could also see them limping. He picked up the pace, and before he was through Wormwood Scrubs, he had overtaken the South African and made quite an inroad into Dorando's lead. After the race Hayes said, 'I took nothing to eat or drink on the journey. I think to do so is a great mistake. Before starting I partook of a light luncheon consisting of two ounces of beef, two slices of toast and a cup of tea. During the race I merely bathed my face with Florida water and gargled my throat with brandy.'

There was little doubt that the collapse of Dorando at the finish was quite the biggest sensation of the 1908 Games, and at an official banquet for foreign representatives and the Council of the Olympiad in the Grafton Galleries that same night, it was announced by Lord Desborough that Queen Alexandra had expressed a desire to present a cup to Dorando as a mark of her appreciation for his splendid performance. This announcement was greeted with great cheers, as was also Lord Desborough's glowing tribute to the Italian.

The news seemed to be taken rather well by Dorando, too, as he was reported that same night to be making a rapid recovery, despite his collapse, and getting himself fit and well enough to be able to attend the stadium the following day to receive the cup from the Queen.

Johnny Hayes, the official winner, returned to the United States a hero. He had been employed at Bloomingdale's department store in New York, where he did much of his training on a specially constructed cinder track on the roof of the store. When he got back with his Olympic gold medal, he was promoted to manager of the sporting goods department.

In a rematch between Hayes and Dorando over the same distance in the United States shortly after the Games, Dorando won a very close race by about 80 yards in 2:44:20, more than 10 minutes faster than Hayes' victory in London. This race was run indoors on a track at Madison Square Gardens and consisted of more than 260 laps.

Dorando went on to complete a long career as a professional marathon runner, winning many thousands of dollars, mainly in America. The romantic appeal of his collapse at the finish of the London Marathon was such that it was even celebrated in a popular song by Irving Berlin.

Until the end of his life, one of Dorando's most treasured possessions was the gold cup presented to him by Queen Alexandra at the prompting of Sir Arthur Conan Doyle, the creator of Sherlock Holmes. The cup is now in a museum in his home town of Carpi. Conan Doyle was a great fan of athletics and organised a collection to pay for the trophy. The cup itself was a replica of the one awarded to the Olympic victor, and the inscription read simply: 'To Pietri Dorando, in remembrance of the marathon race from Windsor to the Stadium, July 24 1908, from Queen Alexandra'.

Such was the outcry that followed Dorando's collapse that the very first spectacular London marathon might easily have been the last. One newspaper report declared, 'It is a question whether public opinion will ever support another marathon race in Britain. Dorando's condition when he finished, and the condition of many of the contestants in today's event, may lead people to think it is worse than prize fighting or bull fighting.'

But the marathon did survive, with a twin legacy from those London Games of 1908 – a distance fixed at 26 miles, 385 yards, and an image fixed in the popular imagination of a feat almost beyond human capability. To tackle something like this around the streets of London after Dorando's performance, you clearly had to be superhuman, brave, obsessive and not a little crazy.

8

The Magnificent Obsession

*The day I retire is the day they drop me
into the fire or bury me.*
Ron Hill

If you think you are obsessive about the marathon, can you remember the last time you took a day off? Ron Hill can. It was 20 December 1964. He has not missed a day's training since.

Christmas Days, birthdays, holidays – for 40 years they have all been running days for him. The last time he had a day without a run, the Tokyo Olympics had just ended and the House of Commons voted to abolish the death penalty.

Hill is a marathon-runner, one of the greatest this country has ever produced. He's nearing 70 now, but when his legs were nearly new he made it to three Olympic Games. He was twice the England Cross Country Champion, he won gold medals in the marathon at the European and Commonwealth Games. He was the only Briton to win the Boston Marathon and he set world records for 10 miles, 15 miles and 25 kilometres.

At the Boston Marathon in 1970, Hill smashed the course record by more than three minutes with 2:10:30. The following July he won the Commonwealth Games marathon in 2:09:28 – at that time the second fastest marathon ever.

'On 21 December in 1964 I set out on what I call a streak,' said Hill. 'My mission was simple. It was to make myself the best athlete I could and to push my physical capabilities to the very limit. In dictionary terms a streak is usually associated with people taking their clothes off and running across the pitch at big sporting events, but tucked away among the dictionary definitions is a more appropriate meaning to which my streak refers. It's "to move forward quickly".

'My streak has come to mean the number of consecutive days running – and my streak is now a recognised Guinness world record.'

Hill first started to keep a serious training log on 3 September 1956 while he was still at school. By 1963 he noted that there were only six days in the year that he hadn't run. 'I was disappointed at the Tokyo Olympics in 1964 when I came nineteenth in the marathon,' he said. 'So I decided to get tough with myself. If I was to fulfil my potential as an athlete I was going to have to get well and truly stuck in and not miss a single day in training.

'On Christmas Eve 1964 I started a twice-a-day and once-on-Sundays streak. That lasted 26.2 years, ending on 6 March 1991. Since then I have carried on running at least once a day and I don't intend to stop. Now I run 30 miles a week with an average of around 4½ miles a day.' Hill had clocked up over 145,000 miles by the fortieth anniversary of his streak in December 2004.

These days Hill even gives lectures on the subject of 'keeping your streak alive', though he always denies that there's anything obsessive about his behaviour. 'Some people, though, think I'm completely mad,' he admits.

Today Ron Hill's face is fuller and more deeply tanned than in the years of gold medals and records. It's deeply etched with the miles of a man who never misses his daily run. He shrugs off illness and injury as if they simply don't exist. Nothing stops him.

He has run with a plaster cast on his foot, and noted in his training diary that he had a broken shoulder merely to point out that the pain came not so much from the running as from lifting his arm high enough to press the button of his stopwatch. Every step has been timed, every session logged; every entry in his neat diaries is evidence of a man in the grip of a deep obsession.

There was the time that Hill had to have surgery on a knee so swollen that it took an hour of warming up to get it to bend. He ran the morning of the operation, of course. The day after, without telling his doctors, he dragged his heavily bandaged leg out for a one-mile shuffle. Three weeks later a doctor doubted if he would ever run on the knee again, 'but I was already up to three miles twice a day,' Hill said. 'I just hadn't told him.'

Crazy and painful – but the unbroken sequence of training endured. Then there was the head-on car crash. 'I was driving on a narrow road when a car coming towards me tried to overtake on a blind bend,' Hill said. 'My car was a write-off. I broke the sternum bone in my chest and my heart was bruised. Fortunately I had already run that morning.

'The hospital released me next day because my wife and my mother were home to look after me, but as soon as they went shopping I was able to sneak out, find a flat stretch of road and hobble a 12-minute mile. Nobody knew I was running for a week.'

He has hopped off trains to run on platforms, and left planes in Paris, Alaska and Tokyo to squeeze in runs between flights. 'Once on the way back from Haiti at a stopover in Barbados they called my flight while I was out running. My wife had to board without me. They were on the tarmac taxiing for takeoff when I reappeared.

'When the morning comes that I can't run any more I'll be dead. Why should people have to stop doing things? I've had to change my ideas and it's taken me a long time to learn because I always thought I was immortal. I thought the body would just heal itself. But there's nothing in the world that says you have to stop doing something because you're 60, is there? People make themselves old by thinking they're old.'

Here is Ron Hill logging a typically defiant training report in 1986:

> My right knee is sore, my left hamstring hurts, my lower back sometimes cracks giving me shooting pains down my legs and most worrying of all, I have this ache in my lower abdomen which I've had for nearly three months. The most likely explanation seems to be a hernia. That could mean a knife job and the end of my streak. So I run on, managing the pain and hoping that one day it will go away.

Somehow through all this, Ron Hill has still found time for work and a happy married life with his wife, May. She fuels his obsession with home-made fruit cake but so strongly disapproves of his running while injured that he sometimes has to hide from her to get out on the road. In the 1980s, Ron Hill Sports was a highly successful business, developing and selling shoes and equipment until the recession bit and the company became overstretched. As the debts mounted Hill's weight dropped from 9½ to 8½ stones. In the end he had to sell the name to another manufacturer to stave off bankruptcy, and using his PhD in textile chemistry he has gone on to set up other businesses dealing in running books and equipment.

So why does Hill go on running so relentlessly now that his glory days are over? What drives him on to perpetual motion? The secret of his obsession may well lie in his earliest sporting inspiration. Hill's boyhood hero was not some famous international star, but a fictional character from a comic strip.

The man who fired his imagination was Alf Tupper, 'the Tough of the Track', who defied all-comers every Thursday in the pages of a popular boys' comic, *The Rover* – living off fish and chips, training in the dark and rain, keeping his tattered kit in a brown paper carrier bag, and above all, never giving up.

'He was the sort of character I could admire,' Hill said. 'An underprivileged lad who could always beat the toffee noses from Oxford and Cambridge. Whatever went wrong he always succeeded and won through because of his own determination.

'From the very start of his career to the finish, Alf Tupper never aged. He set my imagination alight. Everything was against Alf. He lived on disused barges and under railway arches. He trained at night in dimly lit streets and along canal banks.'

Hill's own childhood was spent in the narrow terraced streets of Accrington in Lancashire, and in his imagination he would emulate Alf Tupper, daring to match strides with top Olympic athletes.

Away from the quiet terraced streets, Hill found himself finishing in front of one of the biggest crowds of his life in his first ever marathon. 'It was the Liverpool City Marathon in 1961,' he said. 'There were 51 entrants and I managed to win it. The finish was fantastic because it was at Anfield, the home of Liverpool Football Club, in front of a capacity crowd who were there for a pre-season friendly game. Of course there were no real crowds out on the course but in the London Marathon the crowds are second to none.

'There's a magic about the London Marathon and I've always regretted that I deliberately missed running in the first one. I couldn't see a British marathon ever providing the atmosphere and excitement of a Boston or a New York, but I was wrong.

'I've run in it since and the magic is in the huge size of the field, the London Marathon route itself and the wonderful crowds that line every mile. The crowds are noisiest where they are most needed over those last four miles. When you hear all those spectators, the legs seem lighter and pride somehow speeds up your pace.

'When I ran the London slowly I seemed to be taking part in some mammoth reunion. Everybody knows me and

I know almost everyone else, at least by sight. I was able to pass runners all the way to the finish and short conversations helped the time pass easily. I came across people I had not seen for ages, people I thought had retired years ago. When it comes to marathons, I've seen them all from Turkey to Tokyo, but the London is one race I wouldn't want to miss for any of them.

'The London Marathon is inspiring,' says Hill, 'and inspiration is what first starts people running. Anything is good if it sparks an individual into pulling on a pair of running shoes and experiencing that sense of freedom and independence which only running can give you. For me the inspiration was from quite an unusual hero, and at the age of 13 or 14 I joined my local running club Clayton-le-Moors Harriers.

'Everyone,' Hill reckons, 'needs a dream,' and more than half a century on you get the impression that there is some part of Ron Hill that is forever Alf Tupper.

By the time he turns 70, Hill plans to have competed in 100 different countries. He still protests that he's not obsessive – 'just determined'. He had to be very determined a decade ago when his streak seemed certain to be doomed – by a bunion. 'I had to have it operated on, which meant six weeks in plaster,' he said. 'But my son picked me up from hospital and we went straight to the running track. With a couple of sticks I was able to do a mile, though it was difficult to get the running action going.'

Even the creators who dreamed up Alf Tupper would not have dared this story line, but for six weeks Hill did a mile every day with one foot in a plaster cast. Somewhere during those never-ending miles this remarkable athlete had actually transformed himself into the Tough of the Track.

For a while in my running life I, too, went on a streak. I clocked up 12 years without missing a single day and my boyhood hero, too, was straight out of the pages of comic-book fiction. Wilson of *The Wizard* was one of the great inspirational record-setters of all time.

He was unreal, of course, just a fictional character who romped through the pages of another schoolboy comic in the late 1940s and 50s. I still have a battered volume, its pages faded and browning, splendidly titled *The Truth About Wilson*, by W.S.K. Webb. It was a spin-off book from the weekly serial stories in *The Wizard*. It was bought second-hand for a few pence in the 1960s, and told of the exploits of the character who inspired the dreams of many a schoolboy champion. Wilson was a slight, wiry figure in an old-fashioned black running costume who, according to Webb, 'smashed athletic records like cheap crockery and set standards which will never be equalled let alone surpassed'.

While Wilson's records would have left contemporary sporting pundits scoffing, time and the unstoppable desire of athletes to be faster and stronger mean that even the fairy-tale exploits of Wilson have now become reality.

Take Wilson's first great performance – the mile at Stamford Bridge when he threw off his overcoat and boots and barefoot leaped the trackside barrier to take on a world-class field. Officials looked on helplessly as he reeled off laps in 57 seconds and broke the tape in an unbelievable new world record of 3:48 which everybody supposed would stand for ever. By 1981, however, the real-life Sebastian Coe was running 3:47.33 for the mile, and in 1999, Morocco's Hicham el Guerrouj ran 3:43.13.

It is a great credit to Webb that, however fantastic Wilson's records seemed at the time, they were all realistic enough to come under attack within 30 years. Webb was prescient about the questions that might be asked today after such seemingly superhuman performances. 'I use no drugs or dope,' Wilson said when challenged about his methods, though even in the late 1930s his fictional opponents were already at it.

What Wilson was on, however, was an amazing mixture of herbs. He lived as a hermit, sleeping rough on the Yorkshire moors, and his diet included witch hazel, atropa belladonna, saxifraga, willowherb and digitalis. His spartan, secluded life was in sharp contrast to the style of Ron Hill's great comic-book idol Alf Tupper. Tupper was far more the urban athlete. His greatest feats were achieved after a factory night shift followed by a breakfast of fish and chips, after which he would crush some cheating swarthy foreign competitor, or better still a smooth university type.

Intriguingly, of all Wilson's fictitious records, the marathon is the one that has been left the furthest behind. When he took on the finest the world could offer at a marathon in Athens, Wilson finished well over a mile ahead of his fictional rivals in what was then a world-shattering time of 2:22. In the real world this record fell to Jim Peters, who ran 2:20:42.2 as long ago as 1952. Wilson's best would have placed him well over a mile behind Paula Radcliffe when she ran 2:15.25 in the 2003 London.

The great Wilson was always extremely cagey about his age – for very good reasons, it turns out. As Squadron Leader W. Wilson, DSO DFC and Bar, he was last heard of when shot down as a Spitfire pilot over the English Channel during the Battle of Britain. At the outbreak of war he had been about to reveal his greatest secret of all, that he had found the elixir of life. He realised, however, that to do this he would have to publish his age, which would have ruled him out as a pilot in the RAF. His dark secret was that his date of birth was 1 November 1795.

This meant that he ran his 2:22 marathon when he was around 140 years old. At least that looks certain to be one world record that will never be broken. Unless, of course, Ron Hill manages to keep his streak going.

I discovered that behind these two comic-book heroes there was another astonishing story of obsession. Amazingly, the sporting world's two greatest fictional athletes were found to have been related all along. For they were creations of the same man. The mysterious W.S.K. Webb who brought both Wilson and Tupper's adventures to the world was the pen name of Gilbert Lawford Dalton, a jobbing journalist turned author, born in Leominster in 1903.

The amazing Dalton, who would send off his stories a dozen at a time to his publishers, D. C. Thomson in Dundee, turns out to be almost as astonishing as the great Wilson or Alf Tupper. Dalton's output was prodigious. In a six-week period in 1949, for instance, he wrote 316,000 words of serial fiction, one novel of 80,000 words and three episodes of a radio serial – some 400,000 words in all. A single story for, say, *The Wizard*, featuring the great Wilson, averaged 5,000 words, and Dalton is on record as having completed one such in two hours and twenty minutes.

The true legacy of Wilson, Alf Tupper and Dalton, their creator, could be seen in the packs of boys, the next generation of obsessives, who would try out their plimsolls and their dreams on roads and cinder tracks in the 1950s and 60s.

Many have wondered what it is that makes running quite such an obsessive pastime. One popular theory is that runners simply get hooked on painkilling chemicals, very like opium, that are pumped automatically into the body when an athlete takes exercise. It's a sort of auto drug addiction. After 15 minutes or so of running, the body releases natural opiates that not only kill pain but produce pleasure.

Dr Ian Cockerill, a psychologist from Birmingham University's School of Sport and Exercise Science, reckons there are two forms of exercise addiction – negative and positive. 'Positive addiction means that the individual cannot do without exercise but it enhances the quality of their life,' he says. 'Negative addiction is when your life takes second place to exercise.'

The marathon certainly seems to attract more than its share of pain junkies obsessed by time, distance, food and rest. It seems that once the habit of running gets into the system it can take over. The runner can get hooked, with every detail of life revolving around the unbreakable ritual of the daily run. Nothing is allowed to get in the way of it. Without that fix, the athlete suffers distressing withdrawal symptoms.

Runners will squeeze in a run at a railway station between trains, or at work while others are snatching a sandwich. Sometimes when you return home late at night from a dinner or a party you will catch sight of someone keeping the promises made to their training diary, with miles to run before they sleep.

Exercise, according to Dr Richard Cox, an Edinburgh psychologist who has worked with international sportsmen and women, is an addiction like any other. 'We all have the capacity to be obsessive,' he says. 'We establish a routine and we don't like it to be disrupted. Obsessive exercise can be problematic when it causes health problems. Many long-distance runners used to try to emulate David Bedford, who apparently used to run 200 miles a week. They often ended up in physiotherapy clinics. The first thing to recognise is that it is an obsession.'

The most severe and dangerous form of this compulsion, according to American sports psychologist William Morgan, may well be 'marathon addiction'. 'Initially the addict may withdraw from loved ones,' he said. 'Then his performance at work begins to suffer. In the most serious cases he may continue to run despite serious health problems.'

Certainly the description of a marathon addict withdrawing from loved ones is one that fitted Fred Lebow, president of the New York Road Runners Club and mastermind of the New York City Marathon.

Lebow gave Chris Brasher and his original team a tremendous amount of advice, and no one was more delighted than Fred to be given the number 1 when he came to run in the London Marathon in 1982. Sadly he was forced to drop out at 18 miles because of a knee problem. It was an injury that was almost certainly self-inflicted because of too much running.

Fred Lebow was a fascinating and energetic man, but

when you met him you could be left in no doubt about his obsessive nature. He told me that at various points in his life he trained himself to exist on practically no sleep, weaned himself off regular meals and, in one particularly bizarre experiment, deliberately went without sex for a year to see what effect it would have on his body, his mind and his running.

He also set himself the target of competing in a marathon every month and confessed that a number of his relationships with girlfriends had hit the wall because of his running. Lebow became fixated with counting the number of miles he ran and logging them in a running diary. 'When I was living with one girlfriend,' he said, 'I set myself a goal to run 2,500 miles for the year. It was my New Year's resolution and maybe I was a bit obsessive about it.'

Towards the end of the year Lebow knew that he was getting close. On New Year's Eve he spent the day flying back from the West Coast where he'd been on business and on the plane he checked his running diary, adding up his mileage and concluding that he was 19 miles short of his total for the year.

'My girlfriend and I were off to a dinner party in Central Park West,' said Lebow, 'and when I got to her apartment around seven o'clock she had my suit and tie and shoes all ready and she was trying on her evening gown ready for the party. But as soon as I got in I told her that I had just checked my diary and I was still 19 miles short for the year. "I'll have to go and run," I said.'

Two hours or so later, after pounding his way round Central Park in the cold and rain and adding an extra mile just to be on the safe side, Lebow returned to find his girlfriend in tears. He got dressed and ready, fast. They made the party around 10 – too late for dinner but in time for the dancing and New Year resolutions. 'Way after midnight we both danced with other guests,' said Fred. 'Then later, when I looked for her, I couldn't find her. Somebody said she went home.'

Unable to get a taxi at 2 a.m. in New York on New Year's Eve in pouring rain, Lebow ran the couple of miles back to the apartment. When he got there, soaked and frozen, he found a suitcase in the hall outside her door, a bag with his running kit in it and an envelope.

'There was a long note kind of summing up our relationship, saying she was kicking me out,' said Fred. His girlfriend had also added a PS. She had found his running diary, gone through it and added up his mileage. Fred had got that wrong, too. It turned out that he had already run 2,531 miles for the year – over 30 miles more than his target. He didn't need to run at all that night.

Six months later the girl was married – but not to Fred Lebow.

Shortly after the London Marathon of 2001, I had a long lunch with David Bedford during which we cooked up an event that we believed would deter even the most obsessive of runners. We were talking about a book that had been recently written by Peter Radford covering the exploits of the amazing Captain Barclay. In 1809 Barclay won a wager that he could cover 1,000 miles in 1,000 hours on foot – the catch being that he was allowed to run only one mile in any given hour. This meant exercising round the clock, with no more than snatches of sleep, for almost six weeks. No one knew if it was possible, and when Barclay eventually managed it he lost an enormous amount of weight and came close to death.

Bedford and I wondered if modern marathon runners could match Barclay's feat. By the second bottle of wine we had dreamed up a challenge to invite competitors to run one mile every hour, day and night, in the six weeks leading up to the London Marathon. The route would be up and down the marathon course, and in between their 24 runs a day the contestants would be allowed to crash out briefly on a bunk in a double-decker bus. To top it all, the 1,000 miles would end on the start line of the marathon and to decide the winner there would be a final race-off around the marathon's 26 miles.

We wondered if anybody would be mad enough to take up the challenge – but we had underestimated obsession. Bedford had to turn away many eager competitors. Six men and women set out and five completed the 1,000 miles, proving that Captain Barclay's feat was not really as difficult as it had seemed. After 42 days of pounding the streets of London, former jockey Shona Crombie-Hicks won the 1,000-mile challenge and collected prize money of £11,000 along with her blisters.

Among the most committed runners each year in the London Marathon are members of that small group who can claim to have completed every race since 1981. One of them, Jeff Aston, developed an injury just three weeks before the 2000 London Marathon – a back injury that prevented him from running at all. 'Still, I had no real trouble walking, and since I am stubborn, not starting for me was not an option,' he said. 'I walked the whole way to keep my sequence going. I suppose it has become something of an obsession, but it's going to take something extremely serious to stop me.'

Another, Ken Jones, was pulled out of the marathon by paramedics in 1989. 'I was in a bad way and was taken off and put into an ambulance somewhere along the Embankment,' he said, 'but after a few minutes I managed to fight my way off the stretcher and although they tried to stop me I got going again and finished in 4:18.'

Anyone who reckons men like Ken Jones have a compulsive disorder should consider the so-called Marathon Monks of Mount Hiei in Japan. The monks are spiritual athletes from a Buddhist sect near the ancient city of Kyoto. Their ultimate achievement is the completion of the Thousand Day Challenge, which must surely be the most demanding physical and mental feat in the world. They say that only 46 men have ever completed the challenge since 1885 – hardly surprising, since it takes seven years to do it.

The first 300 days are basic training, during which the monks run 26 miles a day for 100 consecutive days. Eventually, in their seventh year, they run two 26-mile marathons back to back every day for a hundred days. They do it at night, over mountain paths, in straw sandals, wearing an all-white outfit and a straw hat, surviving on a diet of vegetables, tofu and miso soup.

Each monk carries a sheath knife, and a rope, known as 'the cord of death', to remind him of his duty to take his own life if he drops out of the challenge.

Such men make the Ron Hills and Fred Lebows of this world seem almost casual. But there are thousands of mid-pack London runners who share a little of Hill's passion for never missing a run.

You see it in their mood and behaviour if love, injury or the demands of everyday living get between them and their magnificent obsession. And it's not just the men who've become addicted to their sport.

'When I cannot run I am the human equivalent of a train crash,' confessed Melanie Henderson, a twenty-first-century marathon obsessive sidelined by injury. 'I lose car keys, bills, letters, mobile phones. I forget to attend dental appointments. I overspend on my credit card. I cannot sustain a proper conversation. I cannot do my job properly. I am a horrible person to know.'

9

Chasing the Men

People used to think I was a freak. Now women of all
shapes and sizes run. And they're not just beautiful and
slim and wearing pink gossamer tights. They jiggle along
at 12-minute miles, or spring along at 6:30s. And
everyone just ignores them because they're part of the
landscape. That's what I love.
Kathrine Switzer

Crystal-ball gazing has always been a high-risk sport. At
the time of the first London Marathon a book was
published very much in tune with the feminist spirit of the
age, entitled *Catching up the Men*. It advanced the thesis
that standards in women's sport were improving so rapidly
that it was only a matter of time before the records set by
men would be matched or bettered by women.

The predictions were engagingly specific. The author,
Dr K.F. Dyer, a social biologist from Adelaide, used graphs,
statistics and complex formulas to put a stopwatch on the
future. By 1995, he asserted, the women's record would
have caught up with the men's in the 1500m. By 2000 both
records would stand at 3:22.2 seconds. Women would
match men in the 3,000m in 1996, Dyer said, and in the
marathon in 1988. Both men and women would be covering
the marathon in 2:05 by the year 2000.

It did not happen. The men's marathon is remarkably
close to Dyer's prediction at 2:04.55, but the women's
record stands with Paula Radcliffe at 2:15:25.

Dyer gazed further into the future, predicting that women
would triumph in the 400m by 2029, the 800m by 2039,
and the 100m by 2071.

By 1990 another academic was pursuing the same point-less fantasy. Ellis Cashmore, Professor of Humanities and Social Sciences at Staffordshire University, suggested that the only reason women did not match men in just about all sports was because they had been brainwashed by nineteenth-century medical myths into believing that they were the weaker sex. 'If we could turn the clock back 120 years and these myths did not exist, then men and women today would be competing at comparable levels,' he claimed in the *British Journal of Sports Medicine*.

And in 2004 Dr Andrew Tatem, a zoologist at Oxford University, took a look at the winning times in Olympic sprint events since the beginning of the twentieth century and concluded that the gap between men and women was narrowing. 'Logically,' he said, 'there will come a time in the not too distant future when women actually overtake men. Should these trends continue,' he wrote in the journal *Nature*, 'the projections will intersect at the 2156 Olympics.'

Such views may be entertaining but in reality they are little more than a load of crystal balls. It is true that the Victorians had a view of women as passive and vulnerable that kept them out of sport. Pierre de Coubertin was a cruel critic of sportswomen and he excluded them from his Games for as long as possible.

After such a hampered start the statistics of women's improvement are impressive. One man who knows just how impressive is Stan Greenberg, the sports statistician. He gets furious at what he sees as statistical abuse in sport. 'How many more times must we endure this so-called scientific nonsense that sportswomen will catch up and surpass men?' he asks. 'All the data and graphs that are trotted out to prove the theory are totally flawed. In most sports, particu-larly athletics, women have been competing in depth only since the 1930s. The men have been doing it for at least double that time, so their graph shows a much more gradual rate of improvement.

'Women have been able to take advantage from the beginning of modern training techniques, diet regimes, improved technology and sports science, so in an event like the pole vault, which women have taken up only recently, they are making marvellous progress using the latest poles and techniques. Women do have obvious advantages in stamina-based events, particularly swimming,' Greenberg says. 'But even there the base data is flawed. True, a woman holds the three-way Channel record, but it is an event not attempted often enough to prove anything.

'In the marathon it is always noted that the female record was 3:40 in 1960. It had been that since 1926 simply because women were not allowed to run the distance until the 1970s. Not surprisingly they made tremendous advances, but any graph constructed prior to there being major participation is ludicrous.' Greenberg emphasises that he does not wish to denigrate women's performances; 'Rather to applaud the wonderful standards they have achieved.' He adds, 'When they fail – and they will – to meet these pseudo-scientific goals they will be decried by the same people who saddled them with these impossible targets.'

Even so, it is in endurance events that a woman will sometimes emerge to prove that she is not only equal but superior to male opponents. In the marathon, women, far from being too frail for the distance, may have physiological advantages. Any man who has run alongside them knows that they often seem far more comfortable than men in the closing stages. Men frequently go to pieces between 18 and 22 miles when they hit the wall, but the wall holds fewer terrors for women, who can draw on reserves of subcutaneous fat as a fuel supply. As with cycling and Channel swimming, it is in that terrifying territory beyond the wall that women can outperform the men.

Take the case of Ann Sayer, a long-distance walker. In 1979, at the age of 42, she broke a record that had defied some of Britain's toughest men. She walked 400 miles from sea level to sea level over the three highest mountains in Scotland, England and Wales. She had already broken a world record by walking 117 miles inside 24 hours. She also broke the Land's End to John O'Groats walking record and made an appearance as an international athlete over 200km at the age of 57.

Hers is the sort of performance that would have baffled Coubertin. 'Women in sport,' he said, 'have but one task – that of the role of crowning the victor with garlands.' He should have tried telling that to Kelly Holmes or Paula Radcliffe!

But his was a view that was common enough in Victorian Britain, where the self-confident pioneers of organised games gave the rules and the ethos of sport to the world, along with their prejudices against professionals and women.

Women's races in Britain can be traced back to the seventeenth century but they were curious affairs. The *Caledonian Mercury*, Scotland's first newspaper, announced two events in April 1661. In the first, 12 pregnant women, all of whom worked in the brewing trade, were lined up to run to the top of Arthur's Seat, a high hill in Edinburgh, for prizes of cheese and whisky. And the next day, 16 fishwives were to race from Musselburgh to Cannon-cross, about seven miles, for 12 pairs of lamb's entrails.

In 1752 a big crowd turned out to watch women race over four miles in London, but many were lured by the rumour that the girls would run 'ancient Greek style' – in other words naked. In the event, they ran clothed and the interest cooled off.

At country sports there were often the so-called 'smock races' among girls, in which the prize was a smock or a shift, but all too often they were regarded as freak shows and the interest in them had little to do with competitive athletics.

In 1896, when the Olympics were reborn in Athens, they were not deemed suitable for women and none was allowed to compete. One Greek woman named Melpomene turned up demanding to enter the marathon, but she was refused. Not easily put off, Melpomene warmed up for the race anyway and when the starter's gun sounded she began to run along the side of the course.

She fell behind the men but plodded on, stopping occasionally for water, and started passing tail-enders who dropped out of the race in exhaustion. She arrived at the stadium about an hour and a half after Spiridon Louis had been declared the winner. Barred from entry into the now empty stadium, she ran round the outside and finished in approximately four and a half hours. One Greek newspaper criticised the Olympic organisers, saying they had been discourteous to refuse her entry.

Better documented was the achievement of England's Violet Piercy, who was the first woman to be timed officially in the marathon when she clocked 3:40:22 in a British race in 1926. Her time was bettered in 1964 by Scotland's Dale Greig, who ran 3:27:45, and later in the same year New Zealander Mildred Sampson recorded 3:19:33.

In other sports women were given more freedom to compete. In 1927 Gertrude Ederle swam the English Channel. Not only that, she did it two hours faster than anybody else, man or woman. But there was a huge prejudice against any sort of distance running by women. It took years for women to elbow their way into the Olympics, and even when they did, there were dramatic setbacks.

There was an uproar when they were allowed to run the 800m at the Amsterdam Games in 1928. It was a fiercely fought race won by Lina Radke of Germany in 2:16.8, but five of the runners, under-trained and inexperienced, dropped out during the race and others fell to the track at the finish. There were howls of protest at the sight of ladies in distress. It was 1960 before the event was again permitted in the Games and 1984 before women got their own Olympic marathon.

The irony is that sporting medicine suggests that it is

precisely in the areas of endurance activity that women have some advantages over men, and despite the restrictions of costume and culture, there were always exceptional women who showed tantalising glimpses of their great potential for endurance.

Take, for example, Lucy Walker, the first woman to climb the Matterhorn. She always set out from her village base clad in her Victorian crinoline, which she took off to climb in a red petticoat. Her stamina, like her dress, was dismissed as amusingly eccentric despite the fact that she seemed able to match any male climber.

Women of a century ago showed that they could run as well as climb if given the chance. In 1905 the Crowhurst Otterhounds acquired a woman master, a Mrs Walter Chessman, who took over the post from her husband. She amazed everyone with her ability to cover up to 20 miles of cross-country every day, running with the hounds and leaving the huntsmen out of sight.

But there were still no distance races for women – officially at least. The most famous marathon outside the Olympics was the Boston Marathon, an annual event established in 1897. Women were barred from entering that race until 1972 but the rules didn't always keep them out.

In 1966, a 23-year-old girl called Bobbi Gibb hid in the bushes at the start and jumped into the race wearing a black nylon bathing suit. Gibb was no joke runner. She was said to have trained by running as much as 40 miles a day. She finished the race untroubled, clocking 3:21:40. It was the start of a marathon revolution. The following year a girl called Kathy Switzer bent the rules even further and got herself entered in the race with a genuine race number.

The years have mellowed Kathy Switzer, but not a lot. On a gentle late summer afternoon jog along the towpath of the Thames near Oxford she seems serene enough, but ask her how she gatecrashed the once all-male preserve of the Boston Marathon and suddenly she's on fire.

While she was a student at America's Syracuse University

in the 1960s, Switzer trained with a running coach called Arnie Briggs. He was an ex marathon runner who had run the Boston Marathon 15 times and who regaled her constantly with tales of the race. During their daily runs Switzer heard so much about men like Johnny Kelley, Clarence de Mar and Tarzan Brown that finally she urged Briggs to let her run it herself.

'But Arnie didn't believe a woman could run the distance,' said Switzer. 'I wanted to prove to him that I could. Arnie said if I could do it in practice he would take me to Boston.' To make her point Switzer trained until she could cover more than 30 miles and ran Briggs to a standstill on a training run.

'Once convinced, Arnie was like an evangelist,' said Switzer. 'He went all over the campus preaching that women have hidden potential and stamina.'

Kathrine Switzer entered the Boston Marathon by using only her initials on the application form. Her entry was accepted and she lined up with the number 261 pinned to her baggy tracksuit. 'The gun went off and down the street we went. I just felt fabulous,' said Switzer. 'But four miles into the race a press truck came by and the photographers just went crazy seeing a woman in the race and a woman wearing a number at that.'

Following the press truck was a busload of marathon officials, including Jock Semple, the manager of the race, and Will Cloney, the Race Director. 'When they saw me,' said Switzer, 'Will jumped off the bus and stood in the road and shook his finger at me. I just went whizzing by him but then I turned just in time to see this official Jock Semple pouncing on me.

'His arms were raised to grab me and his teeth were bared. He was like a snarling dog, just absolutely vicious. He grabbed me by the shoulders, spun me round and snatched at the front of my shirt to rip my number off.'

'Get the hell out of my race and give me those numbers,' roared Semple, grabbing her by the sweatshirt.

Running with Switzer had been Briggs and her new boyfriend, a hammer thrower named Tom Miller. 'All of a sudden,' said Switzer, 'from the periphery of my vision I saw my boyfriend's orange sweatshirt as he moved across my line of vision and hit Jock Semple with a body block that sent Jock flying into the air and on to the side of the road. My boyfriend was a 235-pound hammer thrower and I was more frightened for the official than I was for us. I had never been close to violence before so to hear that kind of crunch scared me to death.

'But Arnie turned to me and said, "Run like hell." We just went flying down the road. It was terrifying and I was crying but I was determined to stay in the race no matter what. I had 22 miles ahead of me to figure out what I was going to do with this experience.

'I decided I would have to work out a system to let other women have the opportunity to feel encouraged, inspired and realise that running is OK for them. By the time I had finished the race I had decided I was going to create opportunities for them, somehow, somewhere, and that I myself was going to become a much better athlete.' Switzer went on to establish a series of women's races around the world sponsored by Avon.

Suddenly women's marathon running was in the headlines. But even after Switzer, the road-running establishment fought a rearguard action. In 1972 the American athletic authorities decreed that women could not start the New York Marathon with the men. The women's start would have to be 10 minutes before the men to set up a separate race.

There were only six women entrants in that early New York Marathon, and when the gun sounded for the women's start, all six of them sat down in a line. They stayed right where they were for the full 10 minutes until the gun sent the men on their way, then they ran together. In the wake of this race the American Amateur Athletic Union, faced with a lawsuit from the women, relented. The women had won the day.

The perfect finish,
Dick Beardsley and Inge Simonsen share
victory in the first London Marathon, 1981

Chris Brasher with Princess Diana, starter for
the 1988 London Marathon

First Olympic champion,
Spiridon Louis of Greece

Roger Bourban,
the Running Waiter, in 1982

Winning line-up in 1982, Hugh Jones and Joyce Smith are flanked by (*left*) Mike Gratton (GB) and Judith Hine (NZ) and (*right*) Lorraine Moller (NZ) and Oyvind Dahl (Norway)

Charlie Spedding, winner 1984   Mike Gratton, winner 1983

Liz McColgan leads Joyce Chepchumba in the 1997 race.
This time Chepchumba won

Jimmy Savile with a youthful Dave Bedford

Veronique Marot, winner 1989

Dorando Pietri, first man home in the 1908 marathon

Allister Hutton,
winner 1990

Ingrid Kristiansen and Steve Jones,
winners 1985

Eamonn Martin, winner 1993

John Disley, the co-founder
of the London Marathon

Nick Bitel, Chief Executive
of the London Marathon

The pick of the charity bunch

Jenny Wood Allen,
outrunning the years

A man in a million,
John Spurling, world-
record fund raiser in 1999

Bearskins and sore
feet on the cobbles

Saving the Rhino
is hot, thirsty work

After such breakthroughs there was no stopping women in the marathon, but it took a track star to show the world just how good they really could be. Greta Waitz, of Norway, never won an Olympic marathon but for more than a decade she was the undisputed queen of the roads – an achievement she crowned with nine straight victories in the New York Marathon and a couple in the London.

Blonde, pale and leggy, with the deceptively fragile look of a Paula Radcliffe, Waitz had decided to retire from competitive track running in 1978 because the longest distance for women in the Olympics at that time was only 1500m. She was working full time as a schoolteacher, running close to 100 miles a week and finding it difficult to keep motivated as an athlete.

But then she got a call from Fred Lebow, who reckoned she might make a useful pacemaker for the women during the early miles of his New York Marathon. 'He decided to invite me only two weeks before the marathon,' said Waitz, 'and the longest run I'd done was only about 11 miles. But it all went much better than I expected. I won the race and I broke the world record. That New York Marathon really changed my running life.'

Waitz returned again and again to conquer New York and over the years she formed a warm friendship with the race promoter. Like many others, she was devastated when Lebow was diagnosed with brain cancer in 1992 and given only six months to live. When he told Waitz that despite his illness he wanted to run in his own marathon, she said she would run it with him to help him through it.

'I was amazed at the support both of us got,' said Waitz. 'We were out there for more than five hours and it was so emotional. I remember I got tears in my eyes and then Fred looked at me as if he was worried and said, "Hey, are you hurting, Grete?" And I said, "No, I'm just so very happy because I know you're going to make it." Then he started to cry too, so we ran the last two miles in tears, both of us.

'At the end he looked at me and said, "When I'm turning

70 we're going to walk this marathon together." He was always positive, always looking ahead. The marathon was his whole life.'

Fred Lebow died at the age of 62 four weeks before the 1994 New York Marathon. Today, a bronze statue of him stands in Central Park not far from the headquarters of the New York Road Runners. Initially one of Fred's brothers objected to the statue, citing the prohibition against graven images. Some Jews believe that since God created man in his image, any representation of a human could be construed as an image of God. So the night before the statue was unveiled, a rabbi slipped under the sheet covering it and chipped away a small piece between the thumb and forefinger of the left hand. Once it was no longer a complete representation, the objections vanished.

The statue of Fred Lebow is now moved for one day each year to overlook the finish line of the marathon he created.

Even after Grete Waitz started her series of marathon breakthroughs in Lebow's race, things were still tough for the woman runner outside New York. When Joyce Smith competed in the women's race in the first London Marathon, she paid her own rail fare to the event and her reward for winning, except for a medal and a trophy, was a wristwatch. Even in the second year, in 1982, when she retained her title, the frills were minimal. After the presentation she was left to walk to the station to get the train home, until a journalist spotted her and paid her taxi fare.

By the time of the third London, in 1983, Grete Waitz was in town to raise the profile and the fortunes of the women runners. Blonde, serene and utterly remorseless in her red gloves and red Adidas strip, she reduced the course record to 2:25.29, a world best time that took more than four minutes off the London record and saw her finish almost three minutes ahead of Mary O'Connor of New Zealand and Britain's Glynis Penny. Greta came back in 1986 to take her second win in London.

The first man to break 2:20 for the marathon was Britain's Jim Peters in the Windsor to Chiswick marathon back in 1953, but by the 1980s there was talk of it being done by a woman. The woman they talked about was the new queen of the London roads, another Norwegian, Ingrid Kristiansen. She was to win the London race four times and set a world record.

Her first sport was cross-country skiing and it wasn't until she was 24 that she opted for a career in running. 'I never really wanted to be a runner,' she said. 'My heart was set on winning an Olympic gold for Norway in cross-country skiing. Every Sunday our whole family packed a picnic and went deep into the forest. We'd ski and run for miles, chasing and playing games with wild animals.'

Then in 1977 she ran her first marathon, using that skiing strength to win in 2:45:15. She went on to stamp an invincibility on distance running which only the likes of Emil Zatopek achieved in men's athletics.

In 1981 Kristiansen, a medical researcher, married a fellow runner from Stavanger and in 1983 they had a son, Gaute. Kristiansen had won the Houston marathon early in 1983 in 2:33.27. 'I did my best marathon time there,' she said. 'But two weeks later I came thirty-fifth in a race that I had hoped to win. I was devastated so I went to the doctor expecting the worst. Imagine my disbelief when he told me that I was five months pregnant.'

Just ten days after her son was born, Ingrid was back jogging again. A month after the birth she was back virtually to full training, and five months later she won the Houston Marathon once more, this time in 2:27:51, several minutes faster than one year and one baby before.

'After my son was born, everyone told me I was mad, that I was too old to carry on,' said Kristiansen. 'But I was breast-feeding him shortly after I won the London in 1984. He was ten months old then and my friends told me that I could never be a mother and a runner, but I proved them all wrong.'

Ingrid was bitterly disappointed when she finished out of the medals at the 1984 Olympic Games, but it made her determined to train harder than ever. She cut out pictures of the Olympic gold medallist Joan Benoit and pasted them up in front of her treadmill. All through the long Norwegian winter Kristiansen ran, haunted by these images of Benoit. Then in the London Marathon of 1985, surrounded by men as she ran, she set a world record of 2:21:06.

She was on schedule for 2:20 at halfway, and still on pace for the first ever 2:20 at 20 miles, reached in 1:46.40. She only slowed marginally in the last few miles before setting a time which would have won every men's Olympic marathon up until 1960.

No man had ducked under 2:20 until 1953. 'But there's no physical reason why a woman shouldn't run that fast,' said Kristiansen. 'The barriers are more mental than physical.' The race to break 2:20 was on, and as women runners began to flirt with the new barrier, a fierce debate began to rage over the question of pacemaking.

In 1998 Kenya's Tegla Loroupe ran 2:20.47 in Rotterdam with the help of two male pacemakers. In December that year the organisers of the London Marathon announced that they would ignore that time. A bonus of $125,000 was offered in London to any woman who could beat the record in a women-only race without the aid of male pacemakers.

Nick Bitel, the Chief Executive of the London Marathon, said, 'We believe that to maintain the integrity of women's marathon running, it is essential to recognise times set in women-only races. We are putting our money where our mouth is.'

It was a controversial stance that attracted plenty of criticism when London claimed that Joyce Chepchumba's winning time of 2:23.22 in 1999 was a world record, even though most experts reckoned it was only the twelfth-fastest time in history.

'They are being ridiculous,' said Jos Hermens, the Race Director of the Rotterdam Marathon. 'Maybe it's jealousy.

Road running is totally different to the track. Ever since women have been allowed to run marathons it's been mixed races. We give our athletes the best possible opportunity to perform to their best, and if that means running against men, that's fine. It's all a little bit silly.'

London Marathon officials defended their position, and promised they would continue to recognise Chepchumba's time unless it was broken in one of the few women-only races. 'We gave Joyce a very special award for a special performance and if other races don't like it they can stick it,' said Alan Storey. Some noted, perhaps a touch cynically, that as long as the row kept news of the marathon in the headlines all the rival race directors seemed happy.

There was no doubting the headline-grabbing abilities of London's next great woman record-breaker, Paula Radcliffe. Radcliffe said she'd always wanted to run in the London since she first watched her father take part in 1985, the year that Ingrid Kristiansen set her own record. 'I remember my brother and I using the Underground to follow my dad's progress and I recall him being very upset that we'd eaten the Mars bars that were intended for him. I always used to say that I'd like to run the marathon with my dad but it never happened.'

In 2002 in London, Radcliffe did not just win the marathon, she demolished a world-class field and put in one of the finest runs in history. Her time of 2:18.56 was the second fastest on record and she finished ahead of the rest by an astonishing margin of more than three minutes. She cruised to halfway and then simply flew away from some of the best runners in the world.

'I regarded Jim Peters as a superman and it was quite impossible to believe any woman eventually running comparable times,' said athletics statistician Mel Watman. 'Indeed one never envisaged a woman running a marathon at all. At the 1952 and 1956 Olympics the longest women's race was 200m, and apart from a handful of experimental races, the mile was as far as women ever raced on track. Now

Paula is running times which only nine British men bettered last year. Indeed she would be close to men's selection for an international vest in the marathon, an unprecedented situation.'

But there was better to come. One year later, Radcliffe annihilated the world record and utterly destroyed the elite women's field in the London. Her time of 2:15:25 beat her own world record set the previous autumn in Chicago by nearly two minutes. She beat her nearest rival by four minutes. This time the London organisers changed their policy on women's racing yet again. While they still insisted on a women-only race for the elite runners, they brought in a number of male pacemakers to guarantee fast times, not just for Radcliffe but for other women in the race as well.

Towed along by two male Kenyan pacemakers, one of whom dropped when the pace got too fierce, Radcliffe led the 2003 race from start to finish. No woman even got close to her. By the end they were so far back they couldn't even see her. Paula had gone from vulnerable to invincible in a run of blazing confidence and blinding self-belief.

It was, she said, 'a good reflection of the training I put in'. The girl with the head-bob and the knee-socks had stolen all the headlines from the men, and left the world wondering how fast she, or any woman, could go.

Wherever they were in the pack, women were liberated and inspired by champions like Paula Radcliffe who dared to match strides with the men. There was nothing now to stop any of them taking up running and tackling the marathon. They were doing it in their hundreds of thousands, some gazelle-like and youthful but many more middle-aged, in baggy T-shirts, running to burn off the calories rather than their opponents.

One of London's finest women runners, Veronique Marot, winner in 1989, returned to the race as a charity fund-raiser, happy to run along with the liberated mid-pack masses. 'Once you become a veteran you need to set yourself completely different goals,' she said. 'Don't try to emulate your old self, don't try to do what you used to do.

'Just getting out is a real positive and anything else is a bonus and better. I've rediscovered what it's like to be out running, whatever the pace.'

And just occasionally a runner will make the leap the other way – from mid-pack plodder to top-class athlete. It's something Dave Bedford believes almost every runner dreams of for a flickering moment at the start of the London. 'A lot of them are thinking, "Why not me? What would happen if everything went better than right and by some fluke, some freak, I had an amazing breakthrough?" It's crazy, but in a marathon anything can happen,' said Bedford.

In the 2004 marathon the breakthrough of Tracey Morris triggered an avalanche of media interest. Here was a 36-year-old optician from Leeds who made it into Britain's women's marathon team for the Olympics in Athens seemingly by leaping from obscurity to stardom in just one race.

In reality she was not quite the novice fun runner that the media like to portray. She had finished thirteenth in the 2003 Great North Run and had prepared well for the London. But it was only her second marathon, and her first had been a fun run. The breakthrough of this delightful housewife, who wondered how she'd manage to get the time off work to train for the Olympic marathon in Athens, was enough to fuel the dreams of hundreds of other hopefuls.

Over a century had passed since a woman was turned away from the start line of that first Olympic marathon. Now the women are welcome at every marathon, and anyone can dream.

On 5 September 2004, Tracey Morris cruised happily round the Flora Lite 5K. With her in the sunshine were

22,000 other women – a moving river of runners and walkers flowing through Hyde Park. Most were running just for fun, but there was nothing to stop any of them dreaming that perhaps they, too, might one day wake up to the headline: 'Mrs Nobody wins the Marathon'.

IO

No Loneliness for the Long-Distance Runner

Here are men and women trying to do something that is incredibly difficult, with thousands willing them on, and it is not the person who is first who is a winner, it is everybody.
Chris Brasher

They used to talk about the loneliness of the long-distance runner. It is a strange idea these days when the parks and pavements so often seem alive with packs of joggers. But there was a time before the age of the big mass marathons when running was an eccentric pastime.

There were runners, of course, but it was an obscure sport pursued by only a handful of lean and grisly eccentrics. Occasionally a Roger Bannister or Gordon Pirie would pop up to hit the news pages, and once every four years the Olympics would remind you that there was a race called the marathon, but the idea of fun-runners, men and women pounding the city pavements on a quest to get fit, to relax, to lose weight or to rejuvenate a flabby, listless body, just didn't exist.

One ageing Cambridge academic, Dr Ulick Evans, used to glory in the tale of how he once trained for the marathon in those far-off days when runners were rarely seen. In skimpy shorts and singlet he set out to try and run 26 miles or so on the outskirts of Cambridge to prepare for the legendary Polytechnic marathon from Windsor to Chiswick. At around 17 miles into his lonely adventure he ran out of energy and hit the wall. The weather turned chill and nasty and he decided that he needed help and shelter.

In increasing desperation he knocked at a number of farmhouse doors. He glimpsed people inside, but no one would answer and every door was locked. Eventually he found one house that took him in and he uncovered the dark cause of his problem. An inmate had escaped from the local mental hospital at Fulbourn, and in those days before the running boom, a tired, bedraggled and rather wild-looking man, in what they took to be his underwear, was easily mistaken for a patient on the run.

Years later, when men in vest and pants were eventually recognised as runners, people watching would still shake their heads and mutter, 'They must be crazy.' But in time the London Marathon and events like it were to change the whole perception of long-distance running. In the decades between the first Olympic marathon in 1896 and the emergence of the big-city marathons, the race had been little more than an obscure ordeal. It was traditionally undertaken only by the most highly trained men, and usually at the end of a distance-running career.

Almost invariably, wherever marathons were run, they were small-scale re-enactments of their Olympic prototype. There were other marathons outside the major championships, but they were all modelled on the Olympics, and competitors went into them seriously and with much the same approach. The fields were small, the standards high. Although the winners would not approach the elite times recorded today, the body of the field would run comparatively faster. It was not unusual for runners clocking slower than three hours either to drop out or to be pulled out by officials.

But towards the end of the 1960s, social developments created a phenomenon unprecedented in the history of sport. Increasing leisure time and huge interest in personal physical fitness created a boom in non-competitive exercise that touched millions. Backpacking, walking, a growing awareness of the environment, together with the knowledge that heart disease and obesity could be relatively easily fought through simple exercise, gave a push to the growing movement for running. In America, government programmes encouraged walking and jogging, and in Britain, newspapers like the *Sunday Times* organised fun runs and low-key races.

Britain also had a long-established and flourishing running club structure that provided very well-trained packs of runners for the front of the field in such events. But soon they were being followed by hundreds of less serious competitors who came into the sport relatively late and who took it up for reasons of health and pleasure rather than with hopes of high athletic distinction.

Instead of a few dozen runners in races there were now hundreds, and the concept of a race began to change. No longer was the majority of the field running to win. Most of these new runners were content merely to finish. Some of them would have personal battles against the clock and almost all of them were running because they said they enjoyed it.

It was not long before entrepreneurs realised these new runners were prepared to spend money on their newfound passion. Running paraphernalia exploded with vastly increased ranges of specialised running shoes; magazines and books devoted to the hows and whys of running appeared. These soon overtook the niche publications that had previously existed merely to give results and race reports.

The surprising realisation for millions of these runners who'd come into the sport for health and recreation was that it was by no means impossible for them to tackle the marathon. For many this became a driving personal ambition. It captured the popular imagination in a vivid way. Soon the very act of completing a marathon, irrespective of the finishing time, became a rite of passage for the new breed of runner.

It was during the 1970s in the United States that the marathon was really taken over by the masses. Events like the New York Marathon, which began with just a handful of runners, mushroomed rapidly to become a giant street carnival that virtually closed the city for a day. By 1980 more than 30,000 had applied to run in it and half of them had to be turned away. New marathon races blossomed throughout America and in Britain, where the marathon boom was unleashed by the inaugural London race in 1981.

Even before this, entries for shorter road races had been growing and new races had been springing up all over the country. Particularly there was the phenomenon of the low-key fun runs. The *Sunday Times* National Fun Run was launched in September 1978 in Hyde Park and attracted 12,000 entries in its first year. There are runners today who have taken part in every London Marathon who first put one foot in front of the other because of the *Sunday Times* Fun Run. Derek Fisher, who is one of them, says that his enthusiasm was sparked by this fun run and that thereafter he became quite obsessive about running the London Marathon and would happily queue all night to get his entry in for the early races.

In May of 1980, just months before the first announcements about the London, a People's Marathon was organised by the Centurion Joggers in Chelmsley Wood near Birmingham. It was open only to runners who had never before tried a marathon or who had tried but failed to break 2:50. The People's Marathon had to turn hundreds of entries away because it was so oversubscribed.

The joggers in their funny hats and stereo headphones had clearly arrived in force. Their aim in life was different to the runners who had gone before them. This new breed seemed quite happy just to run a marathon, however slowly. They didn't care about joining an athletic club or racing shorter distances; they just wanted to jog and take on the marathon.

Paradoxically, the man who did much to produce this

new breed of slow-motion jogger was also a coach who trained some of the fastest men on earth. Arthur Lydiard, who died in 2004, was an athlete turned coach from New Zealand who had long advocated slow distance running as a useful training for serious runners. But, he noted, slow running has benefits for everybody – women, children and the middle-aged alike. 'Running,' he said, 'is not just about racing or preparing for racing. Running is good in itself. Everybody can do it and everybody can benefit.'

Mass jogging became immensely popular in New Zealand and visitors were often impressed by the infectious enthusiasm of the new breed of runner. Brendan Foster, the former world record holder for two miles and 3,000m, whose mid-race surges inspired a generation of athletes in the 70s, was himself inspired by what he encountered in New Zealand. While training there with David Moorcroft, the former 5,000m world record holder, the pair were invited to take part in the Round the Bays race in Auckland.

'There was this race sponsored by the *Auckland Star*,' said Foster. 'It was everything from a fun run, jog, bicycle ride or pushing a pram and something like 60,000 people took part. It was terrific to see everybody having so much fun and I just thought it would be great to try to organise something like it back home. At the end of it there was a huge party on the beach. The place was jumping and I knew I had to try to do something like it in Newcastle.'

Within a year, Foster and a team of enthusiastic helpers had a blueprint for the Great North Run. The Great North Run, a half-marathon, and the London Marathon were announced within months of each other in 1981. 'The jogging boom had taken off,' said Foster, 'and the timing was absolutely right for both events.'

Another former runner who visited New Zealand and was much influenced by Arthur Lydiard and his gospel of jogging for all was the American Bill Bowerman, who had taken up a post as track coach at the University of Oregon in the United States. Bowerman was amazed at the fitness of the middle-aged and even older runners he jogged with in New Zealand, and on his return to America he started to give classes in slow running. His enthusiastic joggers began to hold informal races – fun runs – events where it didn't matter how fast you ran and in which everybody declared themselves a winner.

Suddenly everyone was running and talking about running. Fitness was all the rage and slow, gentle jogging the most efficient way to achieve it. Jim Fixx's *The Complete Book of Running* was overnight a runaway best-seller. Its message was that running was good for everybody. It turned you into a better person, it improved your sex life – Fixx, it seemed, could fix everything.

The benefits of running were clear and enduring. It was a sport accessible to all. No previous athletic ability was demanded; anyone could run a little. The equipment was simple and sexy enough quickly to spill into casual and fashion wear.

Kenneth Cooper, a consultant on physical fitness to the United States Air Force, wrote another best-selling book, called *Aerobics*. He followed it with *The New Aerobics* and *Aerobics for Women*. Cooper's gospel was that for exercise to be an effective contribution to health it had to improve cardiovascular fitness to benefit both the heart and the lungs. This could happen only with sustained exercise. Cooper recommended 15 to 20 minutes' continuous exercise at least three times a week, and decreed that running, fast walking, swimming and cycling were the finest workouts in the world.

To the surprise of many, these three-times-a-week joggers began to enter marathons – and to finish them. Soon thousands of others wanted to prove they could do it too. They found that almost anyone, given patience and persistence, could manage the distance. Completing a marathon, for people who aren't necessarily young or otherwise athletic, is an heroic physical accomplishment, often at a stage in life when few, if any, opportunities for physical accomplishments are within reach. Anyone who has done it will tell you few things in their lives matched the thrill of finishing their first marathon.

The running boom turned a generation of Americans from spectators into participants, and Britain was to follow. That first London Marathon, run in 1981, established an instant tradition. It was as if people had been secretly jogging for years and suddenly they had all signed up to celebrate. Later in that same year, on 23 August, even greater numbers of fun runners turned out for the Pony British Marathon, held in Bolton. Its 8,753 entries, with more than 7,000 of them finishing, made it the biggest marathon in Europe. Five weeks later there were 9,000 entries lining up for the Manchester Charity Marathon.

By the eve of only the second London Marathon, in 1982, the then editor of *Running Magazine*, Andy Etchells, was writing:

> No other event, particularly one with such demanding training and racing conditions, has ever mushroomed with quite such speed in Britain. It is a social phenomenon that is happening across the entire spectrum, male and female, young and old, rich and poor.

By the end of 1982, Etchells noted, Britain would have seen 116 full marathons in that year alone.

> The new breed of citizen runners have taken away the mystique but certainly none of the magic of the marathon. So who are all these thousands, where do they come from, what are their backgrounds and why do they do it? Marathoning is not only a young or even a sporty person's sport. The classic marathon distance has turned many no-hopers into heroes in their own right. The London Marathon is a personal battle and every runner reaching the finish is a winner.

They don't run to beat other people but to challenge themselves.

A few people still yearned for the days when marathon racing was an obscure sport for the chosen few and when there were definitely no women on the start line. An idea of the revolution that had taken place can be gained from the experience of Mike Wilkinson, another of that select band who has run through every London Marathon.

Wilkinson began his athletic career when he was about 10 years old, but it wasn't until he was 26 that he ran in his first marathon. It was very different from the 25 London marathons that were to follow. Wilkinson first lined up for a marathon in the Forres Highland Games. There were just 16 starters and 13 finishers. He remembers battling alone for miles into a head wind, finishing thirteenth and last in 3:15.

These days that time would place him well within the mid-pack – and far from last. These mid-packers are a special breed, often regarded with awe by the champions up front. The fast men are impressed that these part-time runners, who go to work each day and have a family life, somehow manage to fit in enough training to take on the 26-mile distance.

Chris Brasher said, 'There's a completely different perspective in the middle of the pack, for they run just as hard and face challenges just as tough as those out in front. That's one of the things that is great about running. These people can't go out and play tennis with a Wimbledon champion, but they can go out and run with the best in the world. Where else could you get the opportunity to say: I ran in a race with an Olympic champion?'

John Disley believes that it's the mid-pack masses and the huge amounts of money they raise for charity that have made the London invulnerable. 'Nobody can touch it,' he said. 'If anybody tried to say, "We won't close the streets down for you," they would run up against immense opposition. The London Marathon has become an institution in a country where it usually takes centuries rather than decades to become a tradition. It's as much a feature of the sporting year as Henley, Ascot and Wimbledon. Its future is secure. The police and the politicians can't stop it now and that's because of these magnificent masses.'

Brendan Foster says it was apparent as soon as he saw the thousands lining up for the first London Marathon that there had been a revolution in running. 'It was a coming-of-age for the sport of marathon running,' he said. 'When I saw these thousands of runners at the start and at the same time could see the great landmarks around the course, the great sights of London, I knew it was a combination that marked a real turning point in road running, but particularly in marathon running.

'I wish now I had run in that first London Marathon. It would have been a great pinnacle to my own career. That was the race that turned the marathon into a big spectator event, into a spectacle. There was a real sense of occasion and there was a glorious, inspirational side to it all. It showed that for most people athletics, running and sport can be a fun thing. That race also did a huge amount to bridge the gulf between the elite performer and the man or woman in the street. It had a carnival atmosphere and raised millions for charity, but it also allowed for serious competitive running for those at the front.'

Whatever runners felt in that first London Marathon, they were unlikely to feel lonely. Nor were they likely to be considered oddballs, the objects of ridicule from passers-by. The media had turned them into instant heroes for their time. They were running alongside members of parliament, disc jockeys like Jimmy Savile, resplendent in his gold lamé tracksuit, international rugby players, Fleet Street gossip columnists, a blind man roped up to his running companion, a waiter running in full uniform balancing a tray with a glass and a bottle on it.

There were thousands of runners and every runner had

a story to tell. The papers for months were full of them. Wherever you looked and whatever you read, the lonely long-distance runner, shivering in his underwear and terrifying homeowners, had been replaced by the born-again, smiling men and women running in their merry packs through the welcoming streets of London.

I I

Paved with Gold

I've turned down many lucrative offers to run marathons because I want my career to be as good as it can be. I would rather not race for just money. I would rather win little bits of metal at the end of a coloured ribbon.
Charlie Spedding

If you want a measure of how time has changed the London Marathon, ask Joyce Smith. She won't give it to you by looking at the wristwatch that was her prize for winning the first race 25 years ago. She lost that too long ago to remember. But it didn't matter much, since it was worth less than £100.

What she will tell you is that the difference between her win in the women's race in 1981 and Paula Radcliffe's nearly a quarter of a century later was well over half a million pounds. In 1981 Smith paid her own train fare to the race. She collected a medal, a trophy, that watch and then she took the train home.

Paula Radcliffe, by contrast, will have had all her expenses paid, her every wish catered for, and a five-star riverside hotel for the whole of marathon week. In addition, of course, she will have collected a pay-off that sets her well on the road to being a millionaire.

The London Marathon's first-year budget was £75,000. The entry fee was £5 and Dick Beardsley was lured over from the United States to run at the head of the field for just $2,500. These days the budget is £7 million, of which around £2 million goes on assembling and paying for the elite field.

'Good luck to them,' is Beardsley's view 25 years on.

'They should cash in while they can. If they were tennis players or golfers at the top of their sport they would be earning that kind of money every week, and probably with a lot less effort.

'When I was running in the 80s the marathon boom was only just beginning. There wasn't the huge money around that's available today. Times have changed and the marathon has to change with it or become nothing more than a charming everyman's race, without stars and without prestige.'

In 1981 the marathon had a borrowed office in County Hall with just a desk and a couple of chairs. And the practice of paying top athletes appearance and prize money, though it went on in athletics, was strictly against the rules of amateurism that then governed the sport.

A major change took place in the business of running in 1982. An international agreement was finally worked out to allow open prize money. Races could pay a cash purse that would go into a 'trust fund' administered by each national governing body. An athlete could draw from his trust fund 'training expenses', which were loosely defined, and his 'amateur' status would be preserved.

The growth of prize money from illegal to legal, from small amounts to large, was the symbol of the evolution of the marathon in just a few brief years. Fred Lebow's New York Marathon was first held on 13 September 1970. He had only 55 finishers and even fewer spectators. It was just an unpublicised curiosity. Visitors to Central Park that day had no idea what was going on. A decade later the size of marathon fields and marathon budgets had mushroomed. No other sport has witnessed such an incredible spurt in growth.

There was much talk of the then world record holder, Alberto Salazar, who had run 2:08:13, competing in the 1982 London Marathon, but his going rate was too much for Brasher. Salazar wanted £22,000 plus all expenses and Brasher wasn't paying. Salazar turned up in London anyway, brought over by a shoe firm. 'He also presented the prizes to the two London Marathon winners, Hugh Jones and Joyce Smith,' noted one reporter. 'He said not a word to either, made no speech and never smiled. Presumably that costs extra.'

With both Hugh Jones and Joyce Smith announcing they were not running in 1983, the London Marathon looked in danger of losing its elite status. The answer was money. Grete Waitz, who had already won four New York Marathons and set three world records, became the first amateur woman athlete officially to be paid for running in Britain when she agreed to take part in the marathon for appearance money. It was a shrewd move by the race organisers. She won in a world-best time of 2:25:29 and her image guaranteed massive press and TV coverage.

Dave Bedford, now the London Marathon Race Director, knows better than most the value of an image for a sportsman. When he was at the height of his athletic power his shaggy locks, red socks, drooping moustache and wiry physique made him instantly recognisable. He was the wild man of the track, the outrageous rebel who could pack stadiums by daring to predict how he would win races and smash records.

The enduring nature of this image was such that it was still alive and kicking up its heels in advertisements for the 118 directory enquiry service decades later.

But these days the numbers that Bedford worries about are those behind the London Marathon – and impressive numbers they are. With an annual income in excess of £7 million, money is the key to the continuing success of the race. The title sponsors, Flora, spend over £1.6 million a year and BBC Television pays around half a million. The marathon raises further money from publishing and merchandising.

'The London Marathon itself is a charity,' said Bedford, 'that enables runners to raise £35 million a year for various good causes.' The entry fee is £27, and as much as £2.5

million a year is generated by the Golden Bond scheme through which charities and companies can secure guaranteed places in the race. Under the scheme each place in the marathon costs the charities £250 and they have to buy them in five-year blocks. It was an idea dreamed up by Bedford, and has proved a money-spinner for the marathon and the charities alike.

Right from the start the money-generating aspects of the London Marathon have not been without critics. Illtyd Harrington, a former leader of the Greater London Council and a long-serving board member of the London Marathon, said in 1990 that the marathon was 'something which now reflects Wall Street more than ancient Greece. I am worried by the way it is run. It seems to have become a personal piece of property of Brasher and Disley. The marathon is not for the honour, glory or private advancement of anyone.'

Brasher hit back by pointing out that 'No other marathon in the world consistently shows a surplus which is given back to the City.' Under the constitution of the marathon, at the end of every year the company surplus is handed to the London Marathon Charitable Trust.

'The marathon is currently making £2 million a year surplus,' said Bedford, 'which goes into sporting recreational projects around London. In addition we also work with UK Athletics who get about £350,000 a year from us. This includes support for the Endurance Performance Centre at St Mary's College. Some of our surplus also goes into saving playing fields along with the National Playing Fields Association.

'It's true that Chris Brasher had initial concerns about the expansion of the marathon and the commercial direction it was taking. And had the marathon not grasped the nettle of commercialism way back in the late 1980s, then it would probably no longer exist. Even if it had survived, it would certainly not be the greatest marathon in the world.

'What the increased market activity allowed us to do was

to reinvest heavily in the event. So, for example, in the old days there might have been half a dozen pubs along the course who would lay on something special with, say, a band, but now we have a relationship with every single pub and they put out around 90 bands out there. Also we have schools near the course and we give them dedicated places to come and watch. A lot of those things cost money, so we reinvest, and that's why people say the race is incredible.

'Juggling the budgets used to be a lot simpler when payment was relatively modest and easy to work out,' said Bedford. 'Chris Brasher would just phone up a runner and say, "Come along and run the London." These days marathon runners have become superstars, they have agents and an agent's job is to get more money.

'It used, too, to be a hassle to get any kind of sponsor but now the London has more offers than it can consider. It matters a great deal what potential sponsors represent and whether they have the right image for the marathon.'

'The first law of sponsorship is simple,' said Chris Brasher. 'The greater the media exposure generated by an event, the greater the value of that event to your sponsor. When marathons were minority sports media exposure was limited. But when the size and quality of the fields grew, so did the interest of the public and the media.

'Above all the move on to city streets gave the marathon a dramatic stage, and television offered an audience never dreamed of,' he said. 'Television demands two things – top-quality international athletes at the sharp end and a large mass field of runners to give a sense of occasion. That's what we served up for them and they loved it.'

So, too, did the sponsors. Since Gillette, who provided the main sponsorship for the first three years, there have been four title sponsors: Mars from 1984 to 1988, ADT from 1989 to 1992 and Nutrasweet from 1993 to 1995. Flora took over in 1996 and will continue to be official sponsors at least until 2008.

'The world of marathon running has changed enormously

since 1981,' said Bedford 'and the London has changed with it. It was very unsophisticated at the start, whereas now it is as sophisticated and businesslike as any other sport at the elite end.

'We're often asked why we spend so much on the elite. The answer is that it is a fundamental part of the mix of the marathon and how the event is made up.

'What makes the marathon different to the Notting Hill Carnival?' asks Bedford. 'The difference is that the Notting Hill Carnival is a festival of people having a good time for no other purpose than having a good time. If it is lucky it receives 10 or 15 minutes on the TV news that day, and all too often the coverage is about the problems it has had. Without the elite, the Olympic end of the race, the London Marathon would be seen in exactly the same way – people out doing something just for themselves.

'But the TV coverage that comes from the serious end of a serious sport links nicely to the fact that there are then 33,000 other people doing something for personal endeavour, for personal fun and raising money – money for charity.

'You need television coverage and for that you need to attract big names. And for big names you need big money. Three elements have to come together at once – star runners, big sponsors and television. You have to convince them all that the others will deliver. When they do deliver it means that all the runners in the race, fast and slow, the ones who give and the ones who take, they all benefit. That's what makes London the great event it is for everyone.'

12

Out of Africa

Bare feet? Oh, we always take our shoes off for competition. So much more comfortable.
Abebe Bikila, Ethiopia's double Olympic champion

The stick-thin, ebony-black runner, lilting through the bush with ridiculous economy and speed, knows exactly what he wants and where he is going. What he wants is a world record and an education. Where he is going is London, to try to win the marathon.

His name is Josiah Thugwane (pronounced Tug-wan-ee), the 1996 Olympic marathon champion and South Africa's first black Olympic gold medal winner. When you pad breathlessly beside him through the South African bush, he may seem like something out of the past, running with untutored fluency, but this is where the past meets the future.

He may have little English and no education, but Thugwane is a thoroughly professional athlete, consumed with split times and sponsorship and what size bonus he might collect from Nike and Coca-Cola if he breaks the world marathon record.

He drove me to his training camp himself. He drives like he runs – fast. Propped up on cushions like a jockey, he peers over the wheel of his new and powerful 4x4, baseball cap on his head, mobile phone at his side. 'I have a big new house,' he says. 'I have the Olympic medal. I've got money in the bank, I've got this car. What I haven't got is education, that's next. I'm going to get a teacher, I'm going to learn to speak and write good English.'

We are used these days to champion runners tumbling out of Africa, racing in packs and trouncing world records. But even by African standards, Thugwane's is an unusual rags-to-riches saga. Abandoned by his parents as a baby, he spent his early years not in school, but looking after cattle and picking potatoes. The young Thugwane built by hand his family's corrugated-iron shack where he lived and eked out a living in relative squalor until his Olympic triumph.

Before the Atlanta Olympics he was almost unknown outside South Africa. At the time of the Games he was still employed cleaning kitchens and toilets in a South African mine. He made extra money on the side selling beer from a shack. He could not read, write or even sign his own name. He spoke his tribal language of Ndebele, with his tongue clicking wildly in the back of his mouth.

But he could run. And once he had scraped together enough money to buy his first pair of second-hand running shoes, he knew that he could pick up prize money. His first love, though, was football. 'I was a striker,' he says, 'fast but too small.' He is still only five foot two and needle thin at 99lb. His passion is still football. At the training camp, where there is little time for anything other than running, eating and sleeping, he watches football whenever possible on television, his battered feet propped as high as he can get them.

Outside, giraffe, zebra and wildebeest roam and hunters from Europe come to shoot game. But Thugwane finds more safety in the seclusion of his game park than ever he can in the jungle of Johannesburg. There he bought himself a fortified palace in a traditionally white middle-class area, all swimming-pooled and burglar-alarmed with high fences and threats of armed response to intruders. Thugwane says he has to do this because 'people won't leave me alone. They come all the time, they bang on the door, they climb over the fence, they want money. They won't let me sleep, they won't let me run, they scare my wife.'

He is not kidding. His very appearance at the Olympics was almost ended by a gunman. When he was selected for the Atlanta Games, Thugwane bought a Bakkie (a small van, a Mazda) to celebrate. A fortnight later his vehicle was hijacked by hitch-hikers. One pulled a gun and Thugwane now bears the scar of a bullet that ripped an inch-long furrow from left to right across his chin. He was left with his bullet wound, an injured back from leaping clear and a fear for his safety that haunts him still.

When he returned with Olympic gold he found he was a target for begging neighbours and gangs of criminals eyeing his newly won wealth. He has been subjected since to demands and death threats. To escape he keeps moving house and to train he heads for the bush. His latest move came after his wife was greeted at the gate of their home by the severed head of a monkey impaled on the garden railings.

It was only when Thugwane arrived back in South Africa that the significance of his achievement at the Olympics became clear to him. Nelson Mandela came to meet him at the airport and his success triggered a running boom among Zulus. He tries to help as many as he can. After finishing third in the London Marathon in 1997, he spent some of his prize money buying 50 pairs of running shoes to take home with him. He tours the townships giving them to people he thinks will use them. 'I only help those who are prepared to help themselves,' he says. 'If people say to me, "I can't run because I've no shoes," I say, "When I first started running I never had shoes and look at what I've achieved."'

He prepares for his second London Marathon with a regime of total running at the Gannahoek Game Park, where he shares a lodge with a couple of other world-class runners. They run twice a day, six days a week, sometimes as far as 35km. The runners get out for their first session at 6 a.m. to give them time to recover for another session in the late afternoon. They run on flat dirt roads, a fast surface but kind to the legs. They run at altitude, they run in the heat of a South African summer and they run very fast. Thugwane covered 35km in 2:03 for a first run of the day.

His shrewd manager and coach, Jacques Malan, used a similar formula of running and rest in the seclusion of a high-altitude training camp before the Olympic marathon in Atlanta. He knows it works and predicted with quiet confidence that one of his squad would take a medal that day.

The runners will stay in this training camp until six days before the London Marathon with no distractions, no sex, no shopping. The monastic preparation and their concern with the size of prize purses on offer in the marathons of the world remind you of prize fighters slugging their way out of the ghetto.

In the London Marathon, runners with the potential to challenge the world record stand to make so much money that David Bedford takes out insurance against it happening.

In the event Thugwane comes unstuck, and the best the former Olympic champion has managed in the London is his 2:08:06 for third in 1997. But in its 25-year history there has been no shortage of African champions who have graced the London Marathon.

The first of them was the enigmatic Douglas Wakiihuri in 1989. Wakiihuri, a world champion, was a Kenyan who lived and trained in Japan under the strict regime of his Japanese coach. He was followed by Abdelkader El Mouaziz, of Morocco, who in 1999 lost a course record bonus after slowing down to wave extravagantly at the finish and who won the race again in 2001. The Moroccan Khalid Khannouchi, who now runs for the United States of America, won the race in 2002 with a world record time of 2:05:38, and in 2003 the Ethiopian Gezahegne Abera won. The following year Kenya again claimed victory through Evans Rutto.

In the women's race, too, the Africans have left their mark, with two wins to Joyce Chepchumba of Kenya in 1997 and 1999 and one each to Tegla Loroupe of Kenya in 2000, Derartu Tulu of Ethiopia in 2001, and Margaret Okayo of Kenya in 2004.

With winners like these in the London, we have got used to the idea that Africa produces many champion endurance runners and we have learned to expect them to be at the front of the great mass marathons. But it was not always so. In the 1950s, on the tracks and roads of Europe, African distance runners appeared rarely and were regarded as a bit of a joke. In events where such quintessentially British qualities as discipline, strength of character and cool reserve were at a premium, the ebullient and, at times, reckless running of the Africans was seen as naïve and ridiculous.

The Europeans believed they had perfected the art of marathon preparation. It involved a high volume of well-disciplined training, a sophisticated scientific approach. It was not for nothing that one of the leading inter-war marathon runners was known as 'Treadmill' Cliff Bricker.

In those days Africa did have a great distance runner, one of the finest and most influential of them all – but he was white. His name was Arthur Newton, and before he embarked on the career of a globe-trotting professional athlete, he did most of his running in South Africa and in what, in those days, was still Rhodesia. Newton won the famous Comrades Marathon – 54 miles between Durban and Pietermaritzburg – five times and set a series of amazing world bests for long-distance racing. He once covered more than 152 miles in 24 hours – a record that still looks impressive over 70 years later.

He was a deep thinker and a wise writer about his sport. He knew his Africa and he knew his running, and time has proved the correctness of almost every opinion he held. But in one observation he was completely wrong. Like so many of his generation, he believed that the black Africans would never make great distance runners. Writing in the 1930s he said, 'The average Bantu or Zulu is far and away a more capable distance walker and runner than the average white man, yet he has no sort of hope when the latter gets into real training.' Try telling that to Olympic champion Josiah Thugwane or to the 2004 winner of the London, Evans Rutto.

The high point of the methodically trained European marathon runner came with Emil Zatopek. With year-round dedication never seen before, Zatopek churned out thousands of miles and turned himself into a gold-medal-winning machine. When he won the marathon at the Helsinki Olympics in 1952, it was his third victory of the Games, but trailing behind Zatopek was a man who hinted at the African running revolution to come. He was Alain Mimoun, an Algerian – but in the 50s that meant he ran for France. Eventually Mimoun beat Zatopek in the 1956 Olympic marathon in Melbourne, with his old rival in sixth place.

Four years later a man trotted down from the highlands of Ethiopia to astound the world. Abebe Bikila, grass-blade thin, black-skinned, a silent and dignified member of the palace guard of the Emperor Haile Selassie, was an unknown no-hoper at the start of the Rome Olympic marathon. He had a personal best of 2:21 but he was so African, so much an outsider that he ran without shoes on his feet.

Bikila, the mysterious Abyssinian, seemed to float out of the past – but his times belonged to the future. In 2:15:16, the time he took to win the Olympic marathon, he changed African running for ever.

The idea that an unknown Ethiopian could so easily defeat the best long-distance runners in the world in the hardest race of all sparked the hopes and dreams of every African boy. Bikila's legend spread far beyond his homeland and kindled the enthusiasm for running that in less than a decade swept over East Africa.

Soon the champions were tumbling out of Africa, from Kenya, Tunisia, Ethiopia and Djibouti. In the 1968 Olympics five Africans – Keino, Wolde, Biwott, Temu and Gammoudi – won gold medals. Since then they have hunted in packs for records and medals and you will find them at the front of all the world's great marathons.

The reason behind this African dominance is something that Chris Brasher would ponder over many pints on winter evenings. When he was a boy, and even during his athletic prime, it was generally reckoned that you had to be white and from northern Europe to be a good distance runner. The long-distance events had traditionally been dominated by athletes from these nations, men like Paavo Nurmi, 'the Flying Finn', and Zatopek, the 'human locomotive'. A black long-distance runner was a great rarity.

On the other hand, many, if not most, of the finest sprinters in the world were black. 'Sprinters,' Brasher would declare, 'are born. Distance runners are made – out of hard work.' But suddenly his athletic world seemed to be stood on its head. Almost overnight, it appeared, you had to be black and from Kenya or Ethiopia to be a world-class distance runner. The old idea that black athletes lacked endurance was now shown to be totally ridiculous, and there are all sort of theories as to why this is so.

Brasher was fond of saying that you could draw a line down through Africa, dividing two great gene pools that supplied the world with all its finest runners. West Africa and its sons and daughters transported to the USA or Britain gave us all the best sprinters. And East Africa produced all the best endurance runners.

How did this happen? And why were the distance runners from the east of Africa so dominant? Altitude was the most obvious explanation trotted out. The thin air of the highlands produced men and women with extraordinary adaptations of heart, lung and blood supply. When they brought their bodies down to sea level their birthright enabled them to beat all comers.

Others suggested that there was some athletically blessed gene pool based on natural or cultural selection. Many of the best Kenyan runners come from one locality. Most of the medal winners belong to the Kalenjin group, and more specifically to a group within that group, the Nandi.

Yet others suggested that the abilities are essentially cultural. The Nandi traditions derive from their past lifestyle as cattle rustlers and the theory goes that running prowess came to be prized as part of their tribal traditions. Their inherited capabilities were then set alight by the success of role models such as Kip Keino, the Kenyan who won gold medals at the high-altitude Olympic Games in Mexico in 1968.

It may well be, many believe, that the East African talent lies not so much in the genes as in the minds of those who see what their heroes have done, and who believe that they too can live this dream. The dream may well be what is most important.

If you are born a child in Kenya you run. In rural areas where cars and paved roads are still relatively rare, many still find walking and running the most reliable forms of transport and pace out distances between home and town, home and pasture, by the hours taken rather than the miles covered. Moses Tanui, who twice won the Boston Marathon and has covered the distance in 2:06:16, tells how when he was aged 14 he heard on the radio of an athletics meeting in a distant town. He had no way to get there other than his own two feet and so he decided to run the 37 miles there and the 37 miles back.

'The way there was easy,' he says. 'I was happy and excited. I didn't have money for food. I didn't have shoes but never mind.' When this happy-go-lucky adolescent stepped down to the marathon distance, and was given shoes and dollars to do so, there was no stopping him.

But not all Kenyans are born to be great runners. It's a country with over 40 different tribal groups, and the Nandi, the traditional hunters, who would spend hours, even days, tracking down their prey, make up only a few thousand of the total population. Their traditions, though, are tough and their lifestyle has developed an ability to deal both with pace and with pain.

One of their world-class runners once taunted an American athlete who complained of pain in the knee. 'Pain?' he said contemptuously. 'Pain is when you're 12 years old and they take you out into the bush, cut off your foreskin and beat you for three days. That's pain.'

Whether it's the ability to stand pain, altitude, the secrets of diet or simply the lure of a fortune, running is the way up and the way out for many hundreds of young East African athletes. They can leave Kenya or Ethiopia with little more than a good pair of legs and lungs and come back to buy a farm and a mansion.

The rivalry between Kenya and Ethiopia on the tracks and marathon courses of the world has been intense. By 2004 it looked as if Kenya had edged ahead, with 34-year-old Paul Tergat taking the world record in the marathon down to 2:04:55 in Berlin in September 2003.

Every so often Africa throws up a new champion to kick the legend forward. In Ethiopia Haile Gebrselassie is the new Abebe Bikila. Gebrselassie has won two Olympic and four world championship 10,000m titles and set 15 or more world records. His swansong on the track was in the Olympic Games at Athens where even the help of his team-mates couldn't tow him round to a final medal in the 10,000m.

Gebrselassie was born in 1974, the year that Bikila died, and he is now a legend in Ethiopia. After the 2000 Olympics in Sydney, he was welcomed home with a fly-past of jets, a gaggle of government ministers and a city-centre parade where a million fans cheered and saluted him. He has had a street named after him and a film made about his life.

Even so, the ever-smiling Gebrselassie reckons his greatest running may yet lie ahead of him, in the marathon and in London. Like Bikila and Keino, such men serve as an inspiration for the thousands more who will follow in their footsteps.

The difference is that these days, when they line up for the marathon, they are met not with the disbelief that greeted Bikila's triumph nearly half a century ago, but with the delight and respect that sport now reserves for the men and women who come out of Africa to show the world how to run.

13

Just You Watch

We've got athletes from every part of the world
– and elsewhere.
Brendan Foster, commentating on the
London Marathon 2004

Long after the African superstars have loped their way
through Docklands, you can hear the crowds enthusiastically bellowing, 'Come on, Fairy, come on, girl, you can
do it.' The London crowd are there for the rhinos just as
much as for the record breakers, and somehow you feel
they would never have let a Paula Radcliffe grind to a halt
in despair.

The spectators really can keep you going when your body
screams to stop. Once, while running in New York, I pulled
up briefly at a kerbside in Harlem with a hamstring injury
threatening to tear me out of the marathon. As I rubbed
and pummelled the leg, a lone spectator, a giant of a
gentleman, every inch of him Harlem man, shook his head
and warned, 'Don't stop here, man, nobody stops here.'
Sometimes it's best to do as you're told.

Thousands of marathon runners share such moments,
for no matter how well you've trained, how cautious you've
been with pacing, how often you've sipped at the drink
stations, there comes a time when you need all the help
you can get. And in the London, when you need it, it's
there from the crowd. There are people everywhere, bands
playing, everyone urging you on so that you can't, you
daren't, stop.

The spectators seem to put as much effort into supporting
as the runners do into running. For this one day London

simply stops, stands on the pavement and cheers. The spectators have a seemingly unending supply of sustenance for the runners: chocolate bars, orange slices, jelly babies, apples, bananas, water, fruit juice, Coca Cola or champagne – you can eat and drink every step of the way.

In the inaugural London Marathon the official drink stations were few and dangerously far between. In the pre-race hype Chris Brasher urged the public to get out on to the streets to ply the runners with water and set up refreshment spots along the route.

One such oasis was unforgettable. There, as you rounded a corner in the East End, you were suddenly greeted by half a dozen girls in basques and fishnet stockings, laughing, dancing and offering drinks in the drizzle. They had with them a huge banner. It read, irresistibly, 'Get your Kiss of Life here'.

'It's the interaction with the crowd that keeps you going,' says 73-year-old Jan Hildreth, who's made it through every London. 'You make eye contact a hundred times every mile with people you don't know, you've never seen before, but who are there willing you on to the finish. When these strangers catch your eye and shout, "Come on, don't give up," there's a contact that lifts you through exhaustion.'

It's as if the crowd don't just watch – they're part of the race. They're close enough to touch as you pass and the children love to slap hands and high-five with the runners. The smallest stretch their tiny arms upwards and glow with delight if you dip to touch their fingers.

Sometimes it's more than just fingers that touch. In one race Mike Peace, who's never missed a London, was striding proudly down the Mall to the finish when he was stopped in his tracks by a woman. It was his mother, Christine, who had run into the middle of the road to plant on him a smacking birthday kiss. She was hauled away by the police as Peace ran on and his father hid, red-faced, behind a tree.

For many runners it is the spectators and entertainers around the course that keep them on the move. Crowds of around half a million line the pavements. Pubs on the route link up with charities to provide their own entertainment. Local schools wave home-made banners. Pearly kings and queens rival the runners in the fancy dress parade. Bands beat out the rhythm of thousands of slapping feet as they dance through this 26-mile-long street party.

In among the balloons are the banners waving with their messages of encouragement. 'Pain is Temporary, Pride is for Ever' might inspire you as you shuffle by, but it's the child clutching a piece of battered cardboard with the message 'Come on Mum' that makes you tingle. 'You Start with your Legs but Finish with your Heart' might help you through the ache of those last impossible miles, while some marathon messages can bring a grin to the most pain-racked face. One in the New York Marathon advised simply: 'Run like her husband is coming'.

The first time you experience the cheers of the crowd lining the route can be very moving. 'People get cheered who have never been cheered in their lives before,' said Fred Lebow. 'It can be overwhelming. The effect on the runner can be very positive; after all, if a million people cheer and tell you you're looking great, you'd better believe it.'

The champions up at the front may be used to all the attention, but for the rest of the runners who can never hope to win, crowds are an extra, a precious bonus. When Alastair Campbell, Tony Blair's former spin-doctor, ran the marathon, he said that one of his most abiding memories was the support of the spectators and the sense of community along the course. 'I passed one block of flats,' he said, 'and there were flags out and all the kids were applauding the runners.'

It's been said of the New York Marathon that it's like being in a Broadway show – one with a 26.2-mile standing ovation – and there were plenty who doubted if that sort of crowd reaction could ever be matched in stiff-upper-lip Britain. But the idea that Londoners were too reserved to whoop and cheer did not survive longer than London's first marathon morning.

From the start the spectators claimed as their own the hordes of part-time and once-upon-a-time athletes plodding and laughing their way through the streets. It was as if they realised right away that what made the London Marathon an instant national institution were the thousands of shop assistants, policemen, housewives and accountants all slogging their way round for the simple joy of finishing and raising a few hard-earned pounds for a good cause.

For those who stand and cheer, the marathon has another remarkable effect. Thousands of them, once they've been caught up in the excitement of watching, wonder what it would be like to run it themselves. The event, and especially those final miles, can be a very emotional experience for runner and spectator alike. To watch a man or woman meet pain fairly, take on the challenge and overcome it can be deeply motivating.

'That's it then,' they say, standing on the pavement or sitting by the TV. 'If half a dozen rhinos, a gorilla, a 93-year-old and two blokes dressed as a camel can do it, then I can. And next year I'm going to.'

Once the flickering wish to join in rather than watch is ignited, they can't wait to start training. Soon enough they are obsessed with the idea of running a marathon of their own.

If you want to witness the fiercest crowd participation, turn up early on marathon day and take in the Mini-Marathon. There the mums and dads scream for the children as if everyone is running for Olympic gold.

The Mini-Marathon was dreamed up in 1986 as a competition for children from London boroughs, and in 2000 it started to take entries from all over the country. It has its own wheelchair division, and starters for the Mini-Marathon have included Steve Backley, Jonathan Edwards, Denise Lewis, Sir Steven Redgrave, Jonny Wilkinson and Martin Johnson.

Nicola Okey, one of the guiding hands behind these hordes of happy children, reckons the sight of thousands of boys and girls racing flat out along the last 2.8 miles of the course is one of the most enchanting of all on marathon day. The Mini-Marathon, now directed by former Olympic distance athlete Tim Hutchings, runs along the Embankment, past Big Ben, on to the spectacular finish in the Mall, just as the main race is starting in Greenwich.

Several of the early winners of the Mini-Marathon have gone on to international success. Andrea Whitcombe, who won it twice, subsequently held national cross-country titles and competed in world championships. In 1986, Don Martin, who has run in every London Marathon, encouraged his nephew, Keith Cullen, to have a go in the Mini-Marathon. Cullen won his age group race and since then has gone on to represent Britain as an Olympic marathon runner.

And while they may not dare to dream of the Olympics, these children, like the mums and dads in the main marathon, can all hope that they might be glimpsed on television. A wink at the camera, a crazy outfit, a collapse at the finish are all techniques well known to the marathon runner in the age of TV. That little marathon moment will be shared by millions, for while sport has always attracted spectators, the advent of television was a revolution in viewing habits throughout the world. Today there are many more people who watch their chosen sport on television than they ever do live.

In the first year of the London Marathon, BBC television covered it with just 50 minutes of highlights, but they recognised its potential to bring in a huge audience and the race has been covered by the BBC ever since with hours of uninterrupted live coverage. The London Marathon is one of the highlights of both the sporting year and the television year.

The race is one of the BBC's biggest outside-broadcast operations. The technical effort involves up to 46 cameras,

half a dozen mobile cameras on motorbikes and four helicopters. There is live and uninterrupted coverage on BBC
television, and extensive radio coverage. Capital FM has
long been the official marathon radio station, and both
BBC London and Five Live feature the race, with an
on-line service on the BBC website. The BBC provides
pictures around the world for millions, with live coverage
across Europe, Asia and Africa and with the race being
shown in some 180 countries.

Brendan Foster, now very much the on-screen voice of
the London Marathon, believes that the choice of commentators was a winning team from the start. 'David Coleman
and Ron Pickering were a perfect combination,' he said.
'Ron had a real empathy with people of all shapes and
sizes. He may not have known that much about champion
marathon runners, but he understood ordinary people
around marathons. And David Coleman's commentary has
always been some of the most exciting I have ever listened
to. He loved the London Marathon and he knew the details
of runners' lives and how they had prepared for it.'

In its early years, the London Marathon seemed insep-
arable from the distinctive cadences of Coleman and the
warm authority of Pickering. Coleman had been a talented
athlete himself, and way back in 1949 he had been the first
non-international runner to win the Manchester Mile. But
injury ended his competitive career.

In February 1989, as a recreational runner, Coleman ran
two half-marathons within five days of each other, both in
little more than 1:40. He felt he was in good shape and
was looking forward to running a marathon of his own.
Sadly he was hit by shingles while recovering from his
efforts in these half-marathons and had to give up his ambition of running in the London. But his passion for the event
cried out in his every commentary.

He became a national institution, not just for his gritty
and unforgettable descriptions and insights, but for his ability
to put his foot in it. He inspired a long-running column in

the magazine *Private Eye*, entitled 'Colemanballs', that ridiculed the manic propensity for sports commentators, particularly when unscripted and under pressure, to make memorable gaffes.

Coleman himself always denied that the classic gaffe that launched the column – 'and Juantorena opens his legs and shows his class' – was his. He blamed that one on Ron Pickering. But he could certainly lay claim to some classic originals: 'They're still faster although their times are the same,' he would blurt out, or 'Absolutely right but just a fraction wrong.'

In Ron Pickering, Coleman had the perfect partner in the commentary box for those early marathons. Long before he was one of the great voices of the BBC's athletics coverage, Pickering had been National Athletics Coach in Wales, during which time he coached and inspired 1964 Tokyo gold medallist Lynn Davies in the long jump. In later years he was known for his commitment to the development of sport, particularly at grass-root level.

Pickering's philosophy was that sport was one of the most precious commodities that we can hand on to the next generation, and his contribution to this area of athletics lives on in the form of the Ron Pickering Memorial Fund, which does much to support young athletes.

The trio of Pickering, Coleman and Foster had a particularly tough few hours together during the London Marathon of 1990, when low cloud meant that the BBC helicopters were out of action. They tried bravely to describe the progress of a race that neither they nor the TV viewers could see. There were no pictures being transmitted from the lead vehicles at the front of the race because the helicopters that linked those cameras with the transmitting station just weren't operating. Left struggling with pictures from fixed cameras at the start, the viewers were treated to endless shots of pantomime horses and ostriches leaving Blackheath, followed by scenes of roads being swept and rubbish collected.

The London Marathon

The following year there was a sad shadow over the race following the death of Ron Pickering. His wife Jean was given the honour of acting as starter and David Coleman picked out one of the banners carried by runners at that start. It said simply: 'The London Marathon dedicated to Ron Pickering 30,000 times. We all miss you.'

Today the voices of the marathon are those of two former champion athletes, Brendan Foster and Steve Cram. And while the evergreen Coleman may not be there taking the mike, Foster and Cram can still trot out performances of their own quite worthy of 'Colemanballs'.

In 2004 Foster enthusiastically informed the millions of viewers that here in London were 'athletes from every part of the world – and elsewhere'. While Steve Cram explained the technical ups and downs of marathon running by noting: 'There are no hills on this course, and there's Tower Bridge which is a hill.'

'Over the years,' says Foster, 'the crowds have got bigger and bigger. When you see London with all its landmarks and all those ordinary people somehow ready to take on the toughest event on the Olympic programme, it really is fantastic. My only regret is that I gave up my own running career in November 1980. I didn't know the London Marathon was just around the corner. If it had been announced earlier that they were staging the London, I would have kept running to do it.

'In my day the marathon was a race for older men. It was what good track runners tacked on to the end of their career. But I would have loved to have done that one, perhaps to have won it in front of all those spectators in London. It would have been a fantastic memory. It really is the best free show on earth and that's why, year after year, millions want to watch it.'

14

Eating Up the Miles

You've gotta eatta your pasta to runna mucha fasta.
Anonymous

'The smartest marathon runner could lick them all with honey,' said Chris Brasher, writing in the *Observer* way back in 1969. He explained that Ron Hill, running in the European Championship Marathon in Athens in September 1969, had overtaken Belgium's Gaston Roelants towards the end to win the race after following a secret pre-race diet.

It was one of the first reports of what was to become known in marathon running as carbohydrate loading. 'Ron Hill,' he wrote, 'ran last Sunday's marathon, from Marathon itself to the old 1896 stadium in Athens, with the aid of diet.' The diet, Brasher continued, had been discovered about three years previously by a couple of Swedish scientists called Bengt Saltin and Lars Hermonsen. They showed that a person's capacity for prolonged exercise is limited by the available stores of carbohydrate – which is basically the glycogen contents of his muscles. By messing around with your diet it is possible to alter the percentage of glycogen in your muscles.

But for some peculiar reason which is not yet understood the most effective procedure is to exhaust all the glycogen in the muscles and then keep the glycogen content low for a few days by eating a predominantly fat and protein diet. Then when you switch to a high-carbohydrate diet, your glycogen-starved muscles go through what is known as overcompensation. So much so that the glycogen content of the muscles can become as high as 5 per cent whereas normally it's an average of about 1.5 per cent.

None of this, Brasher pointed out, will do the marathon runner any good at the beginning or in the middle of the race. At those points he has to rely on his fitness, speed and stamina. But after about two hours of really fierce exercise the normal glycogen supplies become exhausted and the runner has to start burning fat for fuel, a slow process. Could carbohydrate loading be the answer to the marathoner's age-old problem of hitting the wall?

It seems that the marathon is really beyond the normal physiological limits of fuel supply for all except extremely well-trained runners. The distance is simply too long, the race is too fast. Metabolically man is a long-distance walker, not a marathon-runner. But the body might be fooled.

Anyway, Hill was convinced that he could outwit his body. He believed his special two-part pre-race diet worked, and he wanted to keep the secret to himself. He began his last week's training before a marathon with a long, exhausting run six days before the race. Next he would go on to a high-protein, low-carbohydrate diet for three days, while still training relatively hard. Then just three days before the race he would dramatically reverse his eating regime, stuffing himself on carbohydrates – bread, pasta and potatoes – while reducing his runs to short, slow jogs of a few miles.

The effects could be dramatic. I was one of the early runners who tried the diet. It was great if you got it right, but it could go horribly wrong. During the high-protein phase you could feel so weak and tired that it was hard to walk upstairs. You would feel light-headed, dizzy sometimes, and find it very difficult to run. Several runners who tried the diet fell ill with colds. When eventually you came through it there would often be a feeling of bloating in the legs before the start of the marathon and you usually felt a little stiff in the early miles. But at 20, when others around you were hitting the wall, your reserve tank would kick in and you might yet be master of the marathon.

The Swedish scientists and Ron Hill were sure that they had come up with a dietary approach to distance running that was completely new. The idea of carbohydrate loading ran counter to centuries of advice that saw sportsmen from boxers to ultra-distance runners gorging themselves on rare steak as a pre-race meal. But in reality there were hints from the past that a pre-event diet might be manipulated using carbohydrate.

The American legend Clarence de Mar, who won a record seven Boston Marathons between 1911 and 1930, used what he called an 'elimination diet'. For one week, during which he continued his normal heavy training (often 100 miles a week), de Mar would eat only fresh non-starchy fruits and vegetables. Then when he switched to reintroducing bread, bananas and potatoes, he was delighted to find he could run long and hard without fatigue.

Even earlier, in the 1880s, Percy Stenning, who, in the colours of the Thames Hare and Hounds, cruised to victory in the first two English cross-country championships run over nine miles, was much criticised by contemporary athletic pundits for stuffing himself with pastries when training hard and in the days leading up to his distance races.

Since Ron Hill's early days experimenting in Athens, where he won the marathon, opinion has swung round to the idea that it may not be wise to use the high-protein phase of the diet. It may be both risky and ineffective. It makes training difficult and it can increase susceptibility to infection. Anybody in hard training is probably depleting their glycogen enough anyway.

Some fine runners found the results of tinkering with the diet were disastrous. Jim Alder, Commonwealth Games marathon champion in 1966, is said on one occasion to have been given faulty information about what his great rival, Ron Hill, was up to. As a result poor Alder, it was said, got the diet the wrong way round. He carbo-loaded at the beginning of the week but then depleted his fuel supplies by cutting out the carbohydrates and eating only protein going in to his race. He had a very hard time of it.

Timing is certainly crucial. Although pasta parties the night before the marathon are popular, the benefits are probably largely social. In most cases the night before is far too late for effective carbo-loading.

The best fuels for marathon runners to load up on are complex carbohydrates – bread, potatoes, cereals, rice and pasta. The intake of food containing the simple sugars, such as chocolate, sweetened drinks, honey and jam, should not be overdone. Clearly, stuffing yourself with pasta the night before the marathon is not enough. To have any chance of running comfortably and well, you need to pay close attention to how you fuel your body during the many weeks leading up to the race.

The guidelines are simple enough. The runner's diet has to fuel the muscles so that the body can cover the distances required in training. It has to replenish the fluid that is sweated out in vast amounts while exercise is being taken. And it has to supply the vitamins and minerals that everyone needs, and which sometimes can be flushed out by the taking of large amounts of water and depleted by bouts of heavy exercise.

The athlete who runs regularly enough will usually find that the body will dictate its own dietary preferences. He may crave fruit and liquids, find that pasta, potatoes and bread keep the energy levels high, and that foods dripping in fat can stop him running for hours.

Despite all the sound advice about eating and sport, some athletes simply don't eat enough. An alarming initiative was launched in 1999 by the British Olympic Association, UK Athletics and the Eating Disorders Association. They wanted to make athletes and their coaches, family and friends aware of the early-warning signs of eating disorders like anorexia and bulimia nervosa.

Research at the University of Leeds by Angie Hulley, a former cross-country champion and marathon international, had shown that one in ten of Britain's female distance runners had 'some kind of eating disorder' and were obsessively convinced that less fat equals more fitness. It can happen at the highest level. Liz McColgan, who won the London Marathon in 1996, revealed that in 1988 in the run-up to that year's Olympics, her weight fell to seven stone. She was outkicked for gold in the 10,000m in Seoul. 'I was so weak and undernourished I didn't have the energy to sprint for the line,' she said.

Some obsessional athletes reveal that they often exercise in saunas or run or cycle in plastic or rubber clothing to sweat off weight. Others have been known to use such high-risk techniques as jogging in hot showers while wrapped in plastic bags, swallowing diuretics, laxatives or amphetamines, and self-induced vomiting.

There are some, though, who take the opposite view and reckon that running is a licence to eat. They believe that anything is possible in training if they can just get their hands on enough food and drink. Few would want to match the amazing tuna-sandwich-eating champion of Harrogate, one Steven O'Neill, who, when junior 800m champion of Yorkshire, ploughed his way through 25 tuna sandwiches a day: six for breakfast, fifteen in his packed lunch and four for supper. At tea-time he made do with a large plateful of pasta or rice (with the inevitable tuna added), and throughout the day, whenever he was hungry, he topped up with snacks of apples and cakes.

O'Neill, at six feet two inches and eleven stone five pounds, believed he was underweight and that his food intake was the key to his training.

The most prodigious amount of food consumed in what can be classed as a sporting venture led, amazingly, to a loss in weight. The ultimate sporting diet was documented in mouth-watering detail by Dr Mike Stroud, a compulsive explorer and a sport scientist who's put his body through challenges that most would consider crazy. He has journeyed the Himalayas and the length of the Amazon. He has run in the Sahara Marathon of the Sands – billed as the world's toughest foot race – and, most famously, he teamed up with Sir Ranulph Fiennes the explorer to be the first to walk unsupported from coast to coast across the Antarctic continent.

While dragging a sledge across the South Pole, Stroud did detailed research on diet and its link with body weight. The daily mountain of food was enormous and makes O'Neill's 25 sandwiches look like a slimmer's snack.

'I considered an ideal intake should be as much as 6,500 calories each day,' said Stroud. 'But to haul a sledge with 100 days' rations containing that much energy was not a practical proposition. Instead I decided that the best compromise was to eat only 5,500 calories and accept the loss of body weight.'

It was a mistake. On some of their toughest days, Stroud and Fiennes burnt more than 11,000 calories each. Their energy use far exceeded any measurements previously reported in scientific literature. 'When Ran Fiennes and I returned,' Stroud said, 'our weights were down by nearly 25kg (55lb). With this weight loss we were absolutely ravenous but Ran and I were not like famine victims. We remained hungry in the face of great weight loss because, despite eating too little to meet our needs, we had maintained a very large throughput and so had no marked vitamin or trace element deficiencies. Indeed, rather than anorexia, our drive to consume was total and we both ate day and night for several weeks after coming home.'

The message of such research, Stroud believes, is that we are all just a few steps away from the wandering hunter-gatherers who once roamed Africa. We are born to play hard and eat as much as we can get – and trouble starts

Runners hit the cobbles against the backdrop of Tower Bridge

Dave Bedford, long-time
Race Director of the London Marathon

Haile Gebrselassie,
who dreams of a new world record

Steve Redgrave with his son
Zak at the finish in 2001

Grete Waitz dances over the cobbles

And others dance over the sponges

Josiah Thugwane,
Olympic champion,
with the author

The Laughing,
Running Cavalier

How many smiles to the finish?

Steve Cram, champion
turned commentator

Frank Bruno, heavyweight champion
of the marathon

Flat out and finished,
girls at the end of the mini-marathon

Alan Storey, coach
and former Race Director

Fauja Singh, ran the 2004 London
Marathon at the age of 93

Jim Clarke,
long-time Chairman of
the London Marathon

Boxer Michael Watson, the man who never gave up

The greatest show in town, the mass-start of the London Marathon, 1998

Dame Tanni Grey-Thompson, six times a
winner of the London Marathon

Jeffrey Archer lords it over London in 2004

The flying squad of Britain's finest bobbies

The *Cutty Sark*, one of the
great landmarks of the London Marathon

Roger Black, the man they called 'sex on legs'

Running in the Outback,
Chris Moon and the author

only if we miss out on the hard exercise. Almost all of us, he believes, have tremendous sporting potential and can, if we wish, not just finish marathons, but run across deserts or frozen continents provided we are supplied with enough fuel.

And when it comes to fuelling marathon runners, no single ingredient is as important as fluids. An average runner will lose approximately one litre of sweat for every hour spent running in a marathon. It's not uncommon for a competitor to drop between four and five kilos (10–15lb) of body weight during a race. What is lost is all water, and if it isn't replaced, it can lead to dehydration and heat stroke.

So in the London Marathon there are drink stations all along the course. These stations are essential. Between the start line at Blackheath and the finish at Buckingham Palace, the 33,000 competitors will lose something like 120,000 litres of sweat – enough to fill an Olympic-size swimming pool.

Race organisers now know that runners need their water, but it was not always so. Not long ago in international competitions it was illegal for runners to drink anything during the first third of the race. After that fluids could be consumed only every five kilometres.

These days no runner's kit bag is without its sports drink. Sports drinks are big business. They are often weird-tasting, expensive and can make the unwary runner feel sick. Even so, plenty of runners hope that somehow the miracles promised on the bottles and the cartons might some day come true and get them to the finish fresher and faster than ever before.

In 1999 the London Marathon came up with a sports drink of its own. Along with the 600,000 bottles of mineral water given out at drinks stations along the route, around 130,000 squeezy pouches of Liquid Power, London Marathon's own branded isotonic sports drink, were handed out every five miles. I was given vast amounts of the prototype of this drink to try out while running 250km in the outback of Australia with Chris Moon in oven-blasting heat. We found the drink worked fine but tasted foul – and was much more palatable with a dash of gin.

Whether it's Ron Hill with his protein, or Percy Stenning with his pastries, when it comes to food and drink all runners want to believe in magic, and there have been plenty of commercial magicians through the history of sport who have been eager to cash in on that.

'You too can have a body like mine' was the seductive promise of the Charles Atlas mail order physical culture course that proved irresistible to millions of would-be athletes from the 1930s to the 60s. It made much of before-and-after pictures and was an innocent enough regime – a mixture of press-ups, squats, isometric contractions (dynamic tension) and advice to drink gallons of milk. But the sales slogan of Charles Atlas – real name Angelo Siciliano – tapped into a deep longing in the hearts of the young. For the promise that you too might play football or cricket, jump, ski, swim or run and win fame, fortune and immortality has always been a powerful lure.

The fantasy of emulating their heroes has long been the substance that has fuelled great sporting careers. The bare-foot child in Kenya inspired by Kip Keino, the boy from Brazil yearning to be the new Pelé, the young French cyclist dreaming that he is a Jacques Anquetil – they all hitched their fantasies to a star.

That's fine, but ever since the ancient Greek Olympic Games, competitors have been prepared to try anything and risk any health hazard to steal the competitive edge. Much has been made of the survey done in 1995 by the National Academy of Sports Medicine in Chicago. They asked almost 200 athletes of Olympic class the question, 'If you were offered a banned substance that would enable you to win every competition for five years but would kill you, would you take it?' More than half answered yes.

A century or so ago you could take what you liked, and

marathon runners often did. It was your lookout if you put your life in danger. You could take your pick from morphine, strychnine and belladonna, as well as the more innocent beef tea, reckoned to be better than any of them.

In turn-of-the-century Britain, the top coach was Harry Andrews, trainer to Alfred Shrubb, then the greatest distance runner in the world. In his training manual, published in 1903 and endorsed by Oxo, Andrews confessed that he had tried everything to get his men to run further and faster, from a tumbler of champagne to cocaine. 'Strychnine in lozenge form is also used,' Andrews said. 'I tried this once on a man during a bad time and it had no effect at all so I reverted to hot beef tea and got my man home all right.'

In great city marathons like the London, the spectators are always there with the promise of a reviving snack or drink. Mike Wilkinson, one of those men who has run in every London Marathon, remembers the great enthusiasm of the crowds during the first race in 1981, and being handed what he thought was a glass of orange juice. He discovered that it was actually buck's fizz and that he was running fuelled by champagne.

It didn't put him off, though. A few years later, when he was having a particularly bad run just before reaching the Tower Hotel, he saw a family sitting on folding chairs on the pavement. 'Father was drinking a glass of cider and I said that it looked really refreshing,' said Wilkinson. 'He asked if I'd like a glass too. I immediately stopped running and joined the family group. I had some cider and a cigarette and a lot of amused stares and comment from the other runners.'

I know how he felt. During many London Marathons I arranged for a glass or two of champagne to be waiting for me at 21 miles. It was served chilled, on a silver tray, by the staff of the *Times*. It never got me through the wall, but it certainly cheered me up along the cobbles.

For some years, too, I used a variant on the carbohydrate

loading – I called it 'claret loading'. I found that drinking
the best part of a bottle of decent red wine on a Friday
was a very effective way to both relax and load the legs
with glycogen for a race the following day. It was unusual
but it seemed to work. A similarly unusual approach to
sports drinks was used by 'Tarzan' Brown, a member of
the Narragansett tribe from Rhode Island in the United
States, who allegedly did most of his training in saloon
bars. But it didn't stop him from winning the Boston
Marathon in both 1936 and 1939, so maybe there's something to be learned about fluid replacement from these
old-timers.

Perhaps the last word on fuel for running should go to
Alfred Shrubb, the wiry, mustachioed Englishman reckoned
in his time to be the greatest distance man in the world. A
century ago he broke seven world records in one November
evening.

'I think beer is a great aid in training taken of course in
moderation,' said Shrubb. 'An athlete should drink it as he
feels he wants it. During all the time I have been racing I
have found it a great help. Look here, it's no use a man
trying to run races on tea and soft stuff, it does him more
harm than good. You must have something more solid and
muscle-giving in you.'

15

Outrunning the Years

Start slowly then taper off.
Racing advice from Walt Stack, veteran American runner

To take up marathon running when you have been given only six months to live may seem defiant. It may appear even more improbable if you are 70 years old, 40lb overweight, a lifelong smoker and under warning from your doctors that anything as strenuous as mowing the lawn could kill you instantly. But Noel Johnson, given months to live in 1970 because of a heart condition, ignored the medical advice and took to exercise.

Ten years later, having run, walked and weightlifted his way to fitness, he was the oldest finisher at the age of 80 in the New York Marathon. He set age group records at the mile and the half-mile and ran more than 20 marathons, setting world age records for 84-year-olds (5:42:19) and 88-year-olds (7:40:58).

He became a legend, featuring as the oldest runner in marathons and a fitness guru famed for his views on nutrition and training. Way past his eightieth birthday he would run nine miles every other day and work out on an exercise bike. On the days that he rested from running he did weight training. Eventually the medical doom-mongers caught up with him and he died in San Diego. But he was 96.

There was a time when the world of sport belonged firmly to the young, but increasingly these days the oldies are at it. Much of the impetus comes from the United States. Johnson was very much an American hero. In an age that

141

believes in equal opportunities for all, it seems that millions of Americans believe that they were born with the right to life, liberty and the pursuit of a place in the marathon.

One of America's other great legends – John A. Kelley, who ran 61 Boston Marathons, winning two of them – died in 2004 at the age of 97. He ran his last Boston at the age of 84, and came home in under six hours. The veterans don't stop at the marathon. In 1994, at the age of 41, Irishman Eamonn Coghlan became the first human over 40 to run a mile in under four minutes.

Often ageing sportsmen have been considered remarkable not as athletes but as curiosities. There's always been the occasional venerable performer: the evergreen Stanley Matthews still waltzing down the wing at 50; Ken Rosewall reaching the Wimbledon Men's Final as an antique of 40; Willy Carson winning the Derby at 52; Jean Borotra playing Wimbledon at the age of 66; and W.G. Grace captaining England at 50. There are so many these days that we are getting used to it.

Sports medicine experts have traditionally taken a decidedly cool view of the ageing athlete. A sprinter, they tell us, reaches his physical peak at around 25, a tennis player a year or so later. In football the peak comes at about 28; in cricket and golf at, or just after, 30. But increasingly athletes are discovering ways to get more out of their years. Watch the London Marathon and you will see vast numbers of runners in their fifties, sixties and seventies. Some are even older.

Distance runners like these are a group who can face age with equanimity. The Ethiopian Miruts Yifter won the 5,000m and 10,000m at the Moscow Olympics when some say his age was 36 and others 46 or more. 'Yifter the Shifter' was balding, tiny at five feet three inches, his ageing forehead corrugated with wrinkles. He could hardly have been what the founder of the modern Olympic Games Baron de Coubertin had in mind when he called on the youth of the world to gather together every four years. The story goes that Yifter would shrug his bony shoulders when asked his age and reply, 'You can take away my chicken or my sheep so I count them, but no man can take away my years so I don't count the years.'

What sportsmen like Yifter or Johnson do best is to give us a glimpse of our own possibilities. Just as a world record reassures us that the trajectory of human evolution is still moving forward, so the ancient marathoner, skipping through 26 miles, tells us that we can still raise a run.

Johnson wrote a best-selling book entitled *A Dud at Seventy, A Stud at Eighty*. But there was one ambition he didn't fulfil. He wanted to run a marathon at the age of 100. In London I met a man who might dream of it still.

Before the start of the 2004 London Marathon I dived into a tent to shelter from the rain. There in the corner was a face I recognised. The man sat comfortably in his seat, motionless, resting up for the race to come. But as he caught my eye he rose politely to attention to shake my hand. His name was Fauja Singh. He was about to run the marathon. He looked the picture of health. And he was 93 years old.

Singh – all turban, long grey beard, bright eyes and Adidas shoes – was running in his fifth London Marathon. As well as his four previous Londons he had done a marathon in Toronto and another in New York. He had lived most of his life in the Punjab in India where he was a farmer. He came to Redbridge in Essex after his wife's death to join his youngest son and his family. Fauja is father to four children and grandfather to 13.

He had been a casual runner in his younger days in India but he gave it up when he was 36. After a break of 53 years he took up running again, as therapy he said, and to give himself a purpose in life.

'I love it because it is good for my health and it gets me out of the house,' he said. 'Marathons are tough and even when you're ten yards from the finish you can't believe you've put yourself through it. But once you cross the line that changes and it's pure elation. I'm proof that anyone can run a marathon. I might be old, but look at all the people with disabilities who do it. It's difficult but it's only those who haven't run one who say they can't do it.'

Fauja decided to try the London Marathon at the age of 89 after he'd seen it on television, but he discovered that he had missed the closing date for entries. Neighbours put him in touch with Harmander Singh (no relation), who was well known locally for running marathons in fancy dress to raise money for charity. Harmander helped him get a Golden Bond place through the charity BLISS, which helps premature babies, and offered to help him with his training. Since then Harmander has taken on the role of trainer, mentor, adviser and interpreter.

A typical training day for Fauja starts at 6 a.m. with breakfast of toast, glucose-rich syrup and tea and a portion of yoghurt. His running begins around 7 a.m. and he reckons to cover about six miles every morning. His morning session ends with warm-down exercises, stretching and a hot bath. After lunch he walks up to seven miles, and on some days he covers as much as 10 miles jogging.

He is intensely competitive and is proud to have set new records in the London Marathon for runners in their nineties. He weighs in at eight stone, which is float-around light for his height of six feet. He is a vegetarian and he doesn't drink or smoke. Each morning he meditates before training and he prays morning and evening every day.

He usually runs a mile-and-a-quarter loop on the roads several times in training, each lap in around 15 minutes. He runs easily without distress and pauses briefly between each loop to sip water. At 93, Fauja Singh believes he has achieved most of his marathon ambitions, but he says he might make a comeback in 2009. 'I have retired from marathon running at the moment,' he said. 'But the world record for the oldest person to run a marathon is 98. I'd like to beat that.'

Runners like Fauja Singh and Noel Johnson owe their achievements not to the fact that they were outstanding when they were younger but to the determination they have shown to continue to practise the activity they enjoy. Others who run on into old age have simply never stopped.

Gordon Porteous, a Scot who has set a string of world records for distance running in the over-nineties division, and still holds the best British marathon times on record for over-75 and 80-year-olds, said he has missed only three weeks of training since the 1940s. Porteous has been running hard for 70 years. He was an international cross-country runner in 1946 and ran the marathon in 3:23:12 when over 75.

But you don't have to run continuously for 70 years to reach standards like these. The most important factor is how hard you train, which is related to your psychological drive – your motivation. When someone takes up running for the first time, or comes back to it after a long break, he or she will usually improve dramatically in the first year or two, whatever their age. Training will transform the body into that of an athlete given time, patience, hard work and good health. This applies particularly to endurance events – the marathon and beyond. One of the great joys of running is the realisation that the average unfit person can reverse many of the effects of ageing by using a suitable exercise programme, and that remarkable feats are possible at almost any age.

One weekend in Birmingham eight years ago, a 95-year-old carried off three gold medals while competing as a guest in the European Indoor Veterans Athletics Championships. His name was Everett Hosack and he was born in 1902, the year King Edward VII was crowned in Westminster Abbey, and when you could have snapped up 82 acres around Earls Court in London complete with 1,450 houses for just £565,000.

The remarkable Hosack, from Ohio in the United States, took his titles in the long jump (2.00m), 60m (16.96 secs) and shot (4.07m). I caught up with him as he relaxed after his exhausting weekend by flitting around London like any other tourist on foot, bus and tube – his gold medals jangling in his pockets and his fitness and pride in his victories twinkling in his 95-year-old eyes. When he had seen the sights in London and Birmingham he had plans to take in Paris before flying back across the Atlantic.

Hosack said that he first put on running shoes when he was 21. That was back in 1923. He went to the University of Florida, where he was soon a leading hurdler. After university he ran in a team formed by the New York Central Railroad, his employers, but after the Wall Street Crash of 1929 the stockholders were not keen on spending money on sport, so the track meetings ended.

For the next 50 years, Hosack's athletics career went into suspended animation. But he kept himself trim, and his simple exercise and diet regime might serve as a model for anyone who wants to prepare themselves for a long and successful sporting old age.

As well as his tough physical work in the shunting yards of the railroad company, he lived an outdoor life in the country. He said that he had seven acres of land on which he had planted 300 pine trees. 'I mowed a path around the trees and I used to run around it,' he said. 'It wasn't far, just a mile or so, but I would run it in five or ten minutes two or three times a week. It was much better than running on the sidewalk, which is too cruel on your knees.'

It was a perfect example of training that was just hard enough to keep him in good shape and health, but not so tough that it would wear him out or injure him. Add to this half-century of regular light exercise a good marriage and sound nutrition and you may well have the formula for a long life and sporting success.

Hosack said of his wife, 'We have been sweethearts since 1929 and she fills me up with plenty of fresh vegetables and fruits and we keep well away from anything in cans. I eat simple food but I do have a big weakness for pies – blueberry pie is my favourite.'

Perhaps, I suggested to Hosack, his secret lay in extra

vitamins? 'I do take an odourless substitute for garlic,' he said, 'a one-a-day multivitamin pill and some vitamin E.' However, when asked if he believed that this was the recipe for long life, he said, 'It's too soon to say, I've only been taking them for the past six months.'

After his long mid-career break from competitive sport, Hosack made his comeback at the age of 77 when he joined the Over The Hill Track Club. The secret, he said, was that his legs were still strong and not worn out. It's a pattern that has been echoed by Fauja Singh and by one of Britain's greatest runners, Sir Christopher Chataway.

Chataway was world class when young in the 1950s, pacing Roger Bannister in the first sub-four-minute mile and defeating the Russian, Vladimir Kuts, to set a world 5,000m record. He kept fit, though not competitively so, during his middle years, and now he is enjoying a renaissance as a veteran athlete. At the age of 73 he ran 1:39 for a half-marathon in Brendan Foster's Great North Run.

Such men as Chataway and Hosack make time their friend. They defy the years and, like younger world record breakers, give us a glimpse of what is possible and of hope for the future. But even they are sometimes guilty of a backward glance at their days of glory. When I told Hosack that he looked in great shape for a man of 95, he smiled nostalgically. 'Ah, sir,' he said with a twinkle, 'you should have seen me when I was 92.'

With the growing numbers of indestructible old-timers tackling the marathon, there has been increasing speculation that in the next few years the world will see the first 100-year-old go the marathon distance. In the 2004 London Marathon there were more than 6,000 runners over the age of 50; well over 1,000 of them past 60; and nearly 200 of them gone 70. There were even 16 runners over 80, with the remarkable Fauja Singh the grand-daddy of them all at 93.

For years now the New York Marathon has been offering a million-dollar prize for anyone who can complete the 26 miles at the age of 100. It was a prize that Noel Johnson had long dreamed of winning.

Johnson ran out of time, but someone will do it soon according to Craig Sharp, a sports scientist from Brunel University who has studied sport and ageing. 'We are going to get centenarian runners,' said Sharp. 'Some day someone over 100 will run the marathon and it will be quite soon. You are literally never too old to run.'

It's a dream shared by Derek Fisher, who has run in and finished every London Marathon and who plans to run for a long time yet. 'My father,' he said, 'lived to be almost 102 and I see no reason to stop doing the London Marathon just because I'm getting older. It's a great event and I don't intend to miss it. What I'd really like to do is to run the London on my one hundredth birthday.'

16

Goody-Bag Hunting

I seem to be taking part in a mammoth reunion.
Everybody knows me and I know almost everyone else.
Ron Hill, on the magic of the London Marathon

However old he may be, there is often something mysteriously childlike about a marathon runner. Watching the thousands queuing to register for the London Marathon, you realise that they have all the enthusiasm of children turning up for a birthday party.

What excites them is not the thought of running 26 miles – that is terrifying. Nor is it the prospect of getting the race over with – that leaves them in pain for days. What makes them so enthusiastic is a simple secret known to everyone who has ever organised a children's birthday party: waiting for them is a bag full of free goodies – and if they are lucky there is another bag of goodies when they go home.

The goody bag for runners is something that appeared with the mass-participation folk festivals that are now the big-city marathons. The men who got them underway in the 1970s and 80s were living embodiments of childlike enthusiasm. Men such as Fred Lebow in New York and Chris Brasher in London, it seemed, grew old but wonderfully never quite grew up.

There are runners who perpetually globe-trot, running marathons in New York, London, Paris, Berlin or Boston, caring not which are the fastest courses, but which have the best-stuffed goody bags. So what is in these mysterious bags that send full-grown and finely trained men and women on their way with such childlike grins? What delights do sponsors like Flora and the team behind the London Marathon come up with?

Along with their race numbers, the thousands who check in carry away with them a bag that gives a remarkable insight into the strange and obsessive world of the marathon runner. The most essential item apparently is the tub of Vaseline. Marathon runners are meant to be well-oiled machines. The preferred lubricant is Vaseline and it goes on all moving parts – between the toes, under the arms and to places only marathon runners care about.

Then there are mysterious go-faster nasal strips. These are strange plasters that flare the nostrils and terrify the opposition. They will be hot fashion on the day of the race. There will also be an invitation to a 'Carbo Carnival' for, despite their skinny appearance, marathon runners like to eat their own body weight in carbohydrates before they start.

There is information on heart monitors, disturbing if you are undertrained, and gifts aplenty – sports rubs, magazines, safety pins, mineral water, pasta and sauce. Along with all these essentials come pages of last-minute instructions, the most important of which is advice not to use the gardens of people around Blackheath as loos.

The goody bag at the finish is no less fascinating. Here, for the enthusiastic child of the marathon, is the customised T-shirt, available only if you have covered the whole 26 miles, and, according to David Bedford, 'the most sought-after souvenir'. I have one from the 1996 London Marathon. 'I went through the Wall' boasts the legend on the front, officially endorsing the belief that a mysterious metaphorical barrier exists and that runners must climb, crash through or crawl over it to reach the finish. Also in the finish goody bag is yet more pasta and sauce, an apple, mineral water, a sports drink and a fruit and carbohydrate energy bar.

So sought after are the goody bags that they have even

been the target for thieves. Ten thousand goody bags and at least 1,100 medals went missing during the marathon in 1990. ADT, then the title sponsor, had laid on 35,000 goody bags, but although there were only 24,871 finishers, the bags ran out. Chris Brasher said, 'Ten thousand bags went walkabout. An element of banditry evidently crept in. We fell short. These medals and bags are clearly something everyone wants.'

How anyone ever completed a marathon in the days before the goody bag is, of course, a mystery. But the marathon party is not over for the runners until they collect their medal. In the long-ago mists of marathoning you had to finish first, second or third to win a medal. Nowadays there are medals for all.

On the back of one I have is an inspirational thought from Ralph Waldo Emerson, the nineteenth-century American poet and essayist. 'Nothing great,' it says, 'was ever achieved without enthusiasm.'

When you stagger across the finish line, and you wonder at what you have done, they hang this medal on a ribbon round your neck. You know it's cheap enough, and you know there are many thousands of them, but at that aching moment, with 26 miles behind you, you also know that you wouldn't sell it for a fortune.

The annual London Marathon exhibition where the runners check in and collect their goody bags is a strange and challenging maze of stalls, stands and giant television screens – half Aladdin's Cave, half Ideal Running Kit Exhibition. Masses of runners graze around it. Men and women – the short, the tall, the thin and the very thin – wander through it clutching their Flora London Marathon bags, as if afraid that someone might snatch their precious numbers.

The exhibition is stuffed with running shoes, kit, videos, books, gadgets, gels, pills and strange potions all guaranteed to make even the most well-prepared runner feel hopelessly inadequate. Can you really contemplate going to the start line on Sunday without a 'chill band' that refrigerates your head, a magic pain-relieving patch or a velcro clip to strap energy bars to your shorts?

In case the weather is foul on race day, you can even get yourself a pair of waterproof socks called 'Porelle Drys'. There is a guy jogging round and round in an inflatable paddling pool offering to let you feel his feet as proof that they work.

The best advice for any marathon runner, in the days leading up to the race, is don't try anything new and don't buy anything new. But try telling that to the mid-pack runners, nervously sniffing round the shoe-packed stands. These men and women are vulnerable, an at-risk group, ever ready to be seduced by the go-faster promises that lurk in every aisle.

Everywhere there are shoes that must be faster, lighter and more comfortable than the ones that you trusted would get you past Buckingham Palace. Not only that, they are all on special exhibition offer with irresistible discounts.

If you take it slowly you can browse among armfuls of souvenirs – thimbles and T-shirts, tankards and teddy bears. You can arrange to have your photograph taken and blown up as a memento of your finest four hours. You can get your running gait analysed. You can sign up for marathons in far-away places you've never heard of, or even the North Pole. You can pick up an Iron Man Sports Watch with a built-in personal organiser or satellite navigation equipment.

For the foot-weary one shoe company has a team of masseurs and sports injury therapists on standby. They even have a podiatrist, a foot balance specialist who normally works with top athletes, ready to cast his eye over the most battered feet in town. Those who prefer the do-it-yourself approach are encouraged to pummel their own bodies with a Ron Hill massage stick or a small wooden ladybird.

The more energetic can get their bodies wired up and tested on treadmills before renewing depleted stores of glycogen with buckets of pasta and endless free samples of energy bars. They can, and do, preview every step of the coming ordeal on video, and you can buy strange books that ooze enthusiasm for running.

After months of training, some of the runners who haunt the exhibition have incredible reserves of stamina and are quite capable of spending four or five hours on their feet, drinking in the atmosphere and the free samples. Others are so seduced by it that they will put in several guest appearances over the four days that the exhibition runs.

You can spot the ones who have been at it for hours – they look gaunt and desperately in need of a rest and a drink. But they will be there in their new shoes and shiny new kit on marathon morning. If you think they look exhausted, remember it may not have been the race that did it, merely the hours they put in at the Great Exhibition.

Behind the exhibition, as behind the marathon itself, there is an army at work controlling every detail of the great day. It may have started with a desk and two chairs back in 1981, but as the event has grown, so has the number of people behind it. These days, in their new headquarters close to Blackfriars, a full-time team of nearly 20 is lorded over by long-term Chairman Jim Clarke, Chief Executive Nick Bitel and Race Director David Bedford. Calls from around the world are fielded by a press team headed by Nicola Okey.

Huge photographs of all the London Marathon winners dominate the walls, and 25 years of medals dangle with memories of the millions of footsteps run since the event began. 'The organisational team is full of people who run and who have run in the past at the highest level,' said Bedford. 'That means whether you are the Olympic champion or a five-hour charity runner, you will find you are talking to runners who understand your problems.'

Come race week the team call in more than 50 extras to man the marathon machine, and practically the whole circus decants to set up a new race headquarters at the Thistle Hotel in St Katharine's Dock near Tower Bridge. There they are backed up by regiments of helpers.

There is a 100-strong medical team presided over by the evergreen Dr Dan Tunstall Pedoe and Commissioner Seamus Kelly of the St John Ambulance, who have both worked with the marathon since the first London race. St John mobilise around 1,600 volunteers, with doctors, nurses and paramedics armed with defibrillators. They even have half a dozen medics out on mountain bikes patrolling the course.

The numbers needed to keep the marathon moving are staggering. Over 1,000 marshals at the start, 2,500 at the finish and 3,000 more out on the roads. Somehow they all get in place along with the 1,000 or so portable toilets and the 88lb of Vaseline needed every marathon morning.

The race is not the only event masterminded by the London Marathon machine. There are Flora half-marathons in Silverstone and Liverpool, a 5K City Run in the City of London and Hydro Active Women's Challenge races in London, Birmingham and Liverpool.

There is, also, one much greater event that they still hope to mastermind. 'Should London be successful in the bid for the 2012 Olympic Games,' said Dave Bedford, 'we would be responsible for organising the marathon. We have designed the course and it has been approved by the bid committee, which shows the world-class status the London Marathon now has.

'Chris Brasher, who was an Olympic medallist in 1956, would be as proud as punch to think that this organisation would be laying on the Olympic marathon. We decided the Games marathon could start on Tower Bridge and do three laps, taking in the Embankment, the Houses of Parliament, Buckingham Palace, Trafalgar Square, The Strand, Fleet Street, St Paul's, the Mansion House and the Tower of London. Then the runners would head for the Olympic stadium. What a course!

'But John Disley's original route is still a great one,' said Bedford. 'The start in Greenwich, the Cutty Sark, the Tower – and now with the backdrop of Buckingham Palace we have the finest finish in the world. It's like running through all the postcards.'

Weaving through that picture-postcard course, plotted and planned by Disley, is a thin blue painted line. It takes 300 litres of paint and it is laid in the dead of night on the eve of the marathon. It marks the shortest way round, every step from start to finish.

But it's not there for long. The marathon clean-up brigade are out there scrubbing it away before the sweat has dried on the last runners wending their weary way home, before they've had a chance even to empty their treasured goody bags.

17

Defying the Odds

In running it doesn't matter whether you come in first,
in the middle of the pack or last. You can say, 'I have
finished.' There is a lot of satisfaction in that.
Fred Lebow

'One Michael Watson, there's only one Michael Watson,' chanted the crowd gathered to witness London's slowest ever marathon finisher in April 2003.

'That man,' said Dr Peter Hamlyn, 'has no business walking to the end of the road. Just walking a mile for him is the equivalent of a marathon. I think his finish is one of the greatest physical achievements the marathon has ever seen.'

'That man' was the former boxer Michael Watson, whose career was ended after his fight with Chris Eubank at White Hart Lane in 1991 where he suffered horrific brain injuries. He underwent six life-saving brain operations and spent six months in a coma. Peter Hamlyn was the neurosurgeon who saved Watson's life, supervised his rehabilitation and suggested he tackle the marathon.

'Most marathon runners,' said Hamlyn, 'hit the wall after about 20 miles. Michael will hit the wall after about one mile. In fact he will be more or less walking up it. His injuries were colossal, he was on the brink of death for weeks. He's already extraordinary for surviving, extraordinary for recovering his mind, extraordinary for learning to walk again.'

Watson may have taken six days to complete the course, but no runner in the London Marathon achieved a greater impact than the ex-boxer when he crossed the finish line in The Mall. Walking beside him for the last mile was Eubank, his opponent in the fight in 1991 when Watson collapsed into a corner after the twelfth round.

After the fight it seemed unlikely that Watson would live. His brain terribly injured, he was in a coma for 40 days and doctors thought he would never talk or walk again. For Watson, at 38, the idea of completing the marathon was a ferocious dream. Like the dreams of so many marathon runners, it was a feat almost, but not quite, impossible. And for many, like Watson, with the odds stacked against them, the marathon is the challenge that can win them back their self-respect.

Watson's aim was to walk the 26 miles, 385 yards unaided, with no wheelchair. He planned to do a session of about two miles each morning and the same again in the afternoon. It was a brave ambition.

The legacy of his brain injury was paralysis of his left side. When he set out to walk the marathon his left leg would swing outwards, his left heel would bang the road, his left arm bent crazily and his fingers were held crookedly. He walked as if he was dragging a ball and chain – but he walked.

He reached the one-mile marker to a chorus of 'You'll Never Walk Alone', and a few lurching yards further on he was overtaken by the crew sent to scrub the blue line off the road.

A couple of painful miles later a homeless man, who spent his nights in a cardboard box, took 70 pence from his pocket to give to Watson for the Brain and Spine Foundation he was supporting. An ice cream man donated his whole day's takings, and by the finish Michael Watson had raised more than £200,000 for the charity.

Boxing promoters Frank Warren and Frank Maloney walked with him, as did boxer Audley Harrison, former sports minister Kate Hoey, and Dave Bedford. Muhammad Ali sent a good-luck message from the United States.

Six days after the the winner had crossed the line, they

set the finish gantry up again to greet Michael Watson, and the crowds turned out to chant and cheer. He paused on the line, swaying a little, then lurched across it into the arms of his mother, Joan, who hung the finisher's medal round his neck. The clock showed six days, two hours, twenty-seven minutes and six seconds.

'I hope I can inspire people,' said Watson. 'They said I was going to be a cabbage. What a horrible way to describe a person and look how wrong they were.

'They said I would not walk. They said I would not talk, but look at what I have achieved. The longer it has gone on, the stronger I have felt. In truth I didn't want it to end.'

'In terms of sheer endeavour Michael Watson showed everyone what the marathon is all about,' said Bedford. 'I don't want to sound cynical, but over the years we've had masses and masses of contact from people who have been hurt or damaged and it would be fair to say we've become a little bit hardened to it. But when Michael came to us we were stunned by his iron will. I've never seen someone so challenged by so much. The man is a star, no question.'

Twelve months before Watson's painful saga, 40-year-old Lloyd Scott had set the previous slowest time for the London Marathon. Wearing a 120lb antique diving suit, Scott, a leukaemia survivor, completed the course for charity in five days, eight hours, twenty-nine minutes and forty-six seconds. He was greeted with a kiss from Paula Radcliffe, who'd won the women's race.

I first met Lloyd Scott a decade earlier, in a Lakeland pub, when both of us were sheltering from heavy rain. We were both in running gear and he introduced himself. 'Hello,' he said, 'my name is Scott and I plan to walk to the South Pole.'

A former professional goalkeeper and fireman who battled with leukaemia in 1987, Scott has always been up for mad and life-affirming marathon stunts. In 2003 he was one of the six contestants in the Flora 1,000 Mile Challenge organised by the London Marathon and designed to emulate the feat of covering one mile every hour for 1,000 hours achieved by Captain Robert Barclay nearly 200 years before.

Scott failed to finish that one and pulled out vowing to spend more time with his marathon-widowed wife and children, but soon he was to be found walking a marathon in another diving suit – this time underwater at the bottom of Loch Ness. After that it was off to ride a penny-farthing bicycle across Australia. He had already run a marathon in the foothills of Everest, another in the Sahara and completed expeditions to the North and South Poles.

'For me,' he said, 'great marathons like the London are a chance to show to the world that there's life after things like leukaemia, and the money that's raised does wonders for those who are fighting the odds.'

The stories of courage in the marathon are legion. The trail for them was blazed by the arrival of the wheelchair athletes in the London race in 1983. They were welcomed, it must be said, with a mixture of curiosity and sympathy that some found patronising. And their arrival was not without controversy.

Originally Brasher had fiercely opposed them and decreed, 'Wheelchairs will not be allowed in the London Marathon. Let's be quite clear about that, it would be far too dangerous. The first rule of the marathon is that it should be a foot-race – but it's really the danger to everyone including those in the chairs that worries me.'

The Labour-controlled GLC, and particularly the GLC's deputy leader Illtyd Harrington, were having none of it, and threatened to withdraw £100,000 worth of backing and support for the marathon unless the wheelchair athletes were allowed to compete alongside the runners.

In truth there were enough practical problems to cause Brasher and his team concern. The massed field of runners averaged around seven miles an hour, while wheelchair competitors can exceed 30 miles an hour on downhill sections. The potential for dangerous collisions was obvious, and in 1983, when the wheelchairs started at the back of the field, there were three accidents as the chairs collided with runners on foot.

But these problems were resolved once the wheelchair race started 15 minutes ahead of the field. This gave the wheelchair athletes a clear run and allowed many of them to finish before the first of the runners on foot.

There were just 17 finishers in that first London Wheelchair Marathon in 1983 – the men led home by Gordon Perry and the women by Denise Smith. By 1990 the number of wheelchair finishers was up to 60.

No wheelchair champion has been more successful and more popular than Tanni Grey-Thompson. Born with spina bifida, Tanni has won the women's wheelchair event six times, starting in 1992. 'I watched the first race to include wheelchairs on television in 1983 and decided that I wanted to run a marathon and that it would be London,' she said. 'When I first competed in 1989, staring out at thousands of people, I felt sick with nerves. And I always forget how bad the stretches of the course with cobbles can be until I arrive at them.

'But if anybody asks me which marathon to race I always say London. It has done so much for the profile of wheelchair sport.'

Until her triumphs in the Sydney and the Athens Paralympic Games, Tanni was always better known for her appearances in the London Marathon, even though she considered her talent was much greater on the track. Certainly her victories in London have helped turn her into Britain's best-loved wheelchair athlete. With 16 Paralympic medals to add to her six victories in London, she has long since won her battle to be accepted as a serious athlete both on the track and on the streets of London.

The catalogue of the heroes and heroines who defy the odds and tackle the London Marathon is as long as it is inspiring. Four years after she was told her cancer was incurable and she would die within months, Jane Tomlinson was still alive, had raised nearly a million pounds for charity and had completed three London Marathons. The mother of three from Rothwell near Leeds had also cycled from Rome to Leeds on a tandem, completed three London triathlons, two Half Iron Man triathlons, and the Nice Three-Quarter Iron Man triathlon.

She took on these fund-raising marathon feats while living with the knowledge that she might die at any time from the cancer, which started in her breast when she was 26, and then spread to her lungs and her bones. 'There were a couple of things I wanted to do when I was diagnosed as terminally ill,' she said. 'One was to raise money for cancer research, the other was to say to people who might also be facing death, "Yes, it is awful, but you can still have a good time."

'It does feel like a full stop to your life when you are first diagnosed but you can't just sit there and wait to die.'

In January 2001 Jane decided to train for a three-mile race. 'I'd never done any running before,' she said. 'The first time I went out with my husband Mike we got about 400 yards. I was sick when I crossed the finish line but at least I did it.' By October of that year she was feeling well enough to consider doing a London Marathon. 'Instead of thinking, "It's not fair, I'm going to die",' she said, 'I was thinking, "I'm very lucky to be here."

'I was absolutely terrified on the morning of the London. By 23 miles I was hobbling. I was in an awful lot of pain but I knew that unless I collapsed I was going to finish.' As well as a sense of personal achievement, Jane's races are about creating some special memories for her children. 'We've a huge box full of photographs of all my runs, all the cuttings will be put in there so that the children can look at them in the future,' she said.

Some who defy disease and disability in the London Marathon may appear fragile, but Sir Ranulph Fiennes seems hewn from granite. In June 2003 the explorer had double by-pass surgery after suffering a heart attack. Four months later he achieved the incredible feat of completing seven marathons in seven days on seven continents, starting in Patagonia in South America and finishing in New York.

In 2004 Fiennes was there again at the start line of the London Marathon. Six weeks before the marathon his wife had died, and he had completed a marathon at the North Pole just one week before – all of it to raise money for the British Heart Foundation.

Everyone who completes the marathon is a hero for a day, but such men and women as Fiennes, Jane Tomlinson and Michael Watson are among many who show extraordinary determination and overcome colossal odds to get fit enough to cover 26 miles.

I first came across Chris Moon at a London Marathon training camp in Lanzarote. He extended his left hand in greeting. 'Sorry I've got a strange handshake,' he said, glancing at the silver hook on his right arm. 'I'm told you might be able to help me with my running.'

In 1995 Chris Moon stood on a landmine. It blew off his lower right leg and damaged his right hand so badly that he lost that too. But less than a year after leaving hospital he had run his first London Marathon. He approached me because he wanted to run faster.

We went for a run together so that I could assess his form. It was shocking. His relentless rhythmless lurch rocked his body with every step. But he never stopped and he refused to give up.

After that first run I told him he could knock an hour off his marathon time by improving his technique. By the end of April and the London Marathon, we had done just that.

But Moon's desire to conquer his disability didn't stop with the marathon. Soon he was taking on runs in the Sahara Desert and in America's Death Valley, climbing Mount Kilimanjaro or trudging from John O'Groats to Land's End, and I found myself covering 250km with him in the hostile heat of the Australian outback.

'This,' said Moon, happily, 'is definitely the toughest thing I have ever done. It makes the Sahara Marathon look like a picnic.' We carried backpacks with water, electrolyte drinks, emergency rations, flares, whistles, compasses and survival blankets. But the tougher and rougher it comes, the more Moon likes it.

The first day of that run was oven-door hot, up to 35°, with not a hope of a cloud. Within the first two hours Chris was suffering from sickness and diarrhoea. When blood appeared on his stump I began to wonder if the whole venture might be over on the first morning. By the second day his first-choice artificial leg had had enough. We had to fall back on his spare.

He is so gutsy and so driven that as soon as I managed to coax him to run without pain he would feel he was not trying hard enough. 'I just want to show that anything is possible. Never give up. Never give up,' he would mutter over and over.

Moon's is a mantra that could serve for all those who defy the odds in the London Marathon. Each year you see them, out on the long road from Greenwich to Buckingham Palace, defiantly showing, again and again, that anything really is possible.

18

Cheating and Chips

Sadly nobody's ever offered me their body for
a place in the marathon.
Dave Bedford

Chris Brasher and Fred Lebow would delight in telling me colourful tales of the outrageous letters, phone calls and pleas they had from people trying to secure one of the coveted places in their marathons, which are always vastly oversubscribed (98,500 applied for the 2005 London).

Some people will do anything to get themselves a number. Lebow said that an actress who was working for the New York Marathon back-room team as a volunteer once took him outside on to a balcony during a party.

'She started to stroke my beard, then my legs,' said Fred with a chuckle. 'She said that her husband had won the marathon once before but had been rejected from this year's race. She would,' she hinted, 'do anything to get her husband accepted.' Fred rejected her advances and her husband didn't get to race.

There was a letter, too, from a married woman who said that she'd fallen in love with a married man at a marathon training camp. They were desperate to run the marathon together, she pleaded, and if they couldn't she warned they would be driven to suicide. So could Fred Lebow 'save her life'?

'Then there was a nun,' said Lebow, 'who reckoned that running a marathon was a good way to get in touch with the Lord.' One poignant letter Fred received came from a man who wrote that his older brother had run in the New

York the previous year as one of his final acts before dying of cancer. This man had kept his brother's trainers and now wanted to be accepted to run in his 'dead brother's shoes'.

'It was a hell of a letter,' said Fred, 'but the problem was we'd accepted him to run with exactly that same story the year before.'

There were plenty of sob stories in London, too. Mike Peace of Ranelagh Harriers was one of a team of 50 or so volunteers who helped Brasher sift the entries in the early years of the marathon. 'Most of the heart-tugging letters went straight in the bin,' he said. 'If you believed them all, there were mothers about to die all over the place, just clinging to life to see their son run in the London.

'Then there were the bribes – the entries would come in with cash stuffed in the begging letters. Brasher would put the money straight into the marathon funds, but the letters went into the reject box.'

About a month before the 1979 New York Marathon, long after the entries had closed, a girl approached Fred Lebow to ask him if he could fix an entry. It was, she said, for a friend, a girl who was terminally ill with a brain tumour and had not much time to live. Her last wish was to run in the New York Marathon.

Fred said he'd need a letter from the woman's doctor giving her the go-ahead to run, and another from a lawyer saying she wouldn't sue if something went wrong. The letters showed up and he gave her a place in the marathon.

In April the following year Lebow went to watch the Boston Marathon, which was won that year by Bill Rodgers. But when Fred saw the women finish he was amazed. 'The first girl across the line had an inefficient and ugly stride,' he said, 'and she seemed fresher than most of the fast women marathoners I know.'

That woman was wearing the number W50. She crossed the line in 2:31:56 and was whisked away to the winners' podium. Her name, it was announced, was Rosie Ruiz. She was 23, she was from New York, and she was destined to become one of the best-known names in the history of the marathon.

'I knew there was something wrong right away,' said Lebow. 'I had never heard of this woman. She stood there and her T-shirt wasn't even sweaty. She didn't look like a great runner and I didn't believe there was someone this good from New York that I didn't know about.'

Fred was not alone. Charlie Rodgers, brother of Bill, the man who won the race, took one look at Ruiz on the podium and thought she was a fraud. 'The first thing I did was look at her legs, and I said to myself, "Oh, we have a problem here." I mean it was Cellulite City.'

Lebow was then told that Ruiz had qualified to race in the Boston Marathon by running the New York Marathon in 2:56:29. Rosie, it turned out, was the girl who had been given her entry to his race because of her 'brain tumour'.

'So at the press conference in Boston I asked her if she was a member of any running club in New York,' said Lebow. 'But she wasn't. She didn't even have a coach but she said she ran 65 miles a week around the reservoir in Central Park.'

A check with the computer back in New York showed that she had indeed been recorded as finishing in 2:56, but Fred knew there was something wrong. He and his team trawled for hours through videotape film of the finish of their race. Rosie Ruiz didn't appear at her recorded time or anywhere near it. In fact she was simply nowhere to be seen.

The mystery of whether Rosie Ruiz had really won the Boston Marathon sent the press into a frenzy. The day after the race the *Boston Herald* published a huge photograph of the start under the headline, 'Win $1,000: Find Rosie in this Photo'.

The story and the jokes running with it were carried around the world. 'Did you hear Rosie Ruiz is writing a book?' comedians would ask. 'It starts on page 425.' Or, 'Have you seen the Rosie Ruiz panty-hose? Guaranteed not to run.' Her name trotted into the household vocabulary. Rosie Ruiz suddenly became the most famous marathoner in the world. She had her winner's laurel wreath, and her medal – and she was not going to hand them over.

Back in New York, a photographer called Susan Morrow got in touch with Lebow about the Ruiz affair. 'She said that on her way to see the finish of the marathon she got in the subway in Greenwich Village where she saw a woman wearing running clothes and a marathon number,' said Lebow. 'They talked and the woman introduced herself as Rosie Ruiz and said she'd dropped out of the race with a foot injury. Both women got off the subway at Columbus Circle and walked to the finish line area together.'

Susan Morrow said that she watched Rosie, still wearing her number, go through the barricades behind the finish line to tell officials that she'd hurt her leg. First-aid workers took her away for treatment and one of the medical staff, assuming that she was a finisher, had taken the bar code from her number and given it to the scorers.

Lebow held a press conference and declared that Ruiz was disqualified from his race, and after a week's investigation the Boston Marathon officials eventually disqualified her from their race too.

It turned out that because of her apparently high finish in New York, Ruiz's employers had offered to pay her way to the Boston Marathon. Her boss said he looked forward to seeing her name in the papers again, perhaps even further up the field next time. In Boston, eye-witnesses came forward to say that Ruiz had actually joined the Boston race at Kenmore Square, about a mile from the finish.

While the press delighted in peddling Rosie Ruiz jokes, it wasn't so funny for Jackie Gareau, the French-Canadian girl who had run in behind her in Boston. She was baffled. For most of the race she'd been met with loud cheers as the leading woman runner. Then, after 25 miles the cheers and yells were replaced with polite and sympathetic applause. 'You're second,' shouted a man in the crowd. But

Gareau was sure that no woman had passed her. She knew she must be in the lead.

Ruiz, it turned out, had come to the United States in 1961 from Cuba. She had genuinely undergone brain surgery for the removal of benign tumours but had completely recovered. Her employers were a firm called Metal Traders Inc. and she ran in a bright yellow T-shirt with the letters MTI on the front.

MTI fired her after the Boston episode, when it was alleged she had presented fraudulent cheques for $1,000 or so to New York department stores. In 1982 she was arrested for stealing $15,000 in cash and $45,000 in cheques from a subsequent employer. In 1983 she was caught dealing in cocaine worth $52,000.

To many, Rosie's motives were baffling. She made no money from her marathon performances and she never admitted that she'd cheated. But what the episode told Fred Lebow, Chris Brasher and the watching world was that the marathon had become so big, so glamorous, so newsworthy that some would do anything to be part of it and run for a few moments in the limelight.

Rosie was certainly not the only runner to cheat in the marathon. In 1999 Sergio Motsoeneng apparently finished ninth over the 54 miles of the Comrades Marathon in South Africa. In fact he almost pulled off one of the sport's greatest scams, but photographs of the performance showed that he was wearing a pink wristwatch on one arm for some parts of the race, and a yellow one on the other during different stages, though his clothes, race number and timing chip appeared to be the same throughout. He had kept fresh and fast by switching with his brother Sefako during toilet breaks along the way, each running different stages. Sergio was disqualified from the race and the brothers were banned for 10 years.

A similar trick was used in the Brussels Marathon in 1991 when thousands cheered the Algerian Abbes Tehami, who broke the tape with the clock showing 2:18. However, cameras showed that he had started the marathon with a moustache but was clean-shaven when he sprinted over the finishing line 50 yards ahead of the field. His coach had run the first nine miles and the pair had switched vests behind a tree on a remote part of the course.

And when Kenya's Simon Biwott ran the Berlin Marathon in 2:07.42 there were 33 runners behind him who had tried to keep up by leaving the course, taking the underground and rejoining the race near the finish.

The taking of short cuts was quite a problem for the London Marathon, too, before the introduction of the computer chip attached to every runner's shoe. In 1987 Chris Brasher said, 'The only way to stop the cheats is by publicly naming them.' He explained that extra video cameras were to be concealed along the course to pick out people taking taxis, tube trains or motorbikes to cut down on the running distance.

Brasher told of one man who feared ridicule at work after being persuaded to join the office team. He was so overweight that during the early miles of the marathon his thighs rubbed together and began to bleed. The pain tempted him to miss out the Isle of Dogs loop, which saved him 11 miles.

'Then there was a woman,' said Brasher, 'who claimed an impressive finishing time of under three hours. But when she was questioned by race officials she admitted that she'd hidden in the crowd around the halfway mark and only done about 13 miles of the course.'

John Disley said that many cheats did it to impress their friends or through fear often caused by the pressure of sponsorship. 'Some decent people have felt the need to cheat because they were being sponsored for a lot of money and could not live up to expectations,' he said. 'They didn't want to let down the local church or the kids' hospital. It's sad.

'There were also,' he said, 'plenty of pirate runners – who took part without an official entry or an official number. In some cases they used to copy the bar code from a supermarket can of baked beans and fix it to a number painted or drawn with fibre pens to which were attached logos of the sponsors behind the race.

'With such crudely forged numbers pinned to their vests, these pirates were often able to masquerade as accepted entrants and stride with confidence up to the finish on Westminster Bridge. With Big Ben as a backdrop, and waving to the cameras, it made a lovely souvenir picture.'

'We were always pretty aware of these rogue runners,' said Alan Storey. 'We usually let them run along until the last mile, then, when their resistance is low and the field is spread out, we have groups of bandit snatchers to examine their numbers. When we spot a fake we bundle them off the road in quite a vicious way,' he added with a smile.

'We could stop them earlier but it would usually cause more problems. There are sometimes as many as 50 or 60 rogue runners and we have even had runners with no clothes on. One once tried to streak across Westminster Bridge to the finish line naked, but he never made it.'

In 1996 the London Marathon went as far as naming and disqualifying two veteran runners, both over 60, because stewards were not convinced they had completed the course. Race officials spent hours during a six-week enquiry scrutinising videotape taken at an Isle of Dogs checkpoint but they were unable to spot the two runners.

'We had no alternative,' said Storey. 'A lot of people train tremendously hard. We owe it to them to remove anyone from the results when it is obvious that their performances lack credibility. It's not a massive problem, though we did pull out a couple of dozen every year, usually in the last mile, to make an example of them.'

But time and technology were about to overtake the marathon cheats.

Ingeniously, the device that was to solve the problem was developed by a farmer who wanted to keep track of the whereabouts of his pigs. He used a small radio frequency device and realised the potential of adapting it for use on human trotters.

The London Marathon started to use the ChampionChip in the 1996 race. Small enough to be taped to runners' shoes, the chip can be 'read' each time it passes over a specially positioned mat – spread across the width of the road so that no runner can miss it. The ChampionChip relays instant information back to the race organisers and to radio and television commentators.

'The new scheme offers accuracy and immediacy,' said Storey, who added that one of the chip's other main benefits would be to help television commentators identify individual competitors. 'We will also be able to tell who's catching up and who's falling behind at almost any point in the race,' he said.

The chips were originally issued to the leading competitors, while other runners could hire or buy one. They proved so successful and useful that they are now strapped to the shoes of every runner. The chips mean that every finisher can get an accurate time for the marathon no matter how long it takes.

In the days before the chip the time shown on the overhead gantry at the finishing line often didn't correspond to the time shown on the runner's personal stopwatch. That was because with more than 32,000 runners all trying to start the race, it could take up to 20 minutes or more for the whole of the field to cross the starting line.

These days, thanks to the microchip technology, it's almost impossible to take a short cut in the London Marathon. The days when a Rosie Ruiz could hit the headlines are over.

There are still, of course, plenty who will phone or write with unlikely sob stories in a bid to get their hands on a race number. 'Though sadly,' said Dave Bedford, 'nobody's ever offered me their body for a place.'

19

Simply the Best

*The possibility of a two-hour marathon is quite logical. I
cannot believe it will be long before such a time is run.*
Haile Gebrselassie

What Paula Radcliffe noticed as she raced to a world record
in London on 13 April 2003 was the music blasting from
one of the pubs along the route.

It was Tina Turner's 'Simply the Best'. Paula had listened
to the song over and over in the minibus as she was being
driven to the start. It was part of a motivational tape that
her husband, Gary Lough, himself a former elite miler, had
put together to inspire her.

It certainly seemed to work as the girl who had once
been dismissed as a serial loser, a gallant runner-up, turned
on a performance that had marathon experts shaking their
heads in wonder.

Her world record of 2:15:25 was an astonishing display
that marked a quantum leap in women's distance running.
Her time tore almost two minutes off the world record she
herself had set in Chicago the previous October, and saw
her fly home 4½ minutes ahead of Kenya's Catherine
Ndereba in second place.

It was the biggest winning margin in this race since Ingrid
Kristiansen took the last of her four marathon titles in 1988.

Wearing sunglasses and white gloves, along with the
flesh-coloured knee-length socks that had become her trademark, Radcliffe set out at world record pace from the start.
Her first mile took 5:10, her second 5:08, the third was
even faster at 4:57. Her coach Alex Stanton admitted he

was 'a little surprised', and those who know the marathon well believed that she was certain to blow up.

'The crowds at the start and around the course were fabulous,' said Paula. 'They wished me luck and roared me on and their contribution cannot be underestimated. They are one of the reasons the London Marathon is such a great event.'

Before the start Paula asked Gerard Hartmann, her physical therapist, how he thought she should run. He merely advised her to run as she felt. Hartmann was the man who had put Radcliffe back together after she had collided with a young cyclist during one of her long training runs a few weeks before the race, using emu oil to treat the cuts and grazes she suffered in the fall.

Hartmann and the rest of 'Team Radcliffe', her husband Gary and coach Stanton, had left nothing to chance. Paula had had her usual pre-race breakfast of porridge, honey and bananas. She did her stretching in the hotel and then set off for the start.

Once the race was under way, the other women seemed overawed, content to let her take off at breakneck speed. 'The only time I got worried was when I saw on the clock on the lead vehicle that I had run the third mile in 4:57,' she said. 'I felt very strong and played mind games with myself on the way round. At one stage when I had stomach pains I counted slowly to 100 and knew that when I had done that three times another mile would have gone by.

'The last stretch along Birdcage Walk felt wonderful,' she said. 'The crowds were cheering and because I'd studied a video of last year's race I knew exactly how far there was to go. In the last 800 metres I gave it everything, and at the line I thought I was going to be sick with the effort.'

Head bobbing and arms flying wildly, Radcliffe sprinted across the line with a smile. She bent double and then wobbled as if she might faint and fall. She grabbed a water bottle and straightened up to pose for the cameramen by the finish gantry.

After the race, Paula said she was 'feeling rough because of the stomach cramp that came on at around 19 miles'. She had dug deep into pain to run the fastest time in history. At the finish line nausea and fatigue now overtook her. She struggled with the demands of the routine drug testing, carried out on all winners, and the calls for her to talk to the press. She wobbled in and out of the portaloos at the finish, cramping and passing blood.

Back at the hotel she was offered champagne but turned it down in favour of sipping chicken soup. Shivering and exhausted, all she wanted to do was to curl up and lie down. But after a couple of hours crashed out on her hotel bed she was up, refreshed, and ready to enjoy the warm glow of triumph.

'It was one of those days when everything clicked,' she said. 'The sort of day I hoped I'd get. Now it's all over I can relax and tomorrow it's our wedding anniversary.'

Paula could afford to relax. With the cash she had earned in prize money, time bonuses and appearance fees from the race, and from her kit sponsor Nike, she left London around £600,000 richer. Carey Pinkowski, the race director of the Chicago Marathon, said, 'She's turned everyone else into also-rans. I'd have to offer her $1 million just to start a race now.'

Paula's victory was a vindication of one of Chris Brasher's original aims for the London Marathon – to improve the standard of British distance running. But the fact that this 29-year-old woman was faster than any of the British men was staggering.

In three marathons run over 12 months, Radcliffe had exploded the myths surrounding what women could achieve, and Gerard Hartmann said her performance in London 'made even the men's world record look soft'.

The world watched and wondered what this woman might do to the marathon at the Olympic Games in Athens.

Some Olympic images can hang in the folk memory for ever – Dorando Pietri, legs buckling at the finish of the

1908 marathon; Seb Coe on his knees, his fists beating the track after conquering his conqueror, Steve Ovett, in 1980. But for Paula Radcliffe the image that hung over from the Athens Olympics was simply unendurable.

It was of a crumpled, broken, bewildered girl sitting on a kerbside at 22 miles, her head in her hands, tears and despair in her eyes. It was an image that was on every British front page the next day.

Down the road in the stadium at the finish of the marathon, the British contingent had been waving flags, singing and partying. Then the giant screen showed Radcliffe stopping. They saw her stumble on for 50 more metres and then splutter completely to a halt. 'Why didn't she carry on?' they asked over and over in disbelief.

Talking to Steve Cram on the BBC 24 hours later, Radcliffe burst into tears again because she feared she had 'let everyone down' – and everyone had a theory about what had gone wrong.

Dr Dan Tunstall Pedoe, the London Marathon's Medical Director, believed it was psychological. 'Athletes prepare for major races with mental rehearsals,' he said. 'What she probably mentally rehearsed was being in the front, holding off any challenge from behind her, and ultimately winning. When she found she was back in third place and the American came and passed her, mentally there wasn't much point in her going on.

'The fierce heat of Athens, too, was a factor. It becomes a lottery when you run in those conditions. It's not a fair test of running ability, it's a test of how you cope with grossly unhealthy running conditions. You can train a bit in high temperatures but your training suffers. You can only do so much without doing yourself damage.

'The most dangerous risk is heat stroke, which can kill. It can result in renal failure, kidney failure and brain damage. The one time we had someone get heat stroke during the London Marathon, he ended up spending a week in intensive care.

'Running in extreme heat can also increase the chances of exercise-associated collapse and stomach bleeding. It's like sticking your head in an oven and taking a deep breath.'

Paula herself revealed she had been hit by injury in the weeks leading up to the Games. As part of her treatment she had been taking anti-inflammatory pills that had upset her stomach. Food was more or less passing straight through her, and as a result her body was starved of the fuel it needed for the 26 miles.

'I just couldn't go any further,' she said, after dropping out of the Olympic race. 'It was like a car running out of petrol.

'It really hurt that people thought I had given up, because I just wouldn't do that. I don't mind people criticising, but to decide I was a quitter was just wrong.'

To demonstrate she was no quitter, Paula made an audacious, and many thought foolhardy, bid for redemption by announcing that she would run in the New York Marathon just 11 weeks after the pain of her Olympic disaster. She desperately needed to dull the memory of defeat by proving to herself that she could still dare to go the distance.

It was crazy but magnificent. Her duel with Susan Chepkemei of Kenya over the final miles of the race through Central Park was one of the greatest marathon battles ever, and millions watching live on television saw the two women match gut-wrenching strides, each refusing to give an inch.

With around 200 metres to go, Paula finally made a wincing and relentless drive to the finish to win by four seconds in 2:23:10.

'I don't know about redemption,' said Paula, 'but it was important for me to come here and win. I think it's very difficult to make up for Athens. It happened, it's over now, and it's about moving on from there.'

Following her comeback victory in New York, Paula set her sights on a return to the London and perhaps also to 10,000m running, aiming for gold in the World Championships. But she said her ultimate target would be the Beijing

Olympics of 2008 – and redemption there, of course, in the marathon.

When she returns to London, Paula will find the course faster than ever. Gone at last are the leg-wrecking cobbles of the Tower of London and the twists and turns of the diversion around the Tower Hotel. They used to lay a stretch of carpet there to cushion the uneven surface, but even so, cramp lurked in those cobbles, always waiting for weary legs. From 2005 the route will pass instead along a fast stretch of road on the Highway and Tower Hill.

Nick Bitel reckoned the improvements could make the London course as much as a minute faster for an elite runner such as Radcliffe.

'The real problem for Paula,' said Dave Bedford, 'is that there is nothing she can do other than to win in Beijing that will totally obliterate that run in Athens. I would love to think that Paula could wallpaper over Athens but that image will stick in the public's mind.

'We will see Paula at her best again,' he predicted, 'and I think she will go on to run faster than she has ever done before. It's a long way to the next Olympics but I'm sure we will see her there. I still believe she is the best in the world and we will see her justify that after what happened in Athens.

'The problem with the Olympics,' added Bedford, 'is that it is unfair, unreasonable and it is perverse. No other sport gives you one chance in four years. Look at cycling, football, tennis – no other sport does that.

'But with track and field it's just that one chance every four years. It is an absolute lottery.

'We're looking forward to seeing Paula running at her best again in London. After all, that's where she ran her fabulous world record, one of the greatest marathon runs ever seen in Britain.'

But of course there are plenty of other races that could lay claim to the title of being 'the greatest'. For Dave Bedford the 2003 men's London Marathon is his personal favourite.

While Radcliffe was striding unchallenged to a world record, the men's race could not have been closer, with five runners approaching the finish line together.

'In a way it was a dreadful shame that everything got overshadowed by Paula,' said Bedford. 'Because in the men's race there was this bunch together with 600 metres to go. As they turned the corner they were together in a line coming down the Mall sprinting for the finish. Abera, the Ethiopian, just got it but nothing can ever beat a race like that.

'Interestingly, the man who was second in that race, Stefano Baldini, went on to become Olympic champion in Athens, and he was beaten that day in London by the previous Olympic champion – which shows the quality of the event.

'We had all that and a women's world record. If I had been any nearer retirement age,' said Bedford, 'I would have quit happily then. The best doesn't come any better.

'Assembling elite fields like those,' he continued, 'has actually got easier over the years. We now work with agents and the London is these days strong enough to offer realistic money. We pay well, we get the best and we also get incredible good will.

'We are usually the race that top athletes will consider first. We've got the course, we've got the reputation.'

That reputation was built on high-quality fields that produced many thrilling finishes. In 1989 five of the top eight men from the previous year's Seoul Olympic Games lined up in London. They included the silver medallist Douglas Wakiihuri from Kenya, a slim, upright runner with a noble, almost serene bearing; and the bronze medallist Ahmed Salah from Djibouti.

They were fierce rivals, never slow to attack each other on or off the roads. 'Salah said he has come to London with one aim and that is to beat me,' said Wakiihuri. 'He was sore because I beat him in the world championships. Then at the Olympics he took off at 38 kilometres, far too early. I decided to go with him and we both burnt out.'

In the race a trio of Wakiihuri, Salah and Australian Steve Moneghetti crossed Westminster Bridge (the run-up to the finish in those days) together. Wakiihuri kicked and was away. 'Winning the London Marathon,' he said, 'meant as much to me as an Olympic gold medal would have done.'

For Chris Brasher, a great race needed a tough challenge – and he reckoned the most remarkable performance in the London came when the wind howled and the runners shivered.

In 1994, despite the conditions, Mexican Dionicio Ceron won in 2:08.53. Brasher said the run was 'absolutely unbelievable'. Without the high winds Ceron believed he would have broken the world record, and Brasher's verdict was that 'he's the most impressive marathon runner I've seen in my long career'.

The men's world record that had eluded Ceron eventually came to London in 2002. In what many believe was the greatest marathon competition in history, Moroccan-born USA citizen Khalid Khannouchi won in 2:05.38, four seconds faster than the world record he set at the 1999 Chicago Marathon. He won the London race by 10 seconds, beating Paul Tergat of Kenya and Haile Gebrselassie of Ethiopia, with six men in the race running faster than 2:08.

'The race went to the wire,' said Khannouchi. 'I gave everything I had. When I first saw the London course in 2000 I thought it was a world record course, although it is tricky and does have turns that slow you down a little.'

London has always had a reputation of being not quite as fast as some of the other big-city marathons such as Rotterdam or Berlin. But Khannouchi showed what could be done when you have the combination of expert pacemakers, almost perfect weather conditions and a wonderfully talented field. His runs also prompted great speculation about the prospect of a two-hour marathon.

In the world of the marathon the best is always still to come, and there are many who believe that we might yet see runners breaking through the greatest of all distance barriers – the two-hour marathon.

'When will it be done?' wonders Bedford. 'And where?' To answer this question, you need to take a wild run through time into the future of running and the future of the London Marathon . . .

It is 6 May 2024, London Marathon Day, the date set by Lord Bedford of Shaftesbury after detailed discussions with the Ministry of Climate Control – the day when running 42.2 km should be perfect.

Millions are gathered around the course and a battery of television cameras are focused on the bright orange strip of all-weather running track two metres wide that snakes the miles from Blackheath to Buckingham Palace. The crowds and the cameras are there to witness one thing – the latest attempt on the long-awaited two-hour marathon.

Ever since China's Ho Li Futsa failed to beat the barrier by just 12.75 seconds on the newly flattened Boston course, the sporting world had been ablaze with talk of the two-hour marathon. Ho had been disqualified, of course, after failing a routine genetic modification test. But even so he had shown what might be possible.

London had been starved of world records since crowds had flocked to the Campbell Stadium for the far-off Olympics of 2012. But now all eyes are on the 24-year-old Ethiopian, Abebe Tufimu, who has been flown to the start line in Lord Bedford's personal helicopter, recognisable as ever by the giant 118 painted proudly on its side.

Tufimu, the latest product of the Radcliffe Academy of Marathoning, has been programmed using subcutaneous chip implants to cover mile after mile in 4:33.8. His body will be monitored every step of the way by the team of scientists and coaches back in their control room at the Tower Hotel. They will relay analysis from their computers and their instructions via Tufimu's built-in earpiece, which will also take the feed throughout the race from his personal hypnotherapist.

Despite his billion-dollar contract with Bitel Boots, Tufimu is not wearing shoes as such for this marathon. His feet have been painted just 90 minutes before the race with a tough, flexible weatherproof coating – and one of the latest wafer-thin energy-return soles has been laser-glued to the bottom of each foot. Several of the pacemakers, who will run 3,000-metre stretches of the race in a relay, have chosen to take advantage of the specially laid 26-mile synthetic track surface by running in spikes.

Tufimu is confident. He was genetically identified as a distance runner at the age of six, and his years of physical training at altitude guarantee that at sea level he can churn out mile after mile taking exactly 193 steps to the minute with every stride precisely 1.58 metres. He is also an expert in psychological arousal, the technique that enables him to flood his body with naturally produced male hormones, not unlike the steroids so commonly used in the early years of the twenty-first century.

He knows, too, that the rewards for running the world's first two-hour marathon are immeasurable – a guaranteed place in sporting history and, because of his sponsorship contract, a guaranteed million dollars a year for life . . .

So is this how it will be done? Can the marathon's most alluring barrier be broken only by a synthetic superman from East Africa and in the most perfect of conditions?

Half a century ago, back in 1954, a barrier that seemed every bit as daunting and impossible as the two-hour marathon loomed in the world of record-breaking runners – the four-minute mile. Few sporting challenges have ever captured the public imagination in quite the same way. The feat was compared to the scaling of Everest or the landing of a man on the Moon.

Some thought the four-minute mile was simply impossible. It was even suggested that an athlete might collapse and die if he subjected his body to such stress.

But ever since Bannister did it, athletics experts have

been more wary of setting limits to physical feats. When Khannouchi broke the world record in the London Marathon, speculation about the two-hour barrier reached a new level, but Khannouchi himself was quick to pour cold water on the idea that the time might be just around the corner. He said he didn't expect anyone to do it for at least 'another 50 years'.

Similarly, the next record-breaker, Paul Tergat of Kenya, seemed to think that man is getting close to the limit in marathon running. 'I believe records are set to be broken,' he said, 'and to fall lower is possible. But what remains impossible is running a marathon in under two hours.' Then with a smile he added, 'Maybe time will chide me.'

The first marathon runner, amateur or professional, to break the 2:30 barrier was Albert 'Whitey' Michelson of the United States in 1925. Two years later he was beaten in a marathon in New York by a Hopi Indian running in moccasins. The Indian had never before seen an asphalt road, but neither had he ever before been away from altitude.

It took another 28 years before the 2:20 barrier was broken. Then in June 1953 Britain's Jim Peters of Essex Beagles ran 2:18:41 over the famous Polytechnic course from Windsor to Chiswick.

Len 'Buddy' Edelen, an American living and working in England, dipped under 2:15 on the Windsor to Chiswick course in June 1963, chased home by a young Ron Hill. And on 3 December 1967, in Fukuoka, Japan, the ex-Lancastrian Derek Clayton, running for Australia, went three seconds under the 2:10 barrier and started the murmurings about the prospect of a two-hour marathon.

Since then the explosion of big-city marathons, the emergence of professionalism and the lure of big prize money have led to the steady erosion of records. But still, to many, the magic two-hour marathon seems a long way off.

Way back in 1970 Britain's evergreen Ron Hill ran 2:09:28. He believed that a barrier to improved times existed simply because of the problems of fuelling the muscles. 'Unless doctors find a method,' he said, 'or evolution results in bigger people with longer legs, we'll never get down to two hours. I think it's impossible simply because I don't believe the human body is capable of carrying that much energy stored in available glycogen or fat.'

But the man who finished one place behind Ron Hill in the 1972 Olympic marathon, Scotland's Donald Macgregor, predicted, 'The sub-two-hour marathon will be run, and first by a man not a woman, but it could be 30 years before it happens.

'There must be limits to human ability but it is certain that athletes will continue to push back the limits. Clearly there are other factors like fame and money, but these are never the motive for the truly successful runner. They run because they love running.

'The odds,' said Macgregor, 'would have to be on an athlete of African origin doing it, whatever flag he runs under. China, Japan and Korea could be in the running but, much as I hate saying it, I think Europe, as things stand, has had it at that level.'

Hugh Jones, the 1982 London Marathon winner, reckoned the two-hour marathon will come but that it is still half a century away. 'Not in my lifetime,' said Stan Greenberg, one of the world's foremost track statisticians. 'To keep up that pace for 26 miles is unthinkable. It's the mental pressure that will hold them back. It looks impossible at the moment.'

The great Ethiopian Haile Gebrselassie said that he believed the two-hour marathon was a certainty. 'What Paul Tergat did in Berlin,' he said, 'has made the possibility of a two-hour marathon quite logical. I cannot believe it will be long before such a time is run.'

The ever-optimistic Dave Bedford believes we will see it within 20 years. 'We've got the course, we've got the event and we'll get the athletes,' he said. 'It would be wonderful to see the barrier broken and to see it in London. That really would be simply the best.'

20

Dying to Run

An athlete, when racing fit, feels ill, looks ill – wan and drawn. He has stood head bowed and steeled to hear the worst in his doctor's consulting room several times before the crux of the season arrives.
John Disley

Pheidippides, the original marathon runner, so the legends would have it, fell victim to the absence of adequate medical facilities in ancient Athens. He ran, he keeled over and he died.

And Chris Brasher, in the infant days of the London Marathon, gave a chilling description of Boston Marathon runner Alberto Salazar after his neck-and-neck finish with Dick Beardsley in 1982.

> The agony was in his body as they lifted him into the medical centre and put him on a stretcher. He was surrounded by doctors and nurses jabbing tubes into both of his arms, feeding his dehydrated body with pint after pint of saline and dextrose solution. Five and a quarter pints it took before he was able to get to his feet, one hour after he had crossed the finishing line.

Salazar came through the experience alive, though many believed he was never the same runner again, and Dick Beardsley, who finished a footstep behind, says that a little part of his ability perished out there on that marathon course too. Certainly men, even marathon men, have died from time to time, and the most famous runner's

Paula Radcliffe, world record holder
in the London Marathon with 2:15:24 in 2003

Hiromi Taniguchi (Japan, no. 8) on his way to a narrow victory in 1987

Henrik Jorgensen, winner 1988

Toshihiko Seko, winner 1986

Wanda Panfil, winner 1990

Douglas Wakiihuri, winner 1989

Yakov Tolstikov, winner 1991

Dionicio Ceron (winner 1994, '95, '96) and Liz McColgan
on the victory rostrum in 1996

Rosa Mota, winner 1991

Antonio Pinto, winner 1992, '97, 2000

Abel Anton, missed a course record by waving to the crowd in 1998

Katrin Dorre, winner 1992, '93, '94   Malgorzata Sobanska, winner 1995

Khalid Khannouchi, winner 2002

Abdelkader El Mouaziz,
winner 1999, 2001

Gezahegne Abera, winner 2003

El Mouaziz and Joyce Chepchumba (winner 1997, '99) celebrate victory in 1999

Catherina McKiernan, winner 1998

Deratu Tulu, winner 2001

Evans Rutto, winner 2004

Tegla Loroupe, winner 2000

Margaret Okayo, winner 2004

death of all was that of Jim Fixx – the great evangelist of jogging.

In July 1979 Jim Fixx came to Britain on a triumphal tour to promote his runaway best-seller, *The Complete Book of Running*. He bought his Asics marathon shoes with him and he told me how jogging had changed his life.

His book, which had been published in America in 1977, was still top of the best-seller lists nearly two years later, and Fixx had become famously identified with the new wave of jogging and the new way of life linked with it. He had become a household name – the hero of his own book.

It was fascinating to run alongside such a legend, but exactly five years later, on 20 July 1984, Fixx, the man who had sold the idea of jogging for health and fitness to the world, collapsed and died during one of his daily runs in rural Vermont in the United States. He was just 52 years old and he had fallen victim to heart disease – the very danger that he believed a marathon man might outrun.

The irony had the anti-exercise brigade whooping with delight. Newspapers became obsessed with the potential perils of exercise. 'Mr Jogging Dies Going for a Run', rejoiced the headlines.

The scary reports sent a shudder of fear through the massed ranks of runners. The euphoria that had built up around the fitness boom, fuelled to a great extent by Fixx's own book, led many to conclude, mistakenly, that exercise could somehow render you immune to sudden death – and particularly to death related to heart problems.

Americans in particular had flocked to jogging as if it were the elixir of life. Fixx himself, in his *Second Book of Running* – the follow-up to his fortune-making best-seller – said, 'heart attacks, while not unknown in trained runners, are so rare as to be of negligible probability'.

Jim Fixx regularly ran between 60 and 70 miles a week, and he reckoned to 'race' his marathons at a speed of 7½ minutes a mile. He loved his 10 miles a day, but he also told me he hated the strain and pressure of promoting his books and the endless stress and travel that followed in the wake of becoming a famous author. He said the only time he enjoyed being interviewed was if it could be done on the run.

On the day he died, attempting as ever his daily 10 miles, the weather was high-summer hot and his chosen course was hilly. He set off wearing just shorts, his running shoes and a stopwatch.

From the evidence, it looks as if he tried to cut his run back to about four miles. On a steep and grassy hill, just a 50-yard run-in from his hotel, he crumpled and fell. He died in his running shoes.

The post-mortem revealed not only that he died from a heart attack, but that he had suffered three mild heart attacks during the weeks leading up to his last fatal run. It was a shock, but there were explanations.

The simple truth was that Fixx had a family history that doctors believed made him a candidate for heart trouble at an early age. His father, Calvin, suffered a massive heart attack at the age of 36. He was dead by the age of 43. Jim had said he was always aware of the shadow of his father's death and that he welcomed the moment when he himself passed the age of 43. Family history was probably the key factor in Fixx's background propelling him towards his early death.

But sometimes his own behaviour didn't help. He was so anxious before public speeches and appearances on TV that his heartbeat would gallop faster than in any race. He gulped Valium to slow himself down. He had also been a heavy smoker for years before he took up running in his mid thirties. At one point he puffed through 40 a day. Before he took up running he was at least 60lb overweight and regularly stuffed himself with junk food and drink.

Most importantly, perhaps believing his own propaganda, it seems that Fixx resisted undergoing any regular medical examination and, despite being advised to do so, avoided taking a maximum stress test. In fact the only stress test he experienced was in 1973, when he allowed doctors to monitor him on a treadmill because he was writing an article about it. He was 41, and the tests did show some signs of possible heart abnormalities, but Fixx failed to follow up the warning with any further tests.

Of course the big question that hung in the air after Fixx's death was that if such a symbol and icon of fitness could die during a routine run, what hope was there for the rest of us?

Packs of anti-exercisers went on the attack in the wake of Fixx's death. They used his tragedy to snap at the heels of the fitness gurus, relying heavily on fear to highlight the risks of running. But this panic of negative thinking passed, and most doctors now see aerobic activity as an important weapon in the battle against heart disease – but not a panacea.

Inevitably there will always be those who push themselves too far, believing in the myth of invulnerability, the myth that the more we exercise the healthier we become. It's a myth that's particularly strong among long-distance runners.

Some actually believed and preached that just training for and running a marathon would be a guarantee against heart disease. Dr Thomas Bassler, a Californian pathologist, was well known as the proponent of the theory that anyone who finished a marathon in under four hours was immune to death from heart disease. Bassler's views were featured in Fixx's book, but such blind belief, as the author had proved, can be a fatal trap.

In London, the health and well-being of hundreds of thousands of marathon runners came under the scrutiny of Dr Dan Tunstall Pedoe, a consultant cardiologist and himself a fine distance runner.

The remarkable Dr Dan is reckoned by runners and sports scientists alike to be the world's most experienced doctor in marathon medicine. He has been the Chief Medical Officer of the London Marathon since it began in 1981.

Well before the first London Marathon, Dr Dan had met Brasher at ultra-distance-running events, and he shared with him a vision that the London should be a people's marathon – open to all-comers, of all speeds and all ages. Brasher and his team had come under pressure and criticism from some medical authorities alarmed at the dangers of encouraging anyone other than highly trained young athletes to take part in the 'risky' event.

Tunstall Pedoe assured Brasher that with sound advice and sensible warnings, the marathon could be run safely. Since then the medical standards set by the London Marathon have led the world internationally and Dr Dan's formula for safety has stood the test of time.

He advises that anyone with a known heart condition or who experiences shortness of breath during exercise or chest pain at any point should see a doctor before contemplating training for the marathon, and that every entrant should be able to comfortably manage a 15-mile run a month or so before race day.

Each runner in the London Marathon is sent medical advice from Dr Dan as part of the event's regular mailings. It gives guidance on diet and training – and promises that any runner who has to withdraw from starting the marathon on medical grounds is guaranteed an entry the following year. It's an escape clause that works well, unless a runner is under undue pressure to deliver on charity commitments.

Dr Dan fears that charities that buy places in the marathon, using the Golden Bond scheme, understandably have priorities that could conflict with those of the runners. 'Sponsorship is great,' he said, 'but it can bring extra pressure to run even if you're not fit enough. The charities should always be understanding if a runner needs to pull out through illness or injury.'

Tunstall Pedoe originally approached the Royal Army Medical Corps about supplying medical support for the first London Marathon. They seemed alarmed at the prospect of having to man the race on a Sunday, and suggested that St John Ambulance volunteers might be a better bet.

At that first race in 1981, Tunstall Pedoe's medical team was tiny – four doctors, a couple of physiotherapists and podiatrists, backed up by St John volunteers. Some of them, like podiatrist Ralph Graham, physiotherapist Rose Macdonald and Seamus Kelly, of the St John Ambulance, were to become fixtures at the marathon for years to come. That day, though, they gathered in a draughty marquee with bales of hay in place of beds. It was set up on the grass and mud of Green Park as a sort of field hospital for the day.

When Dr Dan ran in to finish his own marathon, in a little over three hours, he was horrified to discover that television and press cameras had invaded the makeshift hospital, looking to film runners in advanced states of exhaustion. He ordered them out, angrily arguing that this was an intrusion into medical privacy, and none of the pictures were broadcast or published. But most of what he and the St John volunteers had to treat during and after that first race were simply blisters, cramp, sprains and skin abrasions.

Twenty-five years on, Dr Dan heads a team of over 100 each marathon day. He has established the London Sports Medicine Institute – a charity to provide research and teaching in sports medicine – and has edited the definitive book on the physiology and sociology of the event, called *Marathon Medicine.*

Clearly Dr Dan is either very wise or very lucky, or both, because, remarkably given the thousands running, it was not until the race was into its tenth year in 1990 that it suffered its first death.

The runner, a 39-year-old from Hampshire, married with a

son, was hoping to raise money for a hospital cancer unit. Chris Brasher said, 'Statistically we had been expecting a death in the race from cardiac failure. We have had about 175,000 people compete over these 10 years since the marathon began and it was inevitable that someone would die.

'I am very sad that coronary disease is the biggest killer in the western world. Someone dies from it in the UK every three or four minutes. It could have happened to this man at home, at work or while driving.'

There have been seven deaths in the London Marathon since then. But, given the millions of running hours covered by the participants, Tunstall Pedoe and the St John volunteers are justifiably proud of the marathon's medical record.

'Our duties,' said Tunstall Pedoe, 'are primarily to keep death off the roads, and prevent what is largely a fun run from swamping hospital A&E departments with tired and collapsed runners.

'We can't medically screen 35,000 runners from all over the world, but we do give them lots of advice. We've had just eight deaths over 25 years – and five of those were runners who were competing with severe heart disease. We've also successfully resuscitated five over the same period.' The statistics show that you are safer running the marathon than riding a motorbike for the same amount of time, and the skill of the marathon team in cardiac resuscitation is now such that some doctors have said that the London Marathon is one of the safest places in Britain to have a heart condition.

Despite Dr Dan's reassurances to Brasher in 1981, though, there were still plenty of doom merchants around to warn of the dangers of the marathon. Before the first race Dr Peter Sperryn, the honorary medical officer to the British Amateur Athletics Board, writing in *Medical News*, said:

I have been disturbed by the number of wounded recruits to running I have seen in the past few weeks training up for this event.

It is distressing to find 40-year-old executives setting themselves such a challenge without taking any advice, having no coach, having no training companions and having, in effect, not the slightest idea where to start.

What does worry me is that in a field of several thousand people with no entry medical certificate or screening, there will be unwise, unfit people putting themselves at risk.

Dr Vernon Coleman warned that running is a remarkably dangerous and damaging activity. 'It is much more like that unexplained madness that took thousands of half-crazed peasants dancing through medieval Europe and beating themselves with twigs,' he said. 'Some called that dancing mania, others referred to it as St Vitus's Dance. Perhaps today's spectacle should be called Brasher's Dance.'

Even Norris McWhirter, the co-founder of the *Guinness Book of Records*, and himself a former international athlete, was busily spreading gloom and doom about the ill effects of the marathon. He suggested that health insurance companies should impose an extra premium on marathon contestants.

He predicted that a high percentage of the runners would need hip and knee replacements and said that marathon runners after 30,000 pounding strides were rendered punch drunk much like veteran boxers.

But even the direst warning fails to put the obsessional marathon runner off his stride. Chris Finill is the youngest member of that group of 29 that has completed every London Marathon. He reckons he can keep up his unbroken streak longer than the others because of his age.

'When I was 28,' he said, 'I was told by my GP to stop running altogether because I had developed an irregular heartbeat when speed training.

'But some doctors don't understand runners, and so for the past 17 years I have been under the guidance of Dr Dan

Tunstall Pedoe. He's always been very supportive of my running and he told me to carry on. He said there was nothing wrong that he could find, and since then I've run at international level. In November 2003 I finished fourteenth in the World 100km Championships in Taiwan. I was the second British athlete home – so much for being told to stop exercising.

'Every run I do now, though, is in defiance of my original doctor's misguided comments – and they still haunt me.' Remarkably, Finill has done every one of his London Marathons in under three hours.

Chris Finill has come to terms with that early health warning, but somewhere in those long, lonely miles beyond Tower Bridge, many London Marathon runners will find doubt cruising at their elbow. 'Should you be doing this at all?' doubt will whisper. 'Is your body up to it? Will it kill you?'

When that happens I think not so much about Pheidippides or Jim Fixx as Sir Ranulph Fiennes.

I sat beside Fiennes in a small tent at the start of the marathon in 2004 and he spoke of how he had run seven marathons in seven days on seven continents. Incredibly he knocked these off just five months after a major heart attack and a by-pass operation at the age of 59.

Fiennes asked if I could help him fix his ChampionChip, the tiny tracking device that every runner must tape to a shoe. He needed a little help since he'd lost so many fingertips to frostbite on death-defying polar expeditions.

'There are two schools of thought about exercise after heart attacks,' he said. 'One school points to people who have tended to overdo it and died, but the other says that people who don't do anything at all after their heart attack often die anyway.

'My cardiologist said running marathons, even seven of them in seven days, might be OK, provided that at all times I kept my heartbeat below 130 beats per minute. He said I'd have to measure it myself.

'Unfortunately,' chuckled Fiennes, 'in the rush to set off round the world to run, I forgot to take the heart monitor with me. So far it's been a story with a happy ending, but we never know what might happen tomorrow.'

21

Tricks of the Trade

*Running is a lot like life. Only 10 per cent of it is
exciting, 90 per cent of it is slog and drudge.*
Dave Bedford

Whether it's heart monitors, nose clips or magic potions,
runners will try anything in the quest to go further and
faster. When Chris Brasher wrote in the *Observer* offering
to take on a few 'guinea pigs' to train for the second London
Marathon, 1,244 applied, offering their bodies, minds and
commitment for nine months.

Among them was a man with an artificial hip, another
who had suffered two heart attacks, a woman expecting a
child in January and wanting to run a marathon in the
spring, an alcoholic who had lost everything and wanted
to rebuild his self-respect, and an inmate of one of Her
Majesty's Prisons.

Brasher and his Ranelagh Harriers clubmate and training
companion, John Hanscomb, read every letter. The two
runners set up rival training schemes and drew up schedules
for their guinea pigs to follow.

'We have excluded,' said Brasher, 'those with artificial
hips or long-term pregnancies. Undoubtedly they could
complete a marathon in May but they need close personal
supervision and you cannot give that at long range.

'I have always liked the story about a Canadian professor
who supervises a cardiac rehabilitation unit. He entered
seven people (six cardiac patients and himself) in the Boston
Marathon,' said Brasher. 'The six patients completed the
course, but the professor dropped out.'

Dropping out was not an option for Brasher and Hanscomb, who were making predictions and laying bets on the outcome of their rival training patterns. Hanscomb was already a veteran of 38 marathons, having run his first one in 1956. Since then he has run in every London and looks like heading for half a century of non-stop marathon running. Brasher, by contrast, was virtually a novice; his one and only pre-London run had been in New York.

Hanscomb advised his guinea pigs to follow the traditional training pattern of the British club runner. This began with a mixture of running and walking, and soon built up to runs of five to seven miles each weekday and a long, steady run of around two hours at the weekend.

Brasher's approach was more rambling. Get out on the mountains, moors or wilderness, he urged. Keep moving for many hours, all day if you can. Walk to get your breath back or to drink in the view, and if you see a pub, never run past it.

The two men dishing out the advice were fiercely competitive and both planned to race themselves. A bet was laid and Brasher called the odds. If he lost to Hanscomb he would stand him two pints of beer. But if Hanscomb lost, he'd owe Brasher 20. They crossed the line two minutes apart, with the experienced Hanscomb the victor.

'The two schedules,' said Brasher, 'may seem very simple, but then "marathon running" is very simple.'

The simplicity of running is something that many fail to come to terms with. They are always hoping that there is some magic training method that will transform them overnight. But the fact is that how fast you can run a marathon is mainly down to the genetic hand you have been dealt by fate.

The measure of how quickly you can cover 26 miles is determined by the greatest amount of oxygen your body can take in, pump around and use to burn the fuel in your body. It's known as your maximum aerobic capacity. It varies with the size of your muscles, the make-up of their fibres and the capacity of your lungs, heart and circulation. It inevitably declines with age, though the decline can be slowed down by exercise.

But the fascination of the marathon is that it is not just the heart, legs and lungs you've inherited that get you through the distance at the front or way down the field. Much depends on how you train and what you eat and drink.

For the novice runner, the number of different training systems to choose from can seem baffling, but what is shared by them all, reckons John Disley, is pain. 'Just as it is logical to worship at the altar of the god that first answers your prayers, so it is natural to pay allegiance to the training system that wins you races,' said Disley.

'Just as there are many different forms of religion, so there are many methods of self-destruction called training schedules. Each one of these demands its own agony of fulfilment. The novice searching for a creed selects the schedule currently in fashion with the top people. He lives by this gospel for at least a season, and if it isn't working he moves on to alternative forms of torture.

'Needless to say, success arrives despite all the changes of systems,' said Disley. 'It comes as a direct result of four or five years of unremitting hard work, and the common factor of all the training methods is pain.'

Novice marathon runners have a host of questions about how to prepare. Some have no idea of the training involved. Others have been terrified by tales of pain and agony. The reassuring truth is that a marathon runner can go further on hard work and less natural ability than in any other sports event. You don't need much talent, but you do need consistency.

These days marathoners – even the mid-pack men and women – train all the year round, some of them twice a day or more and with the best covering well over 100 miles in any week. Hugh Jones, when he won his London Marathon way back in 1982, was running as much as 130 miles a week. These days women like Paula Radcliffe have more than matched that mileage.

For anyone setting out to train for a marathon there are magazines stuffed with advice, and it might be simpler if there were one perfect training method or guaranteed tricks of the trade. But in marathon running the most important thing is commitment and there are no real short cuts.

If you are a complete beginner you may need as long as a year to get into shape to complete a marathon. With some sporting background you might manage it in a matter of weeks. If you just want to finish you might get away with two or three runs a week. If you are aiming to enjoy it and cross the line in good shape you will need to run five or six times a week. Gradual adaptation is the magic key. Build up slowly enough and anything is possible.

Nothing much is new in distance training methods. Most have appeared and reappeared in various guises over the past century. Advice offered to student runners at Cambridge University in 1922 suggested you might get through a marathon on ripe bananas, will power, deep breathing and long walks.

A much tougher approach was served up just half a dozen years later in 1928 in a little book called *Athletic Sports* written by F.A.M. Webster. There you could get the best marathon advice of the day for just sixpence.

The preparation for a marathon race, said Webster, should be long and very gradually progressive – not less than four and preferably six months. The real marathon men appear, however, never to quit training and the book cited as an example the regime of Cliff Bricker.

Bricker, a Canadian, neither drinks nor smokes. He runs strictly to the watch and never worries about the pace or position of his opponents, since he himself can run any one mile of twenty-six in six minutes flat.

He has never broken training since 1924. Each Saturday afternoon he leaves home for a ten-mile run but doubles the distance when a marathon race is in prospect. Sunday at six o'clock in the morning he leaves home without any breakfast and starts on a thirty-mile walk.

The first food he takes that day is a bar of chocolate. He eats a good meal when he gets in and then sleeps until supper time. On Monday he rests, and Tuesday runs five miles at marathon pace. Wednesday he walks ten miles. Thursday evening he skips and does some bag punching. Friday evening he rests in preparation for Saturday's run and Sunday's long walk.

His unwavering schedule has earned for him the nickname of 'Treadmill' Cliff Bricker. He does not diet but eats meat only once a day at noon and he will not touch either tea or coffee.

Webster's book also gave the advice that

the feet must be well conditioned to stand up to hard wear on the roads and perhaps a bath of brine, in which beef has been pickled, is the best preparation for them. Or sheep's gall and oil of camphor mixed in equal parts can be used. For the actual race either a foot dusting powder or tallow should be used. But personal experiment must determine which of these ingredients is best suited to the temperature of the individual's feet.

As a precaution against cold, the body and limbs may be anointed with coconut oil, but an even better unguent is provided by a mixture of whisky and spirits of camphor which will produce a pleasant glow.

'Serious training these days,' said former Olympic marathoner Donald Macgregor, 'could be described as "controlled fanaticism". Apart from a fallow period after big races, training must be carried out consistently and at a high level, even outside the build-up periods. You needn't go to the lengths of "Treadmill" Cliff Bricker, of whom it was said that he "neither drinks, smokes nor favours any form of amusement", but most top runners now cover between 90 and 130 miles a week for long periods of the year. Most of it is run at a moderate pace, between 70 and 90 per cent of maximum, over varied terrain, and includes speedwork, interval and repetition runs and short races.'

The experts say that runners at any level can reap huge training benefits and avoid injuries by following a few simple rules. Alan Storey, in advice to the thousands of mid-pack London runners, stressed the importance of proper warm-up exercises, diet, rest, regular training and good running shoes.

'We advise people to run for four days out of seven for January and February,' he said, 'and then if they can manage that, train for five days a week. It is important to include regular rest days.'

Running magazines are fond of drawing up training schedules for different levels of experience. They label them for 'beginners' or for 'elite' runners. They may or may not work.

One of these schedules was followed in the 1980s, with great success, by Sister Marion Irving, who became known as the Flying Nun from California. But what she had done was to misunderstand the word 'elite'. She thought it meant 'refined and well mannered', so she followed the training schedule for elite runners and topped it up with prayer and meditation. In 1983, at the age of 54, the Flying Nun ran the Californian International Marathon in 2:51:01 and qualified for the 1984 Olympic marathon trials.

Prayer and meditation are not the strangest techniques used by marathon runners, who are always on the lookout for a miracle training method. There are plenty of competitors in every marathon these days who seem to believe that a strip of plaster over the nose can have a similar supernatural effect.

Nasal strips are a sporting aid or gimmick that came out

of the United States, where the market for them is said to be worth more than two billion dollars a year. The marketing men say potential customers include 'anyone who has a nose'. American football players were the first to endorse them, and they spread rapidly to the playing fields of Britain. Half of England's rugby team were seen wearing them, and the enterprising manufacturers have sent 'go faster plasters' to football and rugby clubs, running stores and the Oxford and Cambridge boat race squads. They popped up on noses dipped low over handlebars in the Tour de France, and there were so many in one New York Marathon that an observer said it looked like a plastic surgeons' convention. And when Paula Radcliffe gets her nose in front in the marathon, you'll find she's sporting a nasal strip too.

The principle is simple enough. They supposedly improve breathing by opening up the nasal passages, and consist of a couple of plastic strips, rather like collar stiffeners, in a piece of adhesive tape. Stick it across the bridge of your nose and it acts like a spring, flaring your nostrils until you feel like Kenneth Williams in *Carry On Up the Olympics*. The makers say the strips have been 'clinically shown to reduce nasal air flow resistance an average of 31 per cent'. They were originally developed not to win races, but to stop snoring.

Most experts simply sniff at the claims that nasal strips can improve sporting performance. Peter Sperryn, author of *Sport and Medicine*, dismissed them as 'total rubbish, a mere fashion fetish. Nobody breathes through the nose in sport, and there's no advantage in doing so. It's mumbo-jumbo like most of the stuff that comes out of America about sports diet.'

Alan Storey agreed. 'The amount of air that you can take in through your nose is irrelevant,' he said. 'It's not what you can get in, it's what you can absorb that matters. The strips may help psychologically but opening your mouth when you exercise is a reflex action, you don't have to decide to do it.' Storey said that none of the athletes he coached used the strips. 'If they did,' he added, 'I'd send them home for being improperly dressed.'

If the marathon runner wants to affect his breathing in a really significant fashion, he might try a far more expensive gimmick. One performance aid for the sportsman who has tried everything is the high-altitude bed chamber. You clamber into what looks like a miniature submarine, slam the hatch and get the effect of sleeping halfway up a mountain.

The idea behind it is simple enough. Training at high altitude is known to boost physical performance and it is considered to be one of the secrets behind the record-breaking athletic achievements of the Kenyans, the Ethiopians and others fortunate enough to have been born where the air is thin.

Altitude training stimulates the body's blood to compensate for the low oxygen level by producing more and more oxygen carrying red blood cells. By the time an athlete returns to sea level to compete there is an oversupply of red blood cells, which means that more oxygen is supplied to the muscles, resulting in a heightened performance.

The chamber, designed by Igor Gamow of the University of Colorado, uses the same principle by producing low pressure while an athlete sleeps, yet allowing training during the day as normal. This means you can train at home near sea level but sleep 'at altitude' like a Kenyan.

'If you enhance the blood capacity to absorb oxygen with drugs, it's illegal,' said Gamow. 'But if you do it by sleeping at high altitude, it's not only legal but a lot more fun.'

The bed does not look too inviting – it is not for the honeymooner or the claustrophobic. It is a large cylinder 8 feet long and 30 inches in diameter. Once inside, a dial enables you to depressurise to an altitude of your choice. Effectively you can spend the night at, say, 14,000 feet above sea level while a complex set of valves flushes out the carbon dioxide and replaces it with fresh air. In the morning, if you are not suffering from mountain sickness, you can climb out and train in the oxygen-rich air of home.

A British cyclist and engineer, Shaun Wallace, tried the chamber but found it too cumbersome to move around. He devised a refinement – a portable tent that can be erected in minutes over any bed at home, in a hotel, or even at the Olympics.

The tent, which folds to the size of a suitcase and weighs less than 70lb, uses hot air balloon technology. It can fit a double or queen-sized bed, and once you have zipped yourself inside, you can look out on the world through three large vinyl windows.

It rapidly proved popular with altitude-obsessed athletes, and among those who have spent their nights in the magic tent are Paula Radcliffe and Mark Steinle, the first Briton to finish in the London Marathon in 2000 and whose run won him a place in Britain's marathon team for the Sydney Olympic Games.

If simulated altitude training doesn't get you a faster marathon, how about trying music? There are those who believe that music is a powerful and underrated secret weapon in sport and that it can help you through those last painful miles by putting some badly needed rhythm in your stride. Rhythm is what goes when all energy and hope drains from your legs and they fill instead with cramp and despair.

Rhythm, as an aid to sporting performance, is a training trick that works, and like most techniques in sport it is not new. Down the years, innovative sportsmen and their coaches have often played with it in the search for the perfect race.

The undisputed ultra-marathon distance running king of the 1920s and 30s was Arthur Newton of Rhodesia. He took up serious running in middle age and trotted round the globe, setting records for 100 miles and 24 hours that still look impressive today. Newton was a compulsive experimenter and was convinced that rhythm was the secret of long-distance running. 'The more perfect your rhythm at anything,' he wrote, 'the more work you are able to turn out for a given expenditure of energy. Imagining a tune to keep time with when running is not only easier than actually whistling it but more economical with energy.'

Newton even went as far as to rule that marching music, with four beats to the bar, would cause injury because 'you are apt to emphasise the beat with one foot at the expense of the other'. The perfect answer, he said, was to run with a waltz playing in your head.

He took a huge-horned gramophone along with him on a trans-continental race from Los Angeles to New York and hoped that one day science might come up with a phonograph small enough to be carried by a runner as an aid to training – foreshadowing the Walkman by a good 40 years. You'll spot dozens of runners in the London who share Newton's views, dancing happily along with headphones clamped to their ears.

Newton knew what generals have known for centuries – that you can make soldiers march twice as far if you have a loud band banging out the rhythm. These days rowing eights use the trick with buzzers beneath their seats, just as the ancient slave galleys had a drummer on the deck. And twenty-first-century sportsmen can buy watches with built-in metronomes that bleep alarmingly with every footfall. There are plenty of runners in the London who swear that it's the rhythm of the bands playing along the route that get them through to the finish.

To keep going through a series of marathons, runners will try everything and anything. The 'ever presents', that group who run in every London Marathon, know most of the tricks. Jeffrey Gordon found that hypnosis helped him get going again after illness and injury and to get back under four hours, while Jan Hildreth discovered that taking a one-minute walk after every ten minutes of running let him cover unlimited miles, and still have enough breath for non-stop talking.

One of them, Derek Fisher, even tried tinkering with his blood to make himself go faster. 'There was a year I tried thinning my blood with aspirin for five days before the race,' he said. 'But this only resulted in terrible stomach upset during the run. I got caught short near Westminster tube station and then again on the M4 on the way home. That was particularly distressing and embarrassing because I was so stiff from running the marathon that I had the greatest difficulty in climbing back up the motorway embankment to get to my car.'

Safer perhaps than aspirin is ingenuity. It is the quality that any sportsman or woman can call on when the odds seem hopelessly stacked against them. Who, for instance, would gamble on a woman from the chilly wastes of Alaska winning a tough marathon in a heatwave?

But it happened at the United States Olympic marathon trials in 2000 when Christine Clark, a 37-year-old mother who did her training in ice-bound Anchorage left her rivals wilting along the course and collapsing into the medical tents. In sweltering heat she won in 2:33:31, knocking seven minutes off her best time and winning a place in the United States team for the Sydney Olympic Games.

The unfancied Clark solved the problem of training through snow and ice by doing most of her running indoors on a treadmill, while watching films or listening to Tina Turner tapes, and with the central heating turned up to 70°. She knew that when it comes to endurance events, heat can be a killer and only the ingenious survive.

One of the earliest examples of the same trick came from Don Thompson, who won gold in the 50km walk at the 1960 Rome Olympics. Thompson was worried that he would be 'one of those Britons who can't take a bit of heat'. Cleverly he turned his bathroom into steamy Italy. 'I got this oil stove and put it in the bath,' he said. 'Then I got a kettle that had been boiled on the gas ring downstairs and put it on top of the stove. I closed the door and window and let the whole thing simmer for 20 minutes.

'When the temperature had reached around 110 I waded in and did exercises for half an hour, by which time I was feeling pretty dizzy.' It may have been the paraffin that caused the dizziness, but the ingenious method of training worked.

The inspired would-be champion will always find a way to train that is smarter than his or her rivals. The gold-medal-winning Emil Zatopek was said to run in heavy combat boots, sometimes holding his breath until he dropped. On occasions he sprinted with his wife on his back or ran on the spot for hours in a bath filled with the family washing.

The legendary footballer Sir Stanley Matthews, dedicated to every detail of fitness, would pace around the family home in Stoke before a match with lead insoles in his shoes. 'It made me feel I was floating when I took them out for the game,' he said. The same trick had been used half a century before by the distance-running record breaker Alf Shrubb.

One performance-enhancing technique that is not available to everyone is getting pregnant. In 1984 Ingrid Kristiansen surprised the experts by running one of the fastest marathons ever by a woman just five months after the birth of her first son.

Kristiansen was convinced that motherhood had made her faster and stronger as an athlete. 'It could be that a woman who has given birth increases her threshold for pain,' she conjectured, whilst scientists suggested that performance of female athletes in endurance sports improves after childbirth because of the increase of hormones in the body.

Hormone release in marathon runners of both sexes may be quite rampant if research is to be believed. According to an American survey of thousands of long-distance runners, men and women, 82.2 per cent think about sex while running. Revealingly, 18.9 per cent, it was found, also think about running during sex, and 26.5 per cent would rather give up sex than running.

In 1995 a charity runner from Bishop's Stortford named John Williams announced that he had given up sex for the London Marathon, and inevitably his declaration raised the question of whether sexual activity improves or detracts from sporting performance.

Several studies had suggested that improved fitness produced increased libido, but what the obsessional marathon runner needed to know was whether abstaining would increase performance over 26 miles. Professor Craig Sharp conducted a study, between 1980 and 1983, which found that sexual activity before sporting performance made no difference either way. His conclusion resulted in him being nominated as Man of the Year in Italy in 1983.

Asked for a ruling on the delicate point, one leading American coach, Bob Giegengack, famous for churning out champion runners from Yale, growled, 'It ain't the sex that wrecks my athletes – it's the staying up all night looking for it.'

22

The Greatest Show in Town

If I had my way, all these lovely guys and gals in the London Marathon would be winners.
Jimmy Savile

When Chris Brasher ran New York, in the race that inspired him to get the London Marathon rolling, he told of how he'd overtaken a dinner-jacketed waiter. That waiter's name was Roger Bourban. He was Swiss but he worked in restaurants in Los Angeles. In 1981 Bourban flew over for that first London Marathon complete with bottle, glass and tray. I watched him as he finished in just a shade under three hours. He crossed the line and calmly poured himself a drink.

Three years later, when the Olympic Games were on in Los Angeles, I met and ran with the flying waiter. Beneath the fancy dress there was a fine athlete. We'd bang out 10- and 15-mile runs and he would tell me of the fun he'd had around the world and the attention he had received because he ran marathons in his waiter's outfit.

'I have good friends everywhere,' he said, 'like a dog in a bowling alley. But I found London friendly beyond belief. London was the big one. In fact you could say it was the place where my legend was created. They really appreciated me running in fancy dress in London. That was where the press and the television first took an interest in the crazy costume I was wearing. After London there was so much interest I had to get a manager to handle things.'

What Roger Bourban did in that very first London was to catch the eye because of his outfit, and it was not long before thousands of runners realised they could do the same. They could wear fancy dress, raise sponsorship money for good causes, perhaps even get themselves glimpsed on TV, and so they joined the pantomime that many thought mass marathoning had become.

Turn on the television along with four or five million others at 9.30 on marathon morning and you will hear Brendan Foster or Sue Barker telling you about the waiters, the chefs, the clowns tossing pancakes, the giraffes and the rhinos bumping into penguins. The charities they represent benefit by millions, of course, but some wonder if sport hasn't been overtaken by the circus.

Setting the standard for fancy dress, the London Marathon has long been in the forefront. You get a scattering of these costumed clowns in New York, Paris and Berlin, but if you want to see a constant stream of eccentrics running in seemingly impossible costumes, London is the place to be.

On any typical marathon day, you are likely to spot middle-aged men dressed as bananas, students disguised as lottery balls, nine-foot carrots, Viking longboats, centipedes, Supermen, fairies, Elvis Presleys, Prince Charles look-alikes, men carrying stepladders, runners hidden inside Big Ben, and birthday boys going 26 miles with cakes on their heads.

It's a crazy extravaganza that closes half London in the name of sport as behind the tiny hand-picked elite group up front troop 33,000 plodders, many dreaming of their own brief moment in the limelight. Here in the London Marathon, above all, you can see the Hello-Mum-I'm-on-TV-syndrome taken to the extreme.

Fancy-dress running, though, is no easy option, and one of the great mysteries behind the performances of the Teletubbies and the ostriches in their Adidas shoes is how they manage to perform so well. It has surely got to be effort and agony enough to do a marathon in the lightest athletic kit you can buy, but in some of those crazy outfits, it must be close to impossible.

One of the first things that occurs to the average runner is that the fancy-dress brigade must be just a bunch of attention seekers who do it only so that they can grab more than their fair share of time in the limelight or on the TV screen. Others assume they dress up because they can only ever run slow times anyway and it's a good way of disguising it and getting your excuse in first. If you aren't fast you might as well be funny.

But the truth is that sometimes, like Roger Bourban, the people hidden inside a rhino costume or balancing something bizarre on their heads are actually very well-trained athletes. Many of them do it because they've seen other people do it and it looks like fun.

A lot of fancy-dress runners have already run several marathons and want to try something different to push themselves harder. Others are trying to raise the profile of a charity they are running for or a business that's supporting them, or they want to pay a particular tribute to a friend or relative who has fallen ill or who has died. They get the publicity and the charity gets the money. For other runners, it's a very special way of enjoying the race because running in fancy dress does give you a relationship with the crowd which you never get in the anonymity of vest and shorts.

The crowd often stand in the same place for hours, and when they see a competitor in fancy dress it gives them a reason to shout, a focus for their chants and comments. Sometimes they'll have seen the costume picked up by the television cameras at the start, and when they come down to the roads and actually see the rhino rumble by, the feedback is priceless.

Fancy-dress runners get great support from the crowd, but what is it actually like suffocating inside, and how does the training compare to that of a normal runner? The common factor of all the fanciest outfits is that they are bulky, oversized and irritating. They can be very hot, and whether you're running as a gorilla or a camel, you're probably going to pray for a cool and cloudy day.

A lot of charity runners come terribly unstuck if they haven't practised wearing the costume beforehand, however bizarre that might look training in the suburbs on a winter's evening a couple of months before the marathon. The dangers of a costume are similar to the problems of wearing new shoes or untried shorts in a race for the first time. Multiply the chafing from new shorts by a hundred times and you've got an idea of what it might be like if the strap from your gorilla costume rubs you up the wrong way for 26 miles. The outfits can be heavy, too. Some runners devise special weight-training routines to get themselves fit enough to be a camel or a carthorse.

One of the most accomplished of the charity stuntmen is Dale Lyons, who has romped his way through every London setting records for pancake tossing, egg and spoon racing, and three-legged running. He has also run the London course more than once on the same day. In 1987, and again 10 years later, he finished and then ran back to the start. In 1998 he covered the route three times. So Lyons reckons he has clocked up 28 London Marathons in the first 24 years.

In 2004 this 67-year-old, who calls himself the Galloping Gourmet, ran the London in a chef's hat, tossing a pancake in a large frying pan, in 4:19:55. He said he was slowed down by pancake fatigue and thrown off his stride by being passed by Wombles, telephone kiosks, geriatric ladies, Batman and Robin.

Whatever you think of such oddballs, they add plenty of colour and interest to the event, raise bucketloads of money and entertain the crowd.

Brendan Foster is in awe of the fancy-dress runners. 'The marathon,' he says, 'is the hardest event in the Olympic programme. Then you go to London and you see people who've committed months of their time in preparation to get fit enough to do something which, however you do it, is very, very tough. Yet they make it even more difficult for themselves by doing it carrying a stepladder or wearing a rhino suit.

'It's unusually British,' he said. 'It's slightly mad but I don't think you meet many rhinos, emus or runners dressed as double-decker buses in the Berlin marathon or even New York. It's British eccentricity at its best.'

Foster is a serious sports commentator, but during his broadcasts even he can go into fancy-dress overdrive. 'I just saw a Teletubby go through,' he's been known to yell excitedly, 'looking to be the first Teletubby home.'

Foster's broadcasting colleagues are often forced to get out there on the course, not so much to wonder at the world record pace of some Ethiopian or Kenyan up front as to trap the wildlife lurking around Blackheath. 'I've found a bunny here,' you might catch Sue Barker squealing, pointing her microphone at a giant mound of fake fur, or, 'Tell me, gorilla, who you are running for today?'

Alan Storey, when he was Race Director of the London, summed up well the attraction to the spectator of the marathon experience. 'It's free,' he said. 'It lasts for a couple of hours and it is a chance to see some of the world's greatest athletes and some of the world's biggest idiots, all mixing it in the same race.'

The fancy-dress runners may, as Brendan Foster believes, make life difficult for themselves physically and increase the pain and effort needed to complete the 26 miles, but for many of them the experience of being the centre of attention and raising big money for charity can transform their lives.

The reasons they do it can be chokingly moving. They run to mark memories, they run to heal the sick, to buy scanners and dialysis machines, to support the young and the old. They run as a tribute to those they've lost and as a helping hand to those they hope to save.

Brasher recognised the wider significance of the marathon and the motivation it provides for individuals. 'Here are men and women trying to do something that is incredibly difficult,' he said, 'with thousands willing them on. It is not the person who is first who is a winner, it is everybody, and the prizes for charities and good causes add up to millions.'

But the fund-raising fun runners are not without their critics, and in the early days of the marathon, Brasher and Disley were seriously concerned about the fancy-dress clowns taking over their foot-race. In 1982 one club athlete, a grizzled enthusiastic veteran of many an obscure road race, wrote to *Athletics Weekly* to complain about Brasher's London Marathon.

'They won't let me enter,' he said, 'I'm not a member of Equity.' Some of these club athletes were angry because they felt that the achievement of running a marathon was being devalued. There was a time when it would not have entered the heads of actors, journalists and even politicians to attempt the distance. Some club enthusiasts believed that finishing the 26 miles, 385 yards entitled them to be members of an exclusive club – it was akin to being a four-minute miler.

Serious athletes, with their eyes on high-level competitions, were not the only ones to moan. As the runners limped their way round offices, factory floors, football clubs, school common rooms, church halls, bars and shopping centres – hustling forms and seeking pledges – some backers became weary of the sponsorship demands.

'I'm all for good causes,' said one, 'but I draw the line at being expected to sponsor a grown man to run a marathon in a miniskirt with two balloons stuffed up his shirt.'

For most, though, the lure of a good cause, and the spectacle of so many prepared to go through so much, proved irresistible. As a result, the London Marathon is now the largest single-day fund-raising event in the sporting calendar. The amount raised by the runners has grown every year, and it is now around £35 million annually. Surveys show that over 76 per cent of the field raise money for charity.

Out of the 45,000 accepted for the race, 20,000 secure their slots through the annual ballot and another 15,000 places go to charities. The charities can buy a minimum of five places each, guaranteed for five years under the Golden Bond scheme. A further 3,000 go to overseas runners and the remaining places to the elite field, celebrities and club athletes, with reserved places for the London boroughs who support the event.

Each year the London nominates an official charity – in 2005 it was Help the Hospices – and as a fund-raising event there is no marathon in the world that comes close to it. It is estimated that since 1981 over £200 million has been raised for charities worldwide. The London also has its own charitable trust, which distributes all the profits made from its events to fund recreational projects across London. Since 1981 over £16 million has been given in grants by the trust to local community projects in London for sports equipment and improving leisure facilities, and in 1999 it bought its first playing fields as a way of keeping the land for sport rather than allowing development on it.

As well as the money-spinning fancy-dress parade, of course, the London spectators can amuse themselves with a game of Spot the Celebrity, from Steve Redgrave to Gordon Ramsay, from Charlie Dimmock to Jeffrey Archer. Through 25 years there have been legions of them, from show business, sport, broadcasting and politics, but in the early marathons the celebrity turns were led by the headline-grabbing Jimmy Savile.

In his trademark gold lamé suit, waving an outsize cigar and surrounded by a bizarre pack of minders, Jimmy Savile raised £50,000 in the first London Marathon. The following year his sponsorship was up to £200,000 and he went on to run over 200 marathons or fun runs all over the world and to raise millions for charity.

He would trundle round the London course yelling, 'Come on, all you wonderful guys and gals, give us a cheer and give us your money. This London Marathon is a marvellous idea.'

A less likely superstar of the infant London Marathon was Madge Sharples who, at the age of 66, huffed and puffed her way to a new career – as a pensioner who took up the marathon and ran it very, very slowly.

As the oldest woman runner in the early races, 'Marathon Madge' became an instantly recognised personality much in demand by the media. By the time of the third London in 1983, this Glaswegian pensioner had broadcast on television and radio over 100 times and had been photographed for newspapers jumping about in a pair of shorts, in a bikini and once – at a Sports Personality of the Year lunch – in a gold sequined boob tube and a pair of white silk harem trousers.

But taking her first steps as a runner in that same year, 1983, was another Scottish woman who was to make Marathon Madge seem surprisingly young. Jenny Wood Allen from Dundee was 71 when she ran her first marathon. She completed her first London Marathon at the age of 76 in 1987 and kept running it annually for another 14 years. In 2001 Jenny 'Supergran' Allen popped up as the oldest woman in the race when she was almost 90. She set a world record time for women over 70 while running in the London and she finally hung up her shoes in 2002 at the age of 91.

Since the early days, celebrities galore have graced the London. Some of them are alarmingly fast, like *Blue Peter*'s Peter Duncan and Simon Thomas. Others are content to simmer a little more slowly, like chefs Gordon Ramsay and Anthony Worrall-Thompson.

Some are big-name sportsmen – Steve Redgrave, Roger Black, Annabel Croft, Frank Bruno, Graham Taylor, Graham Gooch, Clive Woodward and Seb Coe among them. Others, like Steve Rider, the *Grandstand* presenter, and news presenter Dermot Murnaghan are more used to bringing the deeds of others to the TV screen.

There's the East End charm of actress Lucy Benjamin, the model looks of Nell McAndrew, and the T-shirts of Charlie Dimmock – they all bring glamour to the marathon and the marathon adds glamour to them. And every year there is a fresh supply of famous faces waiting to be pounced on by Sally Gunnell at Tower Bridge.

MPs have been tackling the London Marathon too, right from the start in 1981 when three of them ran it. One of the three was Matthew Parris, now a columnist with *The Times*, who raced through the first five Londons. He holds the record as the fastest MP and is fiercely proud of his 2:32:57 run in 1985.

Dick Douglas and Gary Waller jointly hold the record (10) for the highest number of London Marathons run while an MP, and David Heathcoat-Amory showed amazing consistency running his two London Marathons in 1987 and 2002 in almost identical times.

The man often considered to be more powerful than any MP, Alastair Campbell, Tony Blair's spin doctor, ran the London in under four hours in 2003. He said that thinking about the Prime Minister's speeches had helped him survive and go the distance – an interesting approach to handling pain. Campbell, running to raise money for the Leukaemia Research Fund, was trained by the winner of the 1982 London Marathon, Hugh Jones.

Another wise in the ways of Westminster who has romped around the London course in under three hours is Seb Coe. The double Olympic champion and now a member of the House of Lords said, 'Although only ticking over compared to the two and three training sessions a day which were the routine ingredients of the international competitor, I was able to draw from a 20-year reservoir that allowed me to compete without having to adopt a spartan lifestyle again.

'With an old training partner and a list of sponsors, I set off on a cool and blustery day which also marked the tenth anniversary of the London. Just under two hours and fifty minutes later I crossed the line, mission accomplished. I had successfully seen off the persistent chicken with some devilish surges around the 14-mile mark, finished in one piece, and raised a sackload of money.

'The London Marathon has become one of the great British days out,' said Coe, 'and, more importantly, those watching on television often decide to undertake what previously they considered to be the impossible.'

Another Olympic gold-medal-winning track runner proud to have run the London for charity is Kip Keino, who ran to raise money for Oxfam in Nairobi. And the greatest gold medallist of them all, the five-times Olympian Sir Steve Redgrave, trundled round the course as well as acting as starter in 2001. He set himself an even tougher target for the 2006 race – bidding to break the world record for the largest charitable amount raised by one person at a marathon anywhere in the world.

Life after sport is a serious business for athletes like Redgrave and Coe who have been such great champions. It is often difficult to adjust to the loss of the challenge to body and mind that dominated every hour of the day. Where can you find new roads to travel that will reawaken the buzz of a long sporting career?

One who found the answer in springtime London was Roger Black. The ambition to run the marathon had long lurked in the legs of this Olympic silver medallist. In his autobiography, published in 1998, he included it in his list of goals that had to wait for his retirement.

By the time Black went to the Atlanta Olympic Games in 1996, he had sorted out an approach to racing that could work for any event. He was no longer consumed with the need to win or break records. Instead he carried with him the single, simple goal of running 'my perfect race'.

'Many people feel I've got to win and if I don't win it's not worth doing,' he said after the Olympics. 'But only one person is going to win. If winning is everything to you then ultimately you are going to be disappointed. But you can always win by saying, "I ran my perfect race."' It is a concept that anybody attempting the marathon can share. In the London there can be many 'perfect races'.

When Steve Cram, equipped with a mobile phone to give

a running commentary, loped round the London in 2:38:13 in 1998, he was greeted at one point by a shout of 'Come on, Seb.' 'The marathon was a fantastic experience,' said Cram. 'I even got carried away and thought I was an athlete again. But then a few old injuries came back to haunt me and I remembered that I was retired.

'I'd often watched the race and wondered what it would be like to compete, although I put it off and off. There was nowhere where there wasn't a big crowd cheering us on. My real aim was to raise some money for Macmillan Cancer Relief and the Northumberland Youth Foundation – and of course to try and avoid being overtaken by Mickey Mouse down the Mall.'

In 1999 John Spurling, now the deputy chairman of the London Marathon, set a remarkable world record for the most money raised by an individual in the marathon: £1,126,560. In October 2003 Dave Bedford and I talked with the man who believed he could beat this record.

Lord Jeffrey Archer, his legs well rested after a couple of years in jail for perjury, reckoned he could run the marathon and raise £1 for every inch of the 26 miles, 385 yards. That would total £1,661,220.

Archer had been an international sprinter in his youth but he had never run any distances, let alone a marathon. I agreed to run with him, to pace him and keep him going, and, as Dave Bedford said, to make sure he covered every inch of the course. All donations were to be handled directly by the Charities Aid Foundation, with four selected charities to benefit: The British Heart Foundation, Make a Wish Foundation UK, The Fund for Addenbrookes and the Facial Surgery Research Foundation. Jeffrey hired a personal trainer and set to work knocking his 64-year-old body into shape.

On race day we set out at a sedate 10 minutes a mile, a pace which Archer reckoned he could keep up comfortably. Alarmingly, by 2½ miles he was puffing – and by three, it appeared, he was already hitting the wall.

In the early miles I tried encouragement. 'You're looking

good, Jeffrey,' I shouted. 'Keep that rhythm going, breathe easy, stay loose.' But sadly his face grew ever more ashen, his legs ever more leaden. I gave up on encouragement and tried abuse – which seemed far more effective.

'Archer, you are pathetic. You've been overtaken twice by a camel, and you only passed the camel because it stopped to have its photo taken,' I yelled. It seemed to work. Archer picked it up a little.

By halfway we'd been out for hours and I was starving. I glimpsed a family picnicking on the pavement. They had a table, chairs, baskets of bread and bottles of wine. 'I'm just going to grab a bread roll, Jeffrey,' I muttered. 'Keep running, I'll catch you up.'

'Any chance of a bit of bread?' I pleaded politely. The picnickers carved off a long chunk from their French loaf. 'Fancy something in it?' they asked. 'Salad? Cheese?'

I rejoined the race gripping my well-filled baguette like an oversized relay baton and set out in search of Lord Archer. For a moment I feared he'd escaped but I soon came upon him, head bowed, about to be overtaken by a centipede. I ran alongside him, enjoying my lunch.

'Would you like some, Jeffrey?' I asked. He grunted, too short of breath to speak, and I broke off a piece of bread. He tried to eat it and choked, and for a horrible moment I thought he might be back in the headlines for the worst possible reasons. But I poured water down him and he rose again.

The East End crowd greeted him with gusto. 'Come on, Jeffrey,' they would shout. 'They'll never catch you now.' Or, 'Oi, Archer, do they know you're on the run?' But there were no boos, and Jeffrey plodded on.

At 24 miles we saw former Olympic athlete Alan Pascoe. The night before he'd chuckled, 'I hope you're going to make Jeffrey suffer.' 'In the marathon,' I'd said, 'everyone suffers.' And if Jeffrey Archer gets all his pledged sponsorship in and claims that world record, there's no doubt he will have endured his share of suffering.

For the thousands in the London Marathon wearing their

costumes and raising their few pounds for a good cause, suffering is as much a part of the experience as carbohydrate loading. It's hard work taking on that challenge, and doing it in fancy dress makes it even harder. When I see Batman, Snow White and the Seven Dwarfs, Dennis the Menace or girls in Wonderbras, I'm more than amused – I am impressed.

Anyone who thinks these runners don't earn their charity money the hard way should talk to Billy Wilson. He has a reputation that makes the strongest runners quake. Wilson lays on an annual event of his own in the Midlands called 'The Tough Guy'. It's a crazy cross-country race with fearsome obstacles. One of his favourites is the 'Fiery Pit' – a pool bridged by a single narrow plank. Runners have to balance their way across while oil slicks belch smoke and flames beneath them.

Wilson has completed five London Marathons and recorded his fastest time while running as the back end of a pantomime horse. 'By three miles,' he said, 'I was dehydrated, exhausted and bleeding from where the straps of the costume were chafing me.' But the tough guy and his son made it, and before they finished, they performed an extravagant equine curtsey outside the gates of Buckingham Palace.

They did it, said Wilson, 'as a mark of respect to the Queen – and because the London Marathon is the greatest show in town'.

23

In Search of the Perfect Shoe

No doubt a brain and some shoes are essential for marathon success, although if it comes down to a choice, pick the shoes. More people finish marathons with no brains than with no shoes.
Don Kardong, Olympic marathon runner

Somewhere early in every marathon, often at around three miles, you become convinced that you've made a terrible and race-threatening mistake – you've worn the wrong shoes.

I once changed my shoes after 21 miles in the London and the feeling was wonderful. As my feet grow ever more battered I often get people to go out to far-flung points on the course with spare shoes just in case I call for a fresh pair. But I confess I am a shoe junkie, the Imelda Marcos of the training shoe. I reckon I have the biggest collection of used running shoes in private hands. For years, if there was a new model on the market I was first in line to buy it. For a while I was even given free shoes by some of the manufacturers, which swelled my collection no end.

I would go anywhere and try on anything in search of the perfect running shoe. Waffles, studs, spikes, air bubbles, pronation plugs – been there, worn that. The best pair of running shoes, the nearest thing to perfection with or without laces, was always going to be the next pair that I bought. I scoured foreign magazines in search of fresh mouth-watering models and even managed to get my feet into some unlikely prototypes that never went into production.

It would be far too painful to try to calculate what this addiction has cost me over the years. Even a spell of coaching the barefoot runner Zola Budd failed to cure me of my compulsion to buy and my belief in the magic powers of the cobbler. Zola may not have needed the benefit of shoes to run like a dream, but I certainly did.

My shoes, laced into my life, exist still. Some in silent slag heaps around my home, others hidden away in vast cardboard boxes, many caked with mud and down at heel, a few, bought in haste, hardly touched.

I can never throw any of them away. They are too full of footprints of the past. They bring back too many memories – happy and painful. They are a testament to countless nights and days lost pounding parks and tracks in search of the perfect run, the perfect race, in the perfect pair of shoes.

These days, though, the prices of second-hand sports shoes have never been higher – especially in Tokyo and Paris, where teenagers trade on the internet and snap up recycled Reebok, Adidas, Puma and Nike shoes in record numbers.

One of the reasons for the craze is said to be the shoes worn by Tom Hanks' character in the film *Forrest Gump*. Nike shoes from around 1970, like those he wore on screen, now have a street value of between $200 and $300. If you have old models of this or any other era squirreled away, you could be in the money, because Nike has now joined that exclusive club of brand names that Japanese collectors find irresistible.

While the perfect pair of shoes may never exist, the reality is that choosing a pair of shoes is one of the most important decisions a runner will ever make. Think what you're asking of your poor overburdened feet every time you run. The wonder is that you can do it at all. Your shoes hit the ground around 1,200 times a mile. Do 10 miles and that's 12,000 times.

Multiply that by your body weight and you will find that your legs are soaking up an impact of over 500 tons for each foot during every hour. That's quite a hammering on your ankles, knees, hips and spine. You need shoes that give you the kindest possible ride.

Not unreasonably, runners will pay a small fortune for the promise of pain-free miles. But strangely, and despite what the shoe manufacturers tell you, the best shoes may not be the most padded – or the most expensive.

Some researchers claim that 60 per cent of those who get injured while out pounding the streets can blame their footwear. Too many runners simply choose the wrong shoes and end up causing Achilles tendon injuries, shin splints, knee pain, or lower back problems.

Anyone tempted to try serious marathon training should buy their running shoes from specialist shops, rather than high-street sportswear chains, and try them out, either on the pavement outside or on a treadmill, before they buy. Some shops offer a biomechanical 'movement analysis' with a physiotherapist standing by to search for potential problems, though some runners think this is commercially led mumbo-jumbo.

Bill Adcocks, who held the record for the classic course from Marathon to Athens for 35 years, said, 'In the past 10 years all sorts of changes have been made to the technology of running shoes, such as greater cushioning and use of different materials, all of which were meant to improve protection against injury. But just as many people are getting injured – often because, even with these innovations, they are wearing trainers that just aren't right for them.'

The 33,000 runners who line up each year to run the London may be dressed as a fairy Superman or Mr Blobby – but in the eyes of Adidas, Reebok, Asics and Nike, they are all potential customers.

And when it comes to trainer wars, the shoe companies conduct their reconnaissance with deadly seriousness. As soon as you cross the finish line at the London Marathon, happy that at last you can get your bruised and blistered feet out of those shoes, there are spotters, market researchers, with clipboards noting down the brand and model of the trainers you are wearing.

One year, because of a foot injury I was nursing, I ran with a Nike shoe on my right foot and an Adidas on my left. The girl with the clipboard froze, her pencil in mid air, and she looked close to a nervous breakdown.

But the shoes that really matter to the big companies are up at the front, on the feet of the winners. As early as the 1920s, enterprising sports shoe peddlers were beginning to learn the value of putting their shoes on high-profile stars. When Jesse Owens won four gold medals at the Berlin Olympics in 1936, he was wearing shoes produced by the German Dassler family, cobblers in the small town of Herzogenaurach, whose two sons, Adi and Rudolph, quarrelled and set up rival shoe businesses – Adidas and Puma.

Of course, for every pair of feet that finishes the London Marathon, there are millions more who never use expensive trainers for running, but who are driven to buy them as fashion wear. Brands like Adidas and Nike are very big global business because the running shoe has jumped the gap from the streets of big-city marathons to the pavements and the catwalks of big-city fashion.

More than 20 per cent of the British footwear market is made up of trainers – you are as likely to find them on the feet of pensioners as teenagers. They hint at a lifestyle of youth, fitness and activity.

It's happened before. In the 1960s Dunlop Green Flash tennis shoes – white-canvas rubber-soled period pieces, remembered for their pungent glue-like smell and their propensity to produce instant blisters – started to be worn in the world beyond the tennis club. The reason was that they projected an image. They carried with them the whiff of firm thighs and bouncy middle-class prosperity.

Despite the astronomical cost of fashion trainers, a good functional road-running shoe can be bought for between £40 and £80, but a baffling array of new 'improved' models line up on the shelves at the start of every season. To mark the millennium, Adidas brought out a limited edition of its Equipment Gazelle at £80. Only 2,000 pairs were made available, and the design included a marathon route map on the tongue as well as the Flora London Marathon logo. Needless to say, there's a battered pair in my obsessive collection.

In the early days of the London Marathon, the enterprising Brasher opened his own running store – The Sweat Shop – and had his own tame consultant shoemaker to whom he would refer problem runners. John 'the Boot' Ellis, a happy chain-smoker who never ran a step, could rebuild a running shoe to cure almost any exercise-related injury. He would savagely rip them apart, cut out the gimmicky features and sew them back together – lighter, more comfortable and faster. 'Most of the companies,' he said contemptuously, 'muck them about just to make them look stylish, and all of them cost too much.'

Brasher's original Sweat Shop has grown into a chain of sports stores, these days run by his son Hugh. In its earliest days it was a rarity – a specialist running-shoe shop run entirely by obsessive and top-class runners who both knew and often ran with their customers.

Brasher and Disley were not only the co-founders of the marathon, they were shrewd businessmen and their early enthusiasm for shops and shoe companies soon had them running into taunts of conflict of interest. But any charge of cornering the market was overtaken by the explosion of such shops all over the country.

The London opened one of its own in Covent Garden in 2004. There, in the London Marathon Store, as well as the seductive racks of running shoes, you can find a whole range of clothing branded specially for the marathon. Once lured in by the promise of the perfect shoe, you can empty your wallet for a kitbag full of other technical running accessories. You can get 1,000 Mile socks, said to guarantee blister-free running due to a unique two-layer system. Instead of your old cotton T-shirt, which once it gets wet with sweat is heavy and hard to dry, you can invest in synthetic wicking materials which draw the moisture away from the body and leave you light. And you can get everything covered in logos that announce to the world: I am running the London.

Ron Hill was a pioneer of such wonderful wear. He took to running marathons in a string vest and set up a business hawking running gear using his own designer textiles. At the Munich Olympic marathon in 1972 he turned up in a silver heat-reflecting outfit that made him look like an alien – visiting Planet Earth just to take part in the Games.

You can run into the future yourself with an electronic device monitoring everything from your heart rate to the speed you're running and the calories you're burning. To ensure you don't suffer from dehydration, you can strap on a CamelBak, a bladder full of liquid you carry on your back like a rucksack.

But most enticing of all, of course, are the non-stop innovations you're offered in running shoes at such shops. Paradoxically, one of the latest harks back to man's most distant past.

In the summer of 2004, Nike announced that they had harnessed the sophistication of 'natural technology' to help runners return to those halcyon days when running barefoot was a spontaneous childhood pleasure. Their researchers had discovered that athletes who ran barefoot ran faster and had fewer injuries.

The veteran New Zealand coach Arthur Lydiard had come to much the same conclusion. He reckoned shoes weakened the foot. 'If you support an area it gets weaker; use it extensively it gets stronger,' he said. 'You run barefoot and all the muscles around your feet strengthen. You don't get shin splints and you get flexible power in the ankles.'

A biomechanist and senior researcher at Nike's sports research lab announced that unshod the foot is like an aeroplane coming in for a landing. When it's free the foot works naturally and efficiently, distributing the pressure of landing and launching, actions which are not present when the foot is encased and cushioned by a shoe.

Nike set out to design a shoe that would replicate bare-foot running motion but still keep the protective qualities of footwear. They named it the Nike Free. One of the techniques they used in its manufacture they called 'siping'. It involved deep slices or grooves to allow greater flexibility throughout the forefoot and toes of the shoe.

It's a technique that some runners have known about for decades. Twenty-five years ago I started taking a Stanley knife to my running shoes, slicing deep grooves in the sole to make them more flexible. It took a long time for the highly paid researchers to catch up.

When Jim Peters took minutes off the world marathon record in the 1950s, running times that would still place him high in races today, he did it in canvas plimsolls, the sort that schoolboys used to buy in Woolworths.

His feet were certainly no tougher than those of Abebe Bikila. He was the first great African distance runner, virtu-ally unknown until he amazed everyone by winning the Olympic marathon in Rome in 1960 running over the cobbled streets barefoot. The shoe companies fell over each other to sign him up, and by the time he won his second gold, four years later in Tokyo, he was safely shod.

There has been a long list of athletes who have reckoned that the shoemaker can do little to improve on the perform-ance of the human foot. Bruce Tulloh, Ron Hill and Jim Hogan would often bid for medals without shoes, and I had the unusual experience of helping to negotiate a lucra-tive shoe contract with Brooks for Zola Budd into which was written a clause saying that she could race without wearing the company's (or anyone else's) shoes.

Races have been won in the most unlikely footwear. In 1983 a 61-year-old Australian sheep farmer called Cliff Young turned up at the start line of the 875km Sydney to Melbourne race. Five days, fifteen hours and four minutes later he crossed the finish line as the winner – still running in the rubber Wellington boots he had started in.

Ten years later, in 1993, a group of American researchers brought a small team of Tarahumara Indians from the highlands of Mexico to run the Leadville Trail 100-mile race in Colorado. The Tarahumaras subsist on rice and beans and the legend of their prodigious endurance was confirmed by anthropologists as early as 1902. The prize money on offer for the Leadville Trail race would have made any of them instantly rich back in their village.

One of them, Victoriano Churro, was already 55 years old. Like his Indian team-mates he passed up the invitation to compete in expensive designer running shoes. Instead he raced in home-made flip-flop sandals, fashioned from leather thongs and rubber cut from discarded tyres found at a rubbish dump the night before the event.

This ultra marathon was full of well-trained runners in fancy, high-priced specialised footwear designed to give them a pain-free ride to victory. But the race was won, of course, by the old man in the home-made flip-flops.

Remember that when your feet start killing you in London.

24

Hitting the Wall

*You don't know what pain is until you get up around 21
or 22 miles. You just hurt like hell. You'd give anything
in the world to quit but you just keep going.*
Dr George Sheehan, writer and marathon runner

Emblazoned across the study wall of Mike Troy, one-time
Olympic swimmer, was one word: PAIN. 'It was there,' he
said, 'to remind me to swim until it hurts – and then swim
some more.' The plan worked. By embracing pain, Troy
won his Olympic gold medal in the 200m butterfly.

That was long ago, in Rome in 1960, but pain in sport
can still be a spur and an inspiration, or it can be the enemy,
an ever-present threat that can finish a career.

Marathon runners live with pain. They flirt with pain.
Some even seem to come to love it. It's through pain you
gain fitness in training, and everyone knows the marathon
race is painful, that's the whole point of it. If it didn't hurt,
no one would do it. If it wasn't agony, it wouldn't be interesting. Pain defines its mythology and its reality.

'You have to learn how to suffer in a marathon,' they
say. The runners know it and the crowd know it too.

In the 2002 London Marathon, millions of television
viewers watched Ben Walsgrove grimacing with pain as he
was half carried to the finishing line. He had run the entire
race with a broken hip. For 25 miles he had endured it as
a stress fracture, but then it became a serious break with
just one mile and 385 yards still to go.

'I was determined to complete the race because I had told
people who sponsored me that they would not need to pay
up if I failed,' he said from his bed in University College

Hospital, where he had had pins inserted into his femur. 'I'd raised £8,500 for Whizz Kidz, I couldn't let them down.

'When I got on to the Embankment with four miles to go the pain became excruciating. Two guys helped me to the finish. They were amazing – they gave up their marathon to help me.'

His wife Tor said, 'I'm very proud of him.' But Dr Dan Tunstall Pedoe wasn't so pleased. 'Severe pain,' he said, 'is always a warning to stop.'

But marathon runners don't stop. In the first London Marathon, in 1981, Jeff Aston was hit by crippling cramp 30 or 40 yards from the finish line. 'There was no way I was going to quit,' he said, 'so I hopped on one leg to the finish.' The crowd loved it and Aston's battle with pain was reported the following day in *The Times*. The experience didn't put him off. Aston has run in every London Marathon since.

'It's wonderful when you get to the end and you're dying on your feet,' they say. 'The crowd are all cheering for you, it's fantastic.' Watching the finishers between four and five hours can be an unsettling and moving experience. Here are ordinary people suffering considerable pain to achieve something quite extraordinary. Some compare it to childbirth. 'After the pain, the relief, the tears, the outpouring of emotion at the finish are very like how you feel immediately after birth,' said one four-hour finisher.

Matthew Pinsent, who with Steve Redgrave is a gold medallist in pain, said, 'If you do it right it's going to hurt. It's not something you try to avoid, you feel pain in your legs, your arms, your lungs, but you put it in the background.' He was talking of rowing, but all sportsmen must learn to live with pain.

Sports scientists have found that champion runners often handle pain very differently to the also-rans. The elite athlete tends to associate with pain; like a pilot at the control panel he monitors every flickering warning signal, using the feedback to master his body.

The slower runner will often disassociate, trying to fool

his mind by focusing on other things, filling his head with thoughts of anything except the pain of the run. The champion uses the pain to drive his body. The also-ran fears the pain will stop him dead.

'What is pain and discomfort to a relatively inexperienced runner,' said the American mile champion Marty Liquori, 'is merely information to the elite runner.'

But while a handful of elite athletes are getting ready to tune into their pain on marathon morning, thousands of other runners are scrabbling desperately to avoid it. They tape their feet with sticking plaster, gulp their painkillers, smear their bodies with Vaseline, but it's all in vain. They are about to learn that the human body (theirs anyway) is not made for this.

Marathon runners can get beaten up as badly as any prize-fighter. The punches through the spine, the smashing of the feet and the dehydration can be an appallingly punishing business. Experts tell you that you are likely to be more than a centimetre shorter when you finish because the repetitive pounding causes the muscles and discs in the back to compress.

One group at the University of Innsbruck in Austria has even suggested that the stress of endurance events could provoke the equivalent of a series of mini heart attacks. These scientists looked at cyclists taking part in the Tyrolean Otztaler Radmarathon, a one-day event that covers 213 kilometres with an altitude change of 5,500 metres. They monitored blood levels of an enzyme called cardiac troponin, thought to be associated with heart muscle death. High concentrations of this enzyme are found in people who have suffered a heart attack.

The scientists found that levels of this chemical increased in 13 of the 38 cyclists who completed the race, and the biggest increases were seen in the youngest, fastest cyclists who had trained the hardest. Similar increases in this enzyme have been seen in competitors in the Hawaii Iron Man Triathlon and in cross-country skiers.

John Treacy from Ireland, who came second in the 1984 Olympic marathon, took a blood test three days later to check his enzyme levels. 'My CPK level would normally be about 300,' he said. 'It's a measure of muscle fibre damage. My level after that marathon was 3,500. The lab technicians laughed at the reading. But normally a reading like that would indicate that someone had suffered a massive coronary. I'd run hard but I was fine.'

On the eve of the London Marathon, Chris Brasher would organise a gathering, a ritual, a dinner at which invariably talk of pain was on the menu. The guests were the best of British marathon running. Each of them had won a marathon medal for their country at a major championship, the sole exception being Joyce Smith, who earned her place at the table by winning the first two London events and setting six national records.

Around midnight you would find Ron Hill, winner of so many marathons, downing a large port and giving his verdict. 'I hate the marathon,' he would say, 'a lot of hard work and not much glory. I've always hated it and that's the truth. All that effort, all that suffering, I must have been mad, bloody mad.'

Jim Alder, Jim Hogan, Bill Adcocks would grunt their agreement and mutter that these days it's all about money and the youngsters don't know enough about pain.

'I'm not jealous of the money,' said Jack Holden, who won his gold medals back in 1950, 'but it's not fun any more, there's too much science, not enough laughter. Running used to be the way to physical fitness and fun, now it's just a living.'

Among the legends at those dinners was a man who knew more about the agony of marathon running than anyone who'd ever hit the wall. Jim Peters met pain in a heatwave in the Empire Games marathon in Vancouver in 1954. He collapsed, was helped from the track and disqualified. At the time he was more than three miles ahead of his nearest opponent.

'When I fell over on the track, I just couldn't understand what had happened,' he said. 'I was completely bewildered but made up my mind I was going to finish. I couldn't disgrace my wife and my kiddies. I thought of them and said to myself, "I'm going on, there's a tape to break, don't stop until you hit that tape." But as I got up and ran it didn't seem to get any nearer. It was there in front of me but I just couldn't break it.'

Peters was hauled off unconscious to hospital, put on saline and glucose drips and nursed through his agony. But he did not race again.

For most marathoners the real pain starts when they hit the wall, and sports medicine has now built up a detailed picture of why it hurts so much.

'The classic explanation,' said Dr Dan Tunstall Pedoe, 'is that when you run too fast you burn up all the glycogen in the muscle. You need to store up as much as you can before the race by carbo-loading. If you run too fast too early, or if you don't run at a steady pace, then you'll burn it all up and you'll be reduced to burning fat, which is slow and painful. The muscles ache and you run more slowly.

'The other explanation is simply fatigue, which usually catches up with runners between 18 and 22 miles. That's when you see a lot of runners start walking. They suddenly feel tired, but if you run sensibly you don't hit the wall – at least not physically.'

That may be so, but research has shown that more than half of all non-elite marathon runners report having hit the wall at least once – and that men are significantly more likely to report hitting the wall than women.

David Fereday, who keeps meticulous records of all his runs in the marathon, reports, 'Hitting the wall – a sudden dramatic slowdown – has occurred in 11 of my 24 Londons. Blowing up on the cobbles can be humiliating and agony. It adds up to 11 very painful experiences – I guess rather like a woman giving birth. Being competitive I simply strive to push and push to prevent the pace dropping down to a painful walk. I hate the pain-filled minutes it adds to my time.'

The wall defies definition, but you'll know it when you hit it. Your pace drops, often catastrophically, your legs feel as if they have been filled with wet sand, you find it difficult to think or calculate your speed, your limbs lose all co-ordination, and self-doubt leaves you feeling helpless and hopeless.

When it happens, the best advice is don't panic and don't fight it. You are going to have to slow down anyway, so you might as well accept it. Above all you must use your mind. You've covered more than 20 miles so how can anything stop you now? Keep moving, however slowly, drink, take carbohydrates or glucose if you can get it. Break the distance left down into small chunks. Take it a mile at a time, or if that's too much, a minute at a time – even a footstep at a time.

It's only pain, and thousands of runners learn to live with pain. Not just the excruciating pain of all-out effort that pumps through the body deep into a race, but the everyday pain of muscles that are mangled, joints and tendons that are damaged by overuse. Runners will try anything to ease the ache that can keep up with them every step of every day. The methods they use can be bizarre. They will try anything from faith healers to seaweed baths.

One man who knows all about pain and injury to man and beast is Billy Wilson, the 'tough guy', who runs a horse sanctuary near Wolverhampton. He once sent me a powerful magnet on a wrist strap. 'Put this on and stand back for fireworks in your running,' he instructed. 'All pains will vanish, and I firmly believe that if the front-runners in this year's London Marathon wear them we will see a world record broken.'

The device was called the Bioflow, and it claimed to use a magnetic field 'to put a charge into the blood stream encouraging the blood to accept more oxygen and work more efficiently'.

Chris Brasher was one of those who strapped on a Bioflow

and cast aside his knee braces – but he did find himself suffering from one unusual side effect. While taking part in a combined sailing and long-distance-running competition as part of a crew skippered by Sir Robin Knox-Johnston, he had something of a crisis of self-confidence when he found his legendary navigational skills deserting him as he got horribly lost in the dark on the cliffs of Dorset.

It was only after he had thrown three compasses in the bin, and had a row with the manufacturers, that he realised that a powerful magnet on your wrist may do wonders for your knees but plays hell with your compass.

Perhaps Brasher should have tried an even more unlikely cure for pain, pioneered in the United States. There George Straznitskas apparently fixed his knees using WD40 – the universal lubricant found lurking in toolkits and garages in its familiar blue and yellow spray can.

Straznitskas, who as a runner once qualified for the United States Olympic marathon trials at the age of 36, said that he heard of someone using WD40 'spray therapy' for pain and tried it on a knee that had hobbled him for three years.

'After two days there seemed to be less pain,' he reported. 'I had been taking six to eight 200mg tablets of ibuprofen daily, but after a week I felt so good that I stopped taking any at all.

'After a month,' he said, 'I spray the knee with a light mist three times a day and average one or two tablets of ibuprofen daily. My daily run (four to six miles) is better than at any time in the past three years.'

Whatever tricks you use to get past the pain barrier, if you can get through the wall and endure 20 minutes of agony, you're a winner. Let it stop you, though, as Paula Radcliffe found in Athens, and the pain in your soul can last for years.

Once again I hear the boom of the cannon. I'm on the green start at Blackheath but this time it is different. This time I have steel in my leg and doubts and warnings not to try it in my head.

Hitting the Wall

In June 1987 I took a morning run in bright sunshine. Wimbledon fortnight, with its tennis, strawberries and cream, was about to begin. As I ran across a road, I was hit by a car. Flung in the air, I came down on the windscreen. It shattered and I bounced off.

I was dragged along beneath the car, a mess of oil and blood and the screaming of brakes. When we stopped, for a moment there was silence, and I could hear a bird singing.

In the ambulance I shivered in my shredded running kit, and in the hospital they fought to save my leg. 'Try to make it good,' I said. 'Please, I'm a runner.'

There were too many injuries to count, and too many operations to care about running. They filled me full of blood and drugs and built scaffolding around my legs. Visitors and doctors drifted in and out and the pain stuck around day and night.

One afternoon my son, Matthew, came to see me after school. He was just coming up to 13. As he sat on the bed I saw the tears welling in his eyes.

'What's wrong?' I asked, wondering if something bad might have happened in class.

'They were talking about you when I came in,' he said. 'There was a man who said you'll never run again.'

My fingernails bit hard into my palms. 'We'll see about that,' I said. 'Don't you worry, of course I'll run again.'

It was a tough promise to keep.

Between operations, my mad running friends rigged up an exercise bike with one pedal in an attempt to keep me fit. They lifted me from the bed to the saddle. Within 30 seconds I blacked out, but it was a start.

Somehow I kept coaching the runner Zola Budd, though still on crutches. One day I took her to run in some woods near Guildford. She was deeply depressed, and I wanted her to run, to lift her spirits. But she refused.

'Run easily,' I said, 'just jog, it's easy enough. Anyone can run.'

She turned on me with all the anger of depression. 'You

can't run,' she said, with a withering glance at my crutches.

'Just watch,' I said, as I threw the crutches into a bush. 'Just you watch.'

Two or three lurching steps later she cried enough. 'Stop it,' she said. 'Stop. I'll run, of course, I'll run.'

I learned to walk again in a swimming pool, to jog a few steps by throwing my sticks ahead of me in the park. I walked with books on my head to try to lose my limp. And I dreamed of running the marathon.

In early April I mentioned it to my surgeon. He shook his head. 'Maybe one day in the future,' he said, 'but as your doctor I have to tell you not to try it.'

I had metal in my right leg from knee to ankle and I feared he might be talking good sense. But as I left the room he looked up for a moment. 'Knowing you,' he said, his eyes twinkling above his glasses, 'may I just say good luck.'

I line up at Blackheath with a bumbag full of painkillers, but they don't seem to work. My right knee isn't ready. The metal inside cuts into the tissue with every step right from the start. The swelling looks alarming, so I try to keep my head up and my eyes on the crowd. Through the wall of sound I catch a 'Come on, Dad,' and in my head I play the promise, 'We'll see about that.'

When I eventually cross the line it is my slowest ever, but the sweetest. I am back. And I know that the finish of that marathon is the start of the next.

My two boys take my medal and have it mounted on a plaque. Beneath the date, and my time of 4:11, are the three words they chose to mark my return to the marathon: 'Mind over Metal'.

25

To the Finish

*Get going, get up and walk if you have to, but finish the
damned race.*
Ron Hill

The phone call always comes in the dark, damp days of
early December. 'I really don't think I'll make it this year,
I'd love to do it one more time, but . . .'

The caller is Jan Hildreth. He is well into his seventies
and he has run every London Marathon since the start in
1981. He will be there, as always, padding to the finish
long after the fast, lean men have gone by. I know. I make
him do it.

He is one of an elite, an ever-dwindling group of 'ever-
presents', as they are known – the runners who have taken
part in every London Marathon. They are down to 29 now
– an obsessive group, ranging from the oldest, Reginald
Burbidge, at 80, to Chris Finill, who is 46 and can still run
2:44.

This remarkable group define what is best about the
London Marathon, and their prayer of 'Let me do it one
more time' is the cry of every marathon runner who is hooked
on the quest for the perfect marathon. Because for each 'ever-
present' runner there are a thousand 'ever-hopefuls', all
searching for the perfect run, the big breakthrough that will
leave them at peace with the marathon.

One of the ever-presents, Rainer Burchett, ran that first
marathon 'in the teeth of family opposition'. 'My wife,' he
said, 'had seen me finish very distressed in the 1980 Masters
and Maidens Marathon the previous autumn and she felt

I was running unnecessary risks.' But Burchett has been doing the London Marathon annually ever since.

He is an ever-hopeful too. 'My ambition,' he said, 'is to be the first person to run a marathon at the age of 100. It's easier now I've got a guaranteed entry. I remember queuing up all night outside a designated post office to get my entry in on Guy Fawkes Night in 1983.'

Steve Wehrle, who became chairman of the BBC Running Club, vowed never to run another after that first London Marathon. 'But I was of course back the following year and every year looking for improvements,' he said. In 2003, with a back locked by sciatica, his painful jog ground to a halt in the first couple of miles. He gritted his teeth and walked the rest of the way in.

'I remember in 2000,' he said, 'standing on the start with some of the other ever-presents – Pat Dobbs from Ireland, John Hanscomb, Bill O'Connor, Dale Lyons – they were all there saying, "This is it – this is the twentieth. No more after this." Of course they all came back to run again the following year.'

'Just to run 25 marathons is not in itself a great achievement,' said the ever-present Dave Clarke. 'But starting, and of course finishing, all these consecutive Londons has been a problem for a lot of us. Nearly all of us at some time have run the London with injuries or illness.

'I've run it with a stress fracture of the metatarsal, fractured ribs, strained muscles and the flu – and any one of those should have stopped me exercising at all. But because it was the London I desperately wanted to keep my sequence going, so I ran it anyway.

'I very nearly didn't run the first London at all. I'd come up to town with two of my fellow Newbury AC members. We booked into a Kensington hotel just a few yards from the underground.

'On race morning we took a leisurely stroll to the tube station. Although the ticket office was shut, we reckoned we could pay our fare the other end and we wandered on to the platform along with other groups who were clearly off to the marathon. But then trains rattled through the station, one after the other, without stopping. We were getting a bit worried so I asked a chap who was sweeping the platform, "What time does the next train stop here?"

'"At 9.30," he said. As the race was starting at 9.00 on the other side of London, this piece of news started a panic, and a mass of bodies ran desperately out of the station. We three with five other athletes went charging around trying to find a taxi. There weren't too many around at that time of the morning. Eventually we spotted one.

'He must have wondered what he was letting himself in for,' said Clark, 'as eight frantic, arm-waving, strangely dressed bodies charged towards him. He said, "Sorry, guys, I can only take six of you, I'm only licensed to take six." But then he relented and said, "Two of you must sit on the floor and keep out of sight." We made it to the start.'

These obsessive ever-presents somehow make it year after year because there is something very special about the London. Jeffrey Gordon, a lawyer in his seventies, is an unlikely-looking marathon runner. Nevertheless he'd never miss a London. 'I've actually run over 100 marathons,' he said. 'But people only take notice of you if you mention you've done the London Marathon. Even if you finish high up in other marathons, nobody cares. I was second and third in some at the age of 47 – but the public aren't impressed by that. They're only impressed by the fact that you actually finished in the London.

'Still, nothing can put me off,' said Gordon. 'Not even a death threat.' He explained that he had once lined up at the start beside a suspended policeman. 'He turned to me and said, "I hope you drop dead in this race." It was because I'd organised evidence of perjury against him in the famous Christmas Tree Bribery Case. His wish didn't come true, though, and I ran one of the best times of my life.'

Don Martin confessed he is addicted to running the London Marathon. He's run with a broken toe, a crippled back and a wrecked knee. Martin's background is in football. 'After the first couple of marathons it became a challenge to do as many as possible,' he said. 'The number of people who have run every one of them gets less and less. I suppose it's stupidity that keeps me going but I love it for all the crowds and getting over the line. To run down the Mall and complete the distance is very emotional and the most wonderful feeling.'

'Years ago,' said Jan Hildreth, 'if you ran the streets to keep fit or race, you had to run the gauntlet of schoolboy taunts and abuse. The London Marathon made a big difference to that. The schoolboys aren't so interested in poking fun at you any more. They just look at you and assume that you are training for the London Marathon.

'We are no longer strange eccentrics, we're heroes, and setting out on this odyssey, taking it on, year after year, trying to manage your injuries and get your body geared up to make it, is a bit of an adventure really.'

It's an approach that Chris Brasher would have understood well. Brasher lived his whole life in search of adventure – big adventures in the mountains of the Himalaya and the tracks of the Olympic Games, or small adventures like canoeing the Thames and pounding the paths of Dorset.

'Any great adventure,' said Brasher, 'can be planned on the back of an envelope.' And that's how he and John Disley scribbled out their vision for the London Marathon. They set up an adventure that millions might share.

Everybody is an armchair adventurer, dreaming of what they might do. And here, with the London Marathon, is a ready-made adventure, a challenge on your doorstep neatly packaged, shown on TV and just waiting for you to have a go.

There's no age limit, no talent test. Thousands who worry about their spreading waistlines, or who wonder if they are growing old a little too quickly, answer this call to adventure. Most sports cast off the middle-aged; the marathon beckons them in.

To the Finish

Here the runners revel in their 26-mile adventure what-ever the cost in effort. Watch them at the end – a bobbing stream of limping, wobbling strugglers, finishing with arms aloft, triumphant as if in victory. In how many other events can you celebrate victory when you finish 20,000th?

'But in this race,' said John Disley, 'they all win, and every runner is regarded as important. That applies as much to Joe Jogger as to the elite.'

'That's the great thing about the London,' said Dave Bedford. 'We give as much respect to the chicken as we do to the winner. Obviously the chicken doesn't get paid like the elite athletes, but as far as the system is concerned everyone gets treated the same. In this event you start with the champions and the record holders. And when they all line up there's a moment when no one knows what might happen.

'Maybe someone we've never heard of will suddenly have the race of his life and win. It's a very small chance, but you never know. In life, ridiculous things can happen. There's that millionth of a per cent chance that someone dressed as a chicken will run a blinder.'

Certainly the strangest things can happen when athletes are fuelled by that heady cocktail of hope, fear and adren-alin, and the terrified chicken fuelled with enough adrenalin might just surprise the champion.

Dr Murray Watson, a zoologist, is convinced that a fear-enhanced performance will beat anything assisted by drugs. He used to keep a tooth-torn pair of bush shorts in his office in the Tsavo National Park in Kenya, to remind him of the night that he beat the world high jump record.

You won't find his record in the books because it was achieved far away from the stadium, with the aid of fear and a pack of hyenas. It took place in the National Park one night after Murray's Land Rover broke down two miles from his base camp. Watson was then 26, relatively new to Africa, and he decided to walk back to camp rather than stay with his vehicle. Within a few hundred yards, and with darkness closing in, he was being hunted by the hyenas. When the leading animal snapped at him he decided it was time to run.

In desperation, and with the hyenas snarling at his back – one even took a bite out of his shorts – he jumped for the lowest branch of a tree and swung to safety. He sat it out in the tree. At dawn he was amazed to find that he was more than 12 feet from the ground, and once down, despite repeated attempts, he could not get within four feet of the leap he had achieved the night before. His colleagues, sceptical of his story, had a go at matching his jump, but not one of them could get near it either.

It is not the only story of its kind. Watson's performance echoes that of others who, in moments of high arousal, pull off the seemingly impossible. There is the case of the distraught Florida mother, Maxwell Rogers, who lifted a station wagon off her trapped son and held it long enough for the child to be pulled free. She weighed 123lb and the vehicle 3,600lb. Trained strongmen found it difficult to match her feat. But for her there had been no weight-lifting, no steroids; instead she was just using one of the great resources available to any sportsman – the power of mind over matter.

There are plenty of sports scientists who feel that the limits of physical conditioning have nearly been reached and that the great advances of the future will come from psychology. What they know is that the human who attempts the impossible because he is being hounded by wild animals is mobilising an innate fear or flight reaction and dosing himself up on one of the most powerful and ancient stimulants – adrenalin.

Adrenalin is a remarkable performance enhancer. If athletes were offered a stimulant that promised to increase the rate and depth of their breathing during competition, boost heart rate and mask pain, the International Olympic Committee would want to ban it. Yet it already exists and every runner can use it. When adrenalin kicks in it can fire freak performances from the untrained, or spark barrier-breaking records from sportsmen, providing tantalising glimpses of human potential. Mix it with the excitement and emotion of marathon day and who knows what may be possible.

David Walker knows all about emotion. He is another who has got through every London Marathon. At the finish of the first his family was there to greet him, complete with his new-born daughter Hannah, aged just three months.

Over the years that followed, even when other members of the family couldn't make it, Hannah was always there to see her father run. 'She always said she wanted to try it herself one year,' said Walker.

'So in the year 2000, with the Millennium Marathon, we fulfilled our dream. We ran together. It was very special. Then, perhaps encouraged or shamed by her, her two brothers signed up for the 2002 event and the three of us ran that one together. At the end we vowed that all four of us would be back for the twenty-fifth anniversary. We'll be there.'

Reg Burbidge, coming up to 80, is the oldest of those ever-presents, and when his wife Alice, who'd cheered him on through every step of his lifetime of marathons, died suddenly, he believed he'd run no more. 'I nearly missed one London some years back,' he said. 'I wasn't keen to do it. I'd have stopped my unbroken streak of Londons then, but my wife pushed me through the door and made me do it. I was so glad she did. But you need the will to run.'

Out on the road with his sadness, Reg Burbidge has found that will to run once more. He'll be there again as ever, padding along alone, and this time dedicating his marathon to Alice's memory.

Every April runners like these continue to gather at Greenwich to make their way to Buckingham Palace, still looking for that perfect marathon and for a way to avoid hitting the wall. And long after the last lean men and women have gone through with their effortless strides will come the pounding plodders, creased with cramp, gaunt with exhaustion, but happy to be out there on the streets of London. Very few quit, most battle on, thousands come back for more.

It's part of the calendar now, this morning in springtime. Twenty-five years on, the London Marathon has become the biggest, the best and the most popular of its kind anywhere. It won its place as an institution very quickly. Henley, Wimbledon and Twickenham are famous partly because their roots are deep in sporting history. They gave sport to the world. They were the first. They were founded on the back of an empire that taught other nations how to play.

The London Marathon, by contrast, was an upstart. But it has moved faster than other marathons, outstripping them all in size and organisation. Right from the very first marathon, London's streets were lined as if for a royal occasion. The television coverage was enormous and the next day's press reaction reflected an almost unprecedented unanimity in its acclaim. According to columnist Ian Wooldridge:

> No sports event in British history, not even England's ecstatic victory in the 1966 World Soccer Cup Final, had received such saturation coverage.
>
> It was almost as though the nation and the daily chroniclers of its character had been dying for something good to happen, something untainted by hooliganism, untarnished by the smart snarling recrimination of losers, unspoiled by the cheap rhetoric of those who imply that big sport is somehow beyond the reach of us and diminished by overt commercialism.

The London course is fast and the running climate fine. When the winds whip up the Thames and the rain drizzles over Docklands, that is the weather the runner likes – and so do I.

Along at the Expo, where the runners sign in, the April air is heady with anticipation. Giant banners proclaim: 'The Impossible is Nothing' and you fill your steps with hope. Unlikely record claims are there aplenty, all waiting to be broken: Fastest Time for a Pantomime Horse – 4:37; Fastest Conga – 5:13; Fastest Time Running Backwards – 3:56; Skipping – 5:46; Fastest Playing a Trumpet – 3:06. The runners collect their numbers, tighten their shoes and step out to show London that in the marathon the impossible is possible.

They'll end up exhausted, depleted, but exhilarated, for the marathon makes profound demands of anyone who dares to go the 26 miles. But no one loses, and no one who has ever run a marathon can be quite the same again. Everyone who finishes finds out just a little bit of how it feels to grow and to be a hero. Out there on the road you'll discover for yourself what it means to face otherwise unimaginable mental and physical challenges – what life can be like when you dare to go the distance.

With five miles to go, cramp smacks suddenly across your thighs. Runners slip past you with a glance, a muttered 'Keep going.' You hobble, you panic, you clutch your legs.

As you slow, the cramp fades but you can't risk a second attack. You creep forward, daring to run again with fears of shuddering to a halt, of dropping out, of taking for ever to reach the finish. Somehow you lurch into a rhythm and begin to move once more.

You pass through alleyways of yelling, clapping crowds. People scream names. 'Come on, Dad,' yells a boy of eight or nine.' His father bites his lip and tries to raise the pace.

If you've run the best you can, you're living on borrowed time and the marathon starts to call in its debt. The physical wreckage is now very real. Muscles have been grinding tissue against bone, overstretched tendons are inflamed, cartilage is tenderised by the hammer blows of a thousand footfalls, and joints grate as the damage kicks in.

Every yard beyond the wall is a fight between courage and collapse. You drip-feed your effort and your determination, knowing either can run out at any time. The needle is on red and there's no way to freewheel to the finish.

You try to hold together. Some struggle to hide their weakness. Some groan and surrender. Some keel over. Some simply stop.

The boy who screamed, 'Come on, Dad' is already waiting there beyond the finish. He's silent now, a little frightened. This time it's his turn to bite his lip.

When it's ended he throws his arms around his father's legs and they both know the marathon is won. The pain doesn't matter, the time doesn't matter, this hug is more precious than any medal, and who cares if the tears come now?

The hunt for the perfect marathon is over. Standing there beneath a silver foil blanket, a medal round your neck, you know that it's this one – and every one you'll ever run.

For you have gone way beyond the wall. You've hit the finish. You're home. And you're a marathon runner.

Appendix:

Marathon Champions

1981

Winners: (Men) Dick Beardsley (USA) and Inge Simonsen
(NOR) 2:11:48
             (Women) Joyce Smith (GBR) 2:29:57

Over 20,000 applied to run, and 7,055 started the
Gillette-sponsored race on a warm and humid day. Men and
women lined up together at Greenwich. Although the race
referee disapproved, the hand-holding dead heat by the
winners was warmly received by the public and the media.
The pair had over a minute's lead over Britain's Trevor Wright.

In the women's race, Joyce Smith, who had never dipped
under 2:30 before, won by exactly nine minutes from New
Zealand's Gillian Drake. A future winner, Veronique Marot,
was ninth in 2:46:51. The decision of the BBC to focus
also on those well down the field gave competitors like
66-year-old Madge Sharples a lot more than 15 minutes of
fame.

1982

Winners: (Men) Hugh Jones (GBR) 2:09:24 (Course
Record)
           (Women) Joyce Smith (GBR) 2:29:43 (Course
Record)
London had now overtaken New York in size and there

were 15,758 finishers – including New York Race Director Fred Lebow. Red-haired student Hugh Jones (Ranelagh Harriers) led from start to finish and his time was the fastest ever recorded in the UK. He beat Oyvind Dahl (NOR) by almost three minutes, with a future winner, Mike Gratton (GBR), third in 2:12:30.

Joyce Smith, of Essex Ladies, again a popular winner, lowered the UK record for a second time, winning by over six minutes from New Zealander Lorraine Moller.

1983
Winners: (Men) Mike Gratton (GBR) 2:09:43
　　　　　(Women) Grete Waitz (NOR) 2:25:29 (Course Record)

The final year of Gillette sponsorship saw Grete Waitz, who ran surrounded by a cohort of men, set a new women's world best – even though it lasted less than 24 hours, being beaten at Boston the next day by Joan Benoit (USA).

A large pack disputed the first half of the men's race but the second half developed into a high-speed duel between Gratton and Britain's Gerry Helme, whose pre-race best was 2:14:51. At Tower Bridge Gratton made a successful break and was 29 seconds ahead by the finish. Henrik Jorgensen (DEN) was third in 2:10:47.

1984
Winners: (Men) Charlie Spedding (GBR) 2:09:57
　　　　　(Women) Ingrid Kristiansen (NOR) 2:24:26 (European Record)

The 1984 race was sponsored for the first time by Mars, and it was used as one of the selection races for the British Olympic team. The men's race was a tactical duel between two Tanzanians, Juma Ikangaa and Zakaria Barie, and two runners from Gateshead Harriers, Charlie Spedding and Kevin Forster. The Africans built up a large lead, but the English runners ran a steady 2:10 pace and caught the leaders at 16 miles. Spedding, who later in Los Angeles won an Olympic bronze medal – the only British runner to win a marathon medal since 1964 – pulled away from his clubmate and won by over a minute.

As an experiment, the elite women started 10 minutes ahead of the men, so that Spedding caught the speeding Kristiansen, who had a big lead over Priscilla Welch (GBR) and Sarah Rowell (GBR), at about 20 miles. The Norwegian broke the European record in this first of her four London victories. Welch was second in 2:30:06.

1985
Winners: (Men) Steve Jones (GBR) 2:08:16 (Course Record)
        (Women) Ingrid Kristiansen (NOR) 2:21:06
(World Record)

The previous year's 10-minute start for the elite women was abandoned, and on a warm sunny day Ingrid Kristiansen was able to benefit by running surrounded by a group of men as she raced to a new world best – which was not broken for 13 years. The champion was exactly seven minutes ahead of Sarah Rowell (GBR), who still set a UK record with 2:28:06, just 32 seconds ahead of fellow countrywoman Sally-Ann Hales.

The men's world's fastest, Steve Jones, was favourite to win, and win he did, but only after a prolonged struggle with Charlie Spedding. The early pace was fast, and the leading group was reduced to six by 15 miles. Over the next five miles Jones and Spedding pulled away together. Jones had a stomach problem at the Blackfriars underpass and slowed briefly, but managed to catch Spedding again and win in a new course record – which stood for 12 years. Scotsman Allister Hutton was third in a personal best of 2:09:16.

1986
Winners: (Men) Toshihiko Seko (JAP) 2:10:02
        (Women) Grete Waitz (NOR) 2:24:54

In contrast to 1985, a strong west wind was blowing over the course. Toshihiko Seko set a fierce pace over the first half (63:30) but the last eight miles into the wind were too much for him, and any hope of records disappeared. Hugh Jones (GBR) finished 1 minute and 40 seconds behind – his ninth run inside 2:12 – and Allister Hutton repeated his third place less than another minute back.

Running in a mixed field, Grete Waitz was partly sheltered from the wind by a pack of men, and recorded a lifetime best of 2:24:54. The second runner, Mary O'Connor (NZ), ran 2:30:52 for second place.

1987
Winners: (Men) Hiromi Taniguchi (JAP) 2:09:50
         (Women) Ingrid Kristiansen (NOR) 2:22:48

In one of the most hotly contested Londons, it was not until near the end that Taniguchi managed to shake off the chasing pack. Four men raced for the line behind him, and Nechadi El Mostafa (MOR) was just able to hold off Hugh Jones (GBR) on Westminster Bridge to take second in 2:10:09. Jones was two seconds behind, closely followed by Gianni Poli (ITA) and Geir Kvernmo (NOR).

It was win number three for Ingrid Kristiansen, who had hoped to beat her own world best set in 1985. But she cannot have been too disappointed with a fine 2:22:48, just over four minutes ahead of new British record holder Priscilla Welch (2:26:51). Veronique Marot (also GBR, though born in France) was third in 2:30:15.

1988
Winners: (Men) Henrik Jorgensen (DEN) 2:10:20
         (Women) Ingrid Kristiansen (NOR) 2:25:41

A double triumph for Scandinavia, as Jorgensen – who had been third in 1983 – ran away from the field from the Tower of London. The race was again an Olympic trial for the UK team, and Kevin Forster secured Olympic selection, this time for Seoul, running 2:10:52. Kudo Kazuyoshi (JAP) was third (2:10:59) and Hugh Jones fourth (2:11:08). Britain's Charlie Spedding misjudged his effort and came tenth. Internationally, the result was overshadowed by the 2:06:50 world best set the same day in Rotterdam by Belayneh Densimo (ETH).

Ingrid Kristiansen looked untroubled, winning for the fourth time, nearly five minutes ahead of Ann Ford (GBR). Third was super-veteran Evy Palm (SWE), and fourth marathon debutante Susan Tooby (GBR).

1989
Winners: (Men) Douglas Wakiihuri (2:09:03)

(Women) Veronique Marot (GBR) 2:25:56 (UK Record)

Under new sponsors ADT, the organisers put together a fine post-Olympic field, with five of the top eight male finishers from Seoul on the start line at Greenwich. Six men broke 2:10, but it was the world champion, Douglas Wakiihuri, the Japan-based Kenyan, who won, leaving his effort until he was within sight of the finish gantry on Westminster Bridge. Second and third were Steve Moneghetti (AUS) and Ahmed Salah (DJI).

Eight years after her first appearance in London, Veronique Marot (GBR) was able to catch the leading woman, Aurora Cunha (POR), who had gone too fast too soon, to win in a new UK record – her first ever marathon victory, at the age of 33. Her record stood until Paula Radcliffe came along in 2002. Second was Wanda Panfil (POL) in 2:27:05.

1990
Winners: (Men) Allister Hutton (GBR) 2:10:10

(Women) Wanda Panfil (POL) 2:26:31

The tenth London Marathon had its first British male winner since Steve Jones in 1985. At 35, Allister Hutton from Edinburgh Southern Harriers ran away from his pace-makers with 12 miles still to go, and defied wet and gusty conditions to win by half a minute from Salvatore Bettiol (ITA) and Juan Romera (ESP). World record holder Belayneh Densimo dropped out at 14 miles.

The women's race was more closely fought, with five finishing inside 2:30. Wanda Panfil improved on her previous second place with a win in a personal best 2:26:31, ahead of the American duo of Francie Larrieu-Smith (2:28:01) and Lisa Weidenbach (2:28:16). The world champion, Rosa Mota (POR), ran only the first half of the race, to raise money for charity – and perhaps to have a look at the course for the following year.

1991
Winners: (Men) Yakov Tolstikov (SOV) 2:09:17
(Women) Rosa Mota (POR) 2:26:14

London hosted the IAAF/ADT World Marathon Cup, and for the first time a major championship was combined with a mass participation race. Peter Nichols was appointed International Race Director. The fact that a team race was included increased the size of the elite field and made the outcome even more uncertain. Thus a previously little-known Russian, Yakov Tolstikov, sixth in 1990, was allowed by a huge pack – who were all watching each other – to make a break at 14 miles, to steal the show and win by over a minute. Manuel Matias (POR) came second in 2:10:21 with Jan Huruk (POL) third in the same time. The men's team title went to Great Britain, with Dave Long the first home finisher, fourth in 2:10:30.

In the women's race, Portugal's Rosa Mota, the reigning World and Olympic champion, made a winning return to London, with Francie Larrieu-Smith (USA) second in 2:27:35. The women's team title was won by the Soviet Union.

1992

Winners: (Men) Antonio Pinto (POR) 2:10:02
             (Women) Katrin Dorre (GER) 2:29:39

Conditions were excellent, and newcomer Antonio Pinto from Portugal had stiff competition from Tena Negere (ETH) and, unexpectedly, from Thomas Robert Naali (TAN), who had started the race as a pacemaker. But Pinto, a former racing cyclist, held them off, while fast-finishing Jan Huruk (POL) caught them to take second place in 2:10:07. Naali, the pacemaker, finished third in 2:10:08.

In the women's race, hot favourite Rosa Mota dropped out in Docklands with a stomach problem, and former East German star Katrin Dorre took her title with a relatively slow time. Second was Renata Kokowska (POL) in 2:29:59, with Britons Andrea Wallace (2:31:33) and Marian Sutton (2:34:38) third and sixth.

1993

Winners: (Men) Eamonn Martin (GBR) 2:10:50
             (Women) Katrin Dorre (GER) 2:27:09

The race had a new sponsor this year in Nutrasweet. The women's race was hyped as a grudge match between Lisa Ondieki (AUS) and Liz McColgan (GBR), with reigning champion Katrin Dorre holding the coats. But it was Dorre who made the break at just the right moment to win in 2:27:09 by 18 seconds from Ondieki, with the Scottish runner McColgan tasting her first marathon defeat another ten seconds down.

Eamonn Martin, the Commonwealth 10,000m champion, brought the smiles back to British faces in his first marathon, outsprinting Isidro Rico (MEX) on Westminster Bridge in 2:10:50. Three days earlier, Martin had endured a sleepless night to witness the birth of his son, Eamonn junior.

1994
Winners: (Men) Dionicio Ceron (MEX) 2:08:53
(Women) Katrin Dorre (GER) 2:32:34

A windy day in London Town meant that Ceron's hoped-for attempt on the world best had to be scrapped. But the Mexican still ran magnificently to defy the weather and get under 2:09. The crucial part of the race was between 35 and 40km, which Ceron covered in 14:41 to open a clear lead. Ethiopian Abebe Mekkonen was second, with another three runners inside 2:10. The first Briton, Eamonn Martin, was eighth in 2:11:05.

Katrin Dorre and Lisa Ondieki again took the first two places in the women's race as the German made it three wins in a row. The pace was moderate and the winning time of 2:32:34 was the slowest in the London Marathon's history.

1995
Winners: (Men) Dionicio Ceron (MEX) 2:08:30
(Women) Malgorzata Sobanska (POL) 2:27:43

The Mexican title-holder returned to win again with a three-second victory over Steve Moneghetti of Australia. The duo were a minute down on Antonio Pinto (POR) with only five miles still to run, but came through strongly at the finish. Pinto was third in 2:08:48.

The pre-race favourite for the women's race was Manuela Machado (POR), but she was defeated by the strong finishing pace of Sobanska, and was only seven seconds from being caught by Ritva Lemettinen (FIN). The race marked the end of the three-year reign of Katrin Dorre (GER), who was seventh, two places behind the runner destined to be the next champion, Scotland's Liz McColgan.

1996
Winners: (Men) Dionicio Ceron (MEX) 2:10:00
(Women) Liz McColgan (GBR) 2:27:54

Olympic year, and, as ever, the London – with its new sponsor Flora – was used by many runners to attempt a qualifying time. The temperature by late morning was 21°C – a very warm day by the standards of London in April. Anita Hakenstad (NOR) took the race by the scruff of the neck in pursuit of 2:30. She was alone in the lead at halfway (73:31) but the strain got to her over the last few miles and she finished fifth in 2:31:07. Spectators were riveted by the spectacle of Britain's Liz McColgan, two minutes down at halfway, working her way through to a victory by over two minutes from Joyce Chepchumba (KEN), 2:30:09.

Ceron's third victory was achieved in classic style: he stuck at the back of the group as it went through halfway at close to record pace, and then went with a potentially decisive move at 35km by the 19-year-old Jackson Kabiga (KEN). The Mexican ran clear for his third win, but Kabiga was caught by Vincent Rousseau (BEL), second in 2:10:26, and Paul Evans (GBR) third in 2:10:40.

1997

Winners: (Men) Antonio Pinto (POR) 2:07:55 (Course Record)

(Women) Joyce Chepchumba (KEN) 2:26:51

In ideal conditions, both races were extremely close, with six men finishing inside 2:09. The men's race included the reigning Olympic champion Josiah Thugwane (RSA) and World Half Marathon champion Stefano Baldini (ITA). British hope Richard Nerurkar took over from the pacemaker at about 15 miles. Three miles on, Baldini went ahead and broke up the pack, and 1992 champion Pinto seemed to have lost contact. However, he gradually overhauled two of the men ahead of him – Nerurkar and Erick Kimaiyo (KEN) – and caught Thugwane and Baldini with just over a mile to go. Thugwane dropped back slightly, and Pinto was able to sprint to a magnificent two-second victory over Baldini, who ran 2:07:57.

The women's race was equally exciting. Pacemaker

Lornah Kiplagat (KEN) led a pack of 11 at halfway in 73:30. Sonja Krolik (GER) then made a break and led by 52 seconds at 20 miles. But the chasing group hunted her down, and after 23 miles Joyce Chepchumba (KEN) and Lidia Simon (ROM) passed her. Liz McColgan, who had looked as if she might finish third, made a great recovery to pass Simon and catch Chepchumba on the Embankment. But the Kenyan just managed to forge ahead again to win by a second amid scenes of great excitement.

1998
Winners: (Men) Abel Anton (ESP) 2:07:57
             (Women) Catherina McKiernan (IRE) 2:26:26

What price glory? If Abel Anton had not waved at the crowd, he might well have been richer by $25,000, the prize for a new course record. But he was so delighted to have caught long-time leader Abdelkader El Mouaziz, who had broken away at 20 miles, that he shared his pleasure with the crowd. The Moroccan finished 10 seconds down and defending champion Antonio Pinto was third in 2:08:13.

McKiernan, winner of the 1997 Berlin Marathon in the fastest ever debut time by a woman, was a clear favourite. The 29-year-old Dublin-based runner started relatively slowly and avoided the early pace of Adriana Fernandez (MEX). From 17 miles onwards her progress was relentless – she overtook previous winners Joyce Chepchumba (KEN) and Liz McColgan (GBR), then Lidia Simon (ROM) and Fernandez. At the finish she was 28 seconds clear of McColgan.

1999
Winners: (Men) Abdelkader El Mouaziz (MOR) 2:07:57
             (Women) Joyce Chepchumba (KEN) 2:23:22
(WR women-only race)

Many of the world's best women's times had been achieved with the help of male pacemaking, and the London organisers stirred up controversy by declaring that as far as they were concerned any world best times not achieved in women-only races would be ignored for ranking purposes. So when Joyce Chepchumba turned in a London performance that broke Lidia Simon's 'women-only' best by two seconds, it secured her a 'world record breaking' bonus from the organisers.

El Mouaziz went one better than in 1998. His winning time was identical to Anton's the year before, but he also missed the record by exuberant waving to the crowd. He built up a big lead during the first half, and despite a late effort by 1997 winner Antonio Pinto (POR), the Moroccan won by over a minute. Abel Anton (POR) was third in 2:09:41, and Britain's Jon Brown fourth in 2:09:44.

2000
Winners: (Men) Antonio Pinto (POR) 2:06:36 (European Record)
(Women) Tegla Loroupe (KEN) 2:24:33

Another Olympic year, and the organisers had enticed the strongest field to date for both races, including the male world record holder Khalid Khannouchi (MOR) and Tegla Loroupe (KEN), the world record holder in mixed races. Loroupe sat in on the slow early pace and along with Lidia Simon (ROM) followed the series of surges from Kerryn McCann (AUS). When McCann finally weakened, Loroupe took over and led Simon across the line by 13 seconds, with Joyce Chepchumba (KEN) a close third.

Pinto ran the second half of the men's race faster than the first. The pack went through halfway in just under 64 minutes, but Pinto made the decisive move during the eighteenth mile – which he ran in 4:32 – to break his own course record as well as Carlos Lopes' (POR) European best. El Mouaziz, 2:07:33, and Khannouchi, 2:08:36, took second and third.

2001

Winners: (Men) Abdelkader El Mouaziz (MOR) 2:07:11
(Women) Derartu Tulu (ETH) 2:23:57

Both races proved tactically fascinating. Most of the world's fastest men were again in the field, but preferred to lay off the initial 2:09 pace set over the first half. As a result the pack was a large one until first El Mouaziz and then Pinto tried to break away. This left a six-strong leading group which also included two Ethiopians, Tesfaye Tola and Tesfaye Jifar, and two Kenyans, Japhet Kosgei and track star Paul Tergat. When El Mouaziz increased the pace, only Tergat could go with him. El Mouaziz won in a personal best and kissed the ground beyond the finish gantry to celebrate.

In the women's race, Lidia Simon (ROM) had confidently asked the pacemakers for a first half of 70 minutes, after which she hoped to burn off Tegla Loroupe (ETH). In the event Loroupe caused a sensation by stopping for some 50 seconds during the second mile to do some stretches. She spent the rest of the race trying to catch up the leaders. By 22 miles she had done so. But the effort was too much, and she fell back again.

Ethiopia's Derartu Tulu took the lead for the first time in Parliament Square and crossed the line in a personal best despite attempts by two interlopers from the crowd to obstruct her. Next were Svetlana Zakharova (RUS) in 2:24:04 and Joyce Chepchumba (KEN) 2:24:12. Simon was fourth, and Loroupe eighth.

2002

Winners: (Men) Khalid Khannouchi (USA) 2:05:38 (World Record)
(Women) Paula Radcliffe (GBR) 2:18:56 (World Record women-only race)

A year of superlatives, with world bests in both races. Weather conditions were ideal, and a great battle between world record holder Khannouchi (now a US citizen), Paul Tergat (KEN) and Haile Gebrselassie (ETH), making his marathon debut, was anticipated. The crowds were not disappointed. After a very fast start (62:47 at halfway) the three favourites fought it out until Khannouchi began a long run for home on the Embankment. Tergat was only ten seconds down at the line – six seconds short of the old world record – while Gebrselassie made the fastest ever debut with 2:06:35. Three others – Abdelkader El Mouaziz (MOR), Ian Syster (RSA) and Stefano Baldini (ITA) finished inside 2:07:30.

The women's race was dominated by Paula Radcliffe, moving up to the marathon for the first time. She broke away from the ninth mile, going through 10 miles in 54:26, and then increased the pace, with individual miles of 5:17 (mile 11) and 5:08 (mile 15). As the finish approached Radcliffe ran even faster – miles 24 and 25 took her only 5:09 and 5:06 – and she crossed the line in 2:18:56, only nine seconds slower than the time set by Catherine Ndereba (KEN) in a mixed race in Chicago (and thus not recognised by London).

The next four runners, though over 3½ minutes behind, all recorded personal bests: Svetlana Zakharova (RUS) 2:22:31, Lyudmila Petrova (RUS) 2:22:33, Reiko Tosa (JAP) 2:22:46, and Susan Chepkemei (KEN) 2:23:19.

2003
Winners: (Men) Gezahegne Abera (ETH) 2:07:56
(Women) Paula Radcliffe (GBR) 2:15:25 (World Record)

The men's race was won in a five-man sprint finish by the world and Olympic champion – but was overshadowed by an amazing new world record by Paula Radcliffe, who ran faster than all the British men. Radcliffe was paced by two Kenyan men – puzzling to some in view of London's long-time insistence on women-only races.

Conditions were cool as Radcliffe followed pacemakers Samson Loywapet and Christopher Kandie at a pace faster than the agreed 2:16. When Radcliffe heard the time for the third mile (4:57), she backed off a little, but still went through halfway in 68:02, 1 minute, 19 seconds ahead of the Romanian Constantina Dita, who later hit the wall. Radcliffe seemed to get stronger as she ran and reached 30km in a new world record of 1:36:39. Shortly after that Kandie retired, leaving Radcliffe with a single pacemaker, who took her through 20 miles in 1:43:34, another record. She finished strongly despite stomach cramps over the last few miles. Catherine Ndereba ran her own race to clock 2:19:55. Deena Drossin (USA) was third in a new American record of 2:21:16.

   The men, too, had a Kenyan pacemaker, Eliud Lagat, and a large group followed him most of the way. Over the last few miles they were whittled down to Lee Bong-Ju (KOR), Gezahegne Abera (ETH), Paul Tergat (KEN), Stefano Baldini (ITA), Joseph Ngolepus (KEN) and Albdelkader El Mouaziz. The Korean was dropped just before the group reached the Mall, but the rest stayed together until the final sprint. Baldini broke away first but Abera was able to outkick him, though both were given the same time. Ngolepus was just one second behind in third, with Tergat fourth another two seconds back. The first eight finished in under 2:09:00.

2004

Winners: (Men) Evans Rutto (KEN) 2:06:18
(Women) Margaret Okayo (KEN) 2:22:35

For the first time there was a Kenyan double in the London Marathon. The weather conditions, wet with a blustery wind, were difficult and, along with other athletes, Rutto took a fall on the cobbles by the Tower of London. He had dropped everyone except his countryman Sammy Korir as the two reached the cobbles. There Rutto fell and slid, knocking over Korir. As they recovered, Rutto pulled away strongly to win, with Korir second in 2:06:48. Jaouad Gharib (MOR), who had also fallen, was third in 2:07:02. First British runner home was Jon Brown, fifteenth in

2:13:39, 14 seconds ahead of the second Briton, Dan Robinson, both achieving the Olympic qualifying time.

In the women's race Okayo struggled both with the weather and with the challenge of Romanian Constantina Tomescu-Dita. The lightweight Okayo, 4ft 11in (1.50m) and 86lb (39kg), with a beautifully balanced pattering action, contrasted dramatically with the powerful Tomescu-Dita and her long, thumping stride. The Romanian built up a lead of 100 metres at one point, but Okayo fought back, and coming into the Docklands tunnel at around 20 miles the Kenyan swept past to go on to win easily. Lyudmila Petrova of Russia took second in 2:26:02. In Paula Radcliffe's absence, first British woman home was Tracey Morris, fifteenth in an Olympic qualifying time of 2:33:52.

Fauja Singh became the oldest athlete to compete in the London Marathon, at the age of 93. He finished in an age-group record of 6:07:13.

2005
Winners: (Men) Martin Lel (KEN) 2:07:26
(Women) Paula Radcliffe 2:17:42 (WR women-only race)

For around 15 seconds, it seemed Paula Radcliffe might be about to repeat her disastrous Olympic performance in Athens. She was well ahead of the field when suddenly she began to slow. Then, around four miles from the finish, she stopped and crouched by the pavement.

But in fact, Radcliffe was answering a call of nature and a few seconds later was back on her way to victory in a new women-only world record of 2:17:42. She finished just over five minutes ahead of Romania's Constantina Tomescu–Dita. Radcliffe said later: 'I've got to apologise to the nation for having to stop but I was losing ten seconds every time my stomach cramped up. I didn't really want to resort to that in front of hundreds of thousands of people. But basically I needed to go.'

David Bedford hailed the 25th London, held in glorious spring weather, as the greatest in the event's history, with close to a million lining the streets to watch the 35,552 starters. 'Paula back on top where she belongs, the biggest number of starters, the biggest number of finishers, the biggest crowds – it's the greatest ever,' said Bedford.

Kenya's Martin Lel surprised many, winning the men's race in 2:07:26, to finish 23 seconds ahead of World Champion Jaouad Gharib of Morocco. Pre-race favourite Paul Tergat was 8th, while 2004 winner Evans Rutto could manage only 10th. Britain's Jon Brown finished 6th in 2:09:31.

British paralympic champion Dame Tanni Grey Thompson was denied a seventh win in the women's wheelchair race after finishing third behind 18-year-old Briton, Shelley Woods. Kenyan Henry Wanyoike set a world record for a blind man of 2:32:51. Paula Radcliffe went on to win the marathon in 2:20:57 at the World Championships in Helsinki in August.

WHEELCHAIR MARATHON CHAMPIONS

Men

1983	Gordon Perry	GBR	3:20:07
			(Back Start)
1984	Kevin Breen	IRL	2:38:40
1985	Chris Hallam	GBR	2:19:55
1986	Gerry O'Rourke	IRL	2:26:38
1987	Chris Hallam	GBR	2:08:34
1988	Ted Vince	CAN	2:01:37
1989	David Holding	GBR	1:59:31
1990	Hakan Ericsson	SWE	1:57:12
1991	Farid Amarouch	FRA	1:52:52
1992	Daniel Wesley	CAN	1:51:42
1993	George Vandamme	BEL	1:44:10
1994	David Holding	GBR	1:46:06
1995	Heinz Frei	SUI	1:39:14
1996	David Holding	GBR	1:43:48

1997	David Holding	GBR	1:42:15
1998	Heinz Frei	SUI	1:35:18
1999	Heinz Frei	SUI	1:35:27
2000	Kevin Papworth	GBR	1:41:50
2001	Dennis Lemeunier	FRA	1:42:37
2002	David Weir	GBR	1:39:44
2003	Joel Jeannot	FRA	1:32:02
2004	Saul Mendoza	MEX	1:36:56
2005	Saul Mendoza	MEX	1:35:51

Women

1983	Denise Smith	GBR	4:29:03 (Back Start)
1984	Kay McShane	IRL	3:10:04
1985	Kay McShane	IRL	2:47:12
1986	Kay McShane	IRL	3:02:40
1987	Karen Davidson	GBR	2:45:30
1988	Karen Davidson	GBR	2:41:45
1989	Jose Cidhockyj	GBR	3:03:54
1990	Connie Hansen	DEN	2:10:25
1991	Connie Hansen	DEN	2:04:40
1992	Tanni Grey	GBR	2:22:23
1993	Rose Hill	GBR	2:03:05
1994	Tanni Grey	GBR	2:08:26
1995	Rose Hill	GBR	2:17:02
1996	Tanni Grey	GBR	2:00:10
1997	Monica Wetterstrom	SWE	1:49:09
1998	Tanni Grey	GBR	2:02:01
1999	Monica Wetterstrom	SWE	1:57:38
2000	Sarah Piercy	GBR	2:23:30
2001	Tanni Grey-Thompson	GBR	2:13:55
2002	Tanni Grey-Thompson	GBR	2:22:51
2003	Francesca Porcellato	ITA	2:04:21
2004	Francesca Porcellato	ITA	2:04:59
2005	Francesca Porcellato	ITA	1:57:00

Index

Index

Hakenstad, Anita 255
Hales, Sally-Ann 249
Hamlyn, Dr Peter 156
Hanscomb, John 194–5, 238
Harlow 4
Harrington, Illtyd 110, 159
Harrison, Audley 157
Hartmann, Gerard 173, 174
Hayes, John J. 62, 63, 64–5, 65
headquarters, London Marathon
153
heart disease 185–8, 191–3
heat stroke 175–6
Heathcoat-Amory, David 215
Helme, Gerry 248
Helsinki 118
Henderson, Melanie 80
Hermens, Joe 92–3
Hermonsen, Lars 131–3
Herodotus 25
high-altitude bed chambers
201–2
Highway, the 177
Hildreth, Jan 124, 203, 237,
240
Hill, May 70
Hill, Ron 67–72, 131–3, 182,
182–3, 225, 226, 231
Hoey, Kate 157
Hogan, Jim 226, 231
Hosack, Everett 145–7, 147
Houston Marathon 91
Hulley, Angie 135
Huruk, Jan 252, 253
Hutchins, Tim 126
Hutton, Allister 41–2, 44, 249,
250, 252
Hyde Park 100
Hydro Active Women's Challenge
154

Hyman, Martin 52
hypnosis 203
hypothermia 12

Ikangaa, Juma 248–9
Innsbruck, University of 230
insurance 116
International Athletes Club 52
Irving, Sister Marion 199

Japan 79–80
Jifar, Tesfaye 258
jogging 99, 100–2
Johnson, Martin 126
Johnson, Noel 141–2, 143, 148
Jones, Hugh 36–9, 44, 109,
183, 196–7, 215, 247–8, 250,
251
Jones, Ken 79
Jones, Steve 40–1, 42, 44, 249
Jorgensen, Henrik 248, 250–1

Kabiga, Jackson 255
Kandie, Christopher 260
Katsimbalis 33
Kazuyoshi, Kudo 251
Kederis, Kostas 24
Keino, Kip 119, 216
Kelley, John A. 87, 142
Kellner, Gyula 28, 30
Kelly, Commissioner Seamus
154, 189
Kenya 116, 117, 118, 120–1
Khannouchi, Khalid 116, 179,
182, 257, 258, 259
Kimaiyo, Erick 256
Kiplagat, Lornah 256
Knox-Johnston, Sir Robin 234
Kokowska, Renata 253
Korir, Sammy 261

Index

Index

Index

Acknowledgements

Like any great venture, the London Marathon is a team effort and my thanks go to the staff and volunteers, past and present, who have kept the London Marathon magnificently on the road.

I have enjoyed the friendship of the late Chris Brasher and John Disley, co-founders of the marathon, through three decades of running, and I am particularly indebted to Jim Clarke, Nick Bitel, Dave Bedford, Dr Dan Tunstall Pedoe, Alan Storey, Nicola Okey and the close-knit team behind the marathon for their help with background to this book.

Andrew Torr guided me through the archive of marathon pictures and I am grateful to the London Marathon for permission to reproduce them here. I have known, and had many friends among the sponsors of the race, and particularly thank Flora, sponsors since 1996, for their endorsement of this book.

Stan Greenberg, one of the world's foremost track statisticians, is the best fact-checker in the business, and my lifelong running companion, Donald Macgregor, Olympic marathon man, is a tireless researcher.

Thanks, too, to the skill and encouragement of my editors at Hutchinson, Paul Sidey and Tiffany Stansfield and my literary agent, Mark Lucas.

Above all, my thanks go to my wife, Carol, and my sons Matthew and William who have helped me through a lifetime of marathons.